BLACK STUDENTS IN THE IVORY TOWER

BLACK

STUDENTS

IN THE IVORY TOWER

AFRICAN AMERICAN STUDENT ACTIVISM AT THE UNIVERSITY OF PENNSYLVANIA, 1967–1990

WAYNE GLASKER

University of Massachusetts Press   *Amherst and Boston*

Copyright © 2002 by
University of Massachusetts Press
All rights reserved

Printed in the United States of America
LC 2001008660
ISBN 1-55849-322-0

Designed by Milenda Nan Ok Lee
Set in Adobe Garamond and Futura by Graphic Composition, Inc.
Printed and bound by
The Maple-Vail Book Manufacturing Group

Library of Congress Cataloging-in-Publication Data

Glasker, Wayne, 1957–
    Black students in the ivory tower : African American student activism at the
University of Pennsylvania, 1967–1990 / Wayne Glasker.
        p. cm.
Includes bibliographical references and index.
    ISBN 1-55849-322-0 (cloth : alk. paper)
    1. University of Pennsylvania—Students—Political activity—History—20th century.
2. African-American college students—Political activity—History—20th century.
3. Student movements—Pennsylvania—Philadelphia—History—20th century.
I. Title.

LD4536 .G53 2002
378.748'11—dc21

                                        2001008660

British Library Cataloguing in Publication data are available.

To my parents,
Morris and Mary Glasker,
who encouraged me in the optimistic belief
that a person can achieve anything
if only he or she will work at it hard enough;

to David B. Rose, my partner and companion;

to Loretta Carlisle,
the lifeline of the History Department
at Rutgers-Camden;

and to the late Samuel Sylvester,
of the School of Social Work at Penn,
who was a tireless advocate
and fearless warrior and champion
on behalf of black students and the black community.

CONTENTS

PREFACE

This book grew out of my encounter with black student activism and the ideology of black nationalism and Black Power at college, and my effort to understand these perspectives. I am a "baby boomer," born in 1957, three years after the historic *Brown v. Board of Education* decision. As such, I am a child of the era of integration, part of the first generation to have come of age since the Civil Rights Act of 1964. I was in the sixth grade in 1968 when Martin Luther King Jr. and Robert Kennedy were assassinated. At the same time, the Black Power movement electrified a decade. In 1974 I graduated from high school, and that summer Richard Nixon resigned in disgrace as President of the United States. I went on to become first an undergraduate, then a graduate student at the University of Pennsylvania, undoubtedly a beneficiary of the gains of the civil rights movement. Doors were open to me that had been closed to my parents and previous cohorts of African Americans.

By the mid-1970s the war in Vietnam was almost over, the national mood had changed, and the turbulence of the 1960s had subsided. In the 1970s many people contrasted the "revolutionary" black student movement of the 1960s with the "bourgeois" students of the "Me" generation who had "sold out" to capitalist materialism. Yet I observed continuing protest and activism by African American students. In March 1978 African American students in the Black Student League (BSL) occupied a building to demand the strengthening of academic support services for minority students, the hiring of more minority faculty members, and the creation of a third world center. Of course, these were "outrageously radical" demands. In the winter and spring of 1985, the BSL occupied the office of the president to protest the failure of the university to fire a lecturer who had referred to the African American students in his legal studies class as "ex-slaves." In January 1986 African American students once again occupied the office of the president to demand that Penn divest its securities of companies doing business in South Africa. At that time Penn had invested $93 million in such companies. The revolutionary image of the 1960s was juxtaposed with both the bourgeois image of the 1970s and the reality of continuing activism into the 1980s and 1990s.

As a product of the desegregation era, I was fascinated by my encounter with so-called separatism at Penn. In 1972 black students agitated for an all-black residence hall. The proponents pointed to the alienation and estrangement that African American students felt, which prevented them from utilizing the services of white resident advisers and academic advising services. To meet the special needs of African American students for counseling and advising, it was argued, a residence with black resident advisers should be created for them. The university did not (and legally could not) meet such a demand. Instead, Penn created a residential "living-learning" program (named after W. E. B. Du Bois) for *any* undergraduate student of any race or ethnicity interested in learning about African American culture and taking advantage of the benefits of black resident advisers. Critics charged that, although in theory any undergraduate of any race could live at the Du Bois Program (and over the years a few whites and other non–African Americans did so), in reality the vast majority of the students at Du Bois were black. To these critics, it was voluntary segregation cleverly hidden behind the guise of "culture" and psychological "special needs."

When, in 1986, the Black Student League denied full membership to a white student, this behavior too seemed a far cry from the color-blind society and Martin Luther King's rhetoric of the nation in which each person would be judged as an individual, by the content of his character and not by the color of his (or her) skin. The critics of the BSL asked how its behavior differed from old-fashioned segregation. Events such as this positively demanded explanation. I was intrigued by the dissonances I witnessed and searched for their deeper meaning. Those of us born after 1954 and coming to adulthood after 1964 were, even in the north, the first postsegregation generation. We stood on uncharted terrain and were negotiating the transition to "integration." But somehow it was not turning out to be what anyone had expected.

Furthermore, the separatist behavior that I observed was not confined to the "politicos" in the BSL. In the late 1960s and early 1970s, several African American student organizations emerged that paralleled "regular" ones: the Black Pre-Law Society, Black Pre-Health Society, the Society of Black Engineers, and the Black Wharton Undergraduate Association. Black fraternities, sororities, and social fellowships emerged as well. These students were not seeking a separate African American nation–state or separation from the dominant culture. On the contrary, they sought to attain their degrees so that they could go on to become doctors, lawyers, engineers, M.B.A.s, and corporate executives. They were busily circulating their résumés to line up summer internships, management trainee positions, and "good jobs" upon graduation. Therefore the BSL and others seemed not so much separatist as self-determinationist.

The more I investigated this "separatism," the more the behavior of African American students seemed to defy the traditional concepts of *both* black nationalism–separatism (on the one hand) and assimilation into the melting pot (on the other). This phenomenon was not unique to Penn. It was not exceptional. It was happening nationwide. Nor was it a stage that people "outgrew." What professional organization today does not have its caucus of African Americans, or Latinos, or women? Even the Congress of the United States has its Black Caucus. This sort of ethnic-group (and interest-group) organization, sometimes called "identity politics," may have become a permanent part of the political and cultural landscape. Perhaps interest-group organization is a reality that we must all learn to understand and cope with, no matter how much some people may deplore it as balkanization and, in Arthur Schesinger's words, the "disuniting of America."

Rather than dismiss separatism, I was convinced that there was an inner logic at work, and I wrestled to find a vocabulary that could describe this seemingly contradictory state. Ultimately, I concluded, as William Van Deburg did in his *New Day in Babylon,* that black students can be understood as assimilationists, cultural pluralists, or separatists. At Penn in the 1970s the legacy of black nationalism and the Black Power movement encountered the discourses of cultural pluralism and ethnicity. Out of this mix black students (and others) created a new synthesis that rejected assimilation. African American students at Penn were caught up in a cultural revolution that rejected monocultural Anglo-conformity and traditional assumptions about individualism and merit and definitions of "qualification." The students were not genuine separatists (such as the territorial nationalists who aspire to create the Republic of New Africa out of five states in the South). Rather, in a word, the students were bicultural. They sought to preserve their own distinctive ethnic culture, identity, and heritage while pursuing economic upward mobility. But upward mobility and cultural assimilation are not the same thing. They aspired to upward mobility without assimilation.

The campus offers a lens through which to understand wider social processes. In this book I set out to document the efforts and actions of African American students and the African American community at the University of Pennsylvania, especially in the period from 1965 to 1978. At a microsociological level, I hope to capture a picture—indeed the narrative—of the actions and experience of African Americans at a predominantly white university.

The trajectory of black student activism at Penn is a microcosm that reflects forces at work in the larger culture and in American society as a whole. It is a mirror, too, in which we might capture a more complete understanding of ourselves and our nation. In examining the sociology of the everyday, we see a trace of macrosociological forces and processes.

It is my hope that this book continues and extends, in a modest way, a line of inquiry into the subject of black nationalism that goes back to E. U. Essien-Udom, Harold Cruse, Frank Broderick, Edwin Redkey, John Bracey Jr., Elliott Rudwick, August Meier, James Turner, Theodore Draper, Rodney Carlisle, Raymond Hall, Clayborne Carson, Manning Marable, and William Van Deburg, among others. It is intended as a contribution to African American intellectual history and American cultural studies. Furthermore, I have striven to record the story of black student activism at Penn knowing full well that there are those who would regard this topic as too specialized and—frankly—not worthy of serious attention. Too often, in the past, African American history was ignored, neglected, dismissed, and devalued because some people considered it inconsequential. Today, however, African American history is one of the most active and productive fields of historical inquiry.

I acknowledge at the outset the limitations and imperfections of my endeavor. Penn's Policy on Access to Restricted Records states that "generally, all administrative records of the University shall be closed to research for twenty-five years." Furthermore, "no photocopying or other reproduction of restricted records shall be permitted." This has rendered all records from after 1976 unavailable today. Therefore, some areas of my research have not had the benefit of restricted sources.

Despite this constraint, I have endeavored to reconstruct a narrative history of the African American student movement at Penn from 1967 to 1978, with selected relevant episodes from the 1980s. I have made ample use of those primary materials that are accessible at the University of Pennsylvania Archives. I have also used the major student newspaper, *The Daily Pennsylvanian,* and the *Almanac,* which is the university's "journal of record, opinion, and news" for the faculty and administration. University documents, resolutions, reports, and policy statements are routinely published in the *Almanac* for dissemination to the university community and for comment. I have also made use of statements, reports, minutes, and memoranda of the central administration, trustees, University Council, and other university bodies. Penn's alumni magazine and city newspapers, such as *The Philadelphia Inquirer* and *The Philadelphia Tribune,* have also been consulted. In deference to the work of my colleague Jacqueline Wade, who included oral history narratives about black students at Penn in her 1983 dissertation, and that of my friend Rasool Berry and others at Penn, who have been conducting an oral history project about black students, I have not made use of oral history. Despite the absence of this dimension, I hope that my narrative based on the documentary and archival record offers a reasonably faithful reconstruction of events.

What follows is an account of the continuing contest between a vision of an assimilated, monocultural, "color-blind" society that seeks to erase consciousness of difference and a pluralistic society that recognizes and respects difference. As we shall see, the American "melting pot" still has not "melted," and the challenge that this country faces is its inability or unwillingness to accept and respect diversity.

CHRONOLOGY OF THE AFRICAN AMERICAN STUDENT MOVEMENT, 1967–1978

August 1, 1967	McGill Report recommends greater diversity in the composition of the undergraduate student body.
February 1968	Black students urge the chairman of the History Department to create a course in black history.
Spring 1968	George Schlekat is hired as Dean of Admissions, and William Adams is hired to recruit African American students.
April 1968	Two demonstrations follow the assassination of Martin Luther King Jr.
September 1968	Of 125 African Americans accepted for admission, 62 matriculate in September.
Fall 1968	Penn offers a course in black history.
Winter 1968–69	January 1 deadline for submitting admissions application is extended to March for African American students.
February 1969	Science Center sit-in opposes expansion by Penn at expense of nearby African American neighborhood.
March 21, 1969	Provost Goddard appoints a committee to study an academic program in Afro-American life and culture (Rieber Committee).

Spring 1969	Ivy League universities issue joint announcement on record number of African American students accepted and admitted.
September 1969	Of 251 African American students accepted for admission, 150 matriculate.
September 1969	House of the Family is established.
December 11, 1969	Demonstration protests admissions policies and funds for recruitment travel. Figures are burned in effigy.
April 16, 1970	Demonstration is held over Black Pre-Freshman Summer Program and political content of Black Student Orientation Program.
April 23, 1970	Six mysterious fires erupt on campus.
April 24–25, 1970	Overnight, two firebombs are thrown into College Hall.
December 1971	John Edgar Wideman is named as director of the Afro-American Studies Program.
January 1972	John Edgar Wideman begins his first full semester as director of the Afro-American Studies Program, and the program considers 1972 the year of its birth at Penn.
Winter 1972	A student committee led by Cathy Barlow urges creation of a voluntary residence for black students.
April 3, 1972	Black students demonstrate on College Green in support of formation of a residence for black students.
Spring 1972	Minority Recruiting Program (MRP) is established by the Admissions Office.
August 31, 1972	W. E. B. Du Bois College House opens for any undergraduate student of any race who wishes to study and foster Afro-American culture.
September 1972	Dr. Robert Engs begins teaching Afro-American history in the History Department.
September 1974	Dr. Houston Baker begins teaching Afro-American literature in the English Department and serves as director of the Afro-American Studies Program.
May 12, 1976	Demonstration at College Hall and at the meeting of the University Council in the Furness Building opposes proposed policy of limiting admission of students with a Predictive Index of 2.0 or lower to 5 percent of the incoming class.

March 3–6, 1978   Black Student League (BSL) occupies the Franklin Building. Growing out of that occupation, on March 4, 1978, racial minority students form the United Minorities Council as an umbrella organization.

BLACK STUDENTS IN THE IVORY TOWER

INTRODUCTION

DUAL ORGANIZATION ON THE
PREDOMINANTLY WHITE CAMPUS

If there is no struggle, there is no progress. Those who profess to favor freedom, and yet deprecate agitation, are men who want crops without plowing up the ground. They want rain without thunder and lightning. They want the ocean without the awful roar of its many waters. This struggle may be a moral one; or it may be a physical one; or it may be both moral and physical; but it must be a struggle.

—Frederick Douglass, "No Progress without Struggle," 1849

We must recapture our heritage and our identity if we are ever to liberate ourselves from the bonds of white supremacy. We need to launch a cultural revolution to unbrainwash an entire people.

—Malcolm X, "Statement of Basic Aims and Objectives of
the Organization of Afro-American Unity," June 1964

O n the morning of Friday, March 3, 1978, African American students at the University of Pennsylvania, led by the Black Student League (BSL), occupied an administration building called the Franklin Building. This action came a day after white students had seized College Hall, where the offices of the president, the provost, and the dean of the School of Arts and Sciences were located. From the perspective of black students, however, the predominantly white student government and the leaders of the College Hall sit-in seemed reluctant to embrace the grievances of African American students. These included demands for strengthening academic support services for minority students, the hiring of more minority faculty members, and creation of a Third World center. In the occupation of the Franklin Building the BSL asserted its capacity for independent action in the service of its own agenda, apart from the white-dominated student government. To some people, however, it also looked like black "separatism." The seizure of the Franklin Building stands as a symbol of African American student activism and this supposed separatism at the University of Pennsylvania.

It is this "separatism," and its relationship to the Black Power movement, black nationalism, and to questions of integration and assimilation, that is the subject of this book. In a narrow sense what follows is a narrative history of black student activism at Penn, with emphasis on the period from 1967 to 1978. Black Student Unions, by a number of names, exist at many colleges. Indeed, the generic name of an organization for black college students is Black Student Union, or "BSU." This book treats the Black Student League at Penn (and any BSU in general) as a "movement organization."[1]

A second example may illustrate what many people regarded as "separatist" behavior on the part of Penn's black students. In the winter and spring of 1972 African American students there demanded a residence hall for black students. In fact, many (though not all) black students at the time wanted an all-black residence. The demand was couched in the language of the special counseling and psychological needs of minority students, who felt alienated from the overwhelmingly white campus and therefore did not seek out assistance from white resident advisers and assistant deans in advising offices. Penn did not (and legally could not) concede to such a demand. Instead, on August 31, 1972, the university inaugurated a residential "living–learning program," which initially was called the W. E. B. Du Bois Residential Program.[2] Any undergraduate student of any race or ethnicity who was interested in studying and fostering Afro-American culture in a residential setting could apply to live in the program. In theory, any white, Latino, Asian, or Native American undergraduate who wished to live at Du Bois College House could have applied for admission, and over the years a few did.

Most of the students who applied to live at the residence, however, were African American. Critics suggested that it was simply a racially exclusionary residence by another name, cleverly hidden behind the facade of equal access for all who desired it and the mask of an interest in African American culture. Many people (both black and white) asked, "Isn't it ironic that black people struggled for decades to integrate predominantly white universities such as Penn and then, when black students were admitted in significant numbers, they quickly demanded a black residence and voluntarily segregated themselves?"[3] The paradox of the residential program, which eventually became W. E. B. Du Bois College House, certainly confounds our usual understanding of "integration."

A third example illustrates the "separatist" (self-determinationist) orientation of the Black Student League at Penn. This is the experience of Sydney Thornbury, a liberal white student who sought admission to the Black Student League in September 1986. The president of the BSL at that time was Conrad Tillard (now Muhammad), who was a member of the Nation of Islam. Indeed, it is instructive that the members of the BSL the previous spring had knowingly elected a student who was an open and avowed member of the Nation of Islam. The BSL denied Thornbury admission as a full (voting) member, but did reluctantly offer her associate (nonvoting) membership. She then declined to accept what she characterized as "tokenism." It may be inferred that Conrad Muhammad opposed the admission of any white person or non–African American to the BSL. It is critical to point out, however, that Conrad Muhammad was not acting simply on the basis of some personal whim or arbitrary impulse.

Rather, Conrad Muhammad was enforcing the long-established policy and practice of the BSL as an organization. The BSL (called the Society of African and Afro-American Students, or SAAS, until 1971) had excluded non–African Americans from full membership since at least 1967. The denial of full membership to Sydney Thornbury was not a reflection of the "sinister hold" that the Nation of Islam or Conrad Muhammad exercised over a helpless, victimized BSL. Rather, it reflected the decades-old self-determinationist orientation and practice of the organization itself and its active members.

Predictably enough, critics charged the BSL with "reverse racism" and "discrimination against whites," and denounced it for "separatism." Some people asked, "What had the civil rights movement been about if African Americans were going back to the very segregation and exclusion that the Civil Rights Act of 1964 was supposed to have ended?" How was the exclusion of whites from an all-black student union any different from the previous exclusion of blacks from segregated "whites-only" organizations in the past?

To historians familiar with earlier black nationalist leaders and ideologies, it might appear that the behavior of the BSL and many African American students represented a continuation of the ideas of Elijah Muhammad, Malcolm X, Kwame Ture, and the Black Panthers. However, since the mid-1970s avowed black nationalism has been in retreat, and today the discourse of nationalism is not nearly so pronounced as it was in the 1960s. Is the behavior of the BSL and other all-black organizations a reflection of the impact of the Black Power movement and black nationalism? Is the behavior separatist? How does one reconcile this seemingly separatist behavior and "voluntary self-segregation" with the civil rights movement? How should we understand what happened to the dream of "integration"? Rhetorically, some people have asked, "What happened to the traditional civil rights movement and where did it go wrong? What happened to the dream of a 'color-blind' society?"

The Black "Cultural Revolution"

As suggested by William Van Deburg, I believe that the direct answer to this question is that, *for many African Americans the underlying assumptions of the civil rights movement were challenged, eclipsed, and superseded by a cultural revolution,* which grew out of a series of movements described variously as Black Power, black nationalism, black pride, black consciousness, the Black Arts movement, and the Black Aesthetic.[4] This book examines the impact of that cultural revolution and ideological "paradigm-shift" on black students at Penn.

In the early 1960s the civil rights movement, most closely identified with the charismatic leadership of Martin Luther King Jr., won important victories. The movement, with support from liberal and moderate white allies, brought an end to formal, state-sponsored segregation and disenfranchisement. The process of dismantling these artificial barriers to equal access to public schools and places of public accommodation, employment, and housing has been called desegregation, or sometimes "integration." The boycotts, sit-ins, freedom rides, and marches (such as those at Birmingham) led to the Civil Rights Act of 1964. It ended legalized segregation in the public schools and universities and places of public accommodation. It banned discrimination on the basis of race and sex in employment and unions, or in any program that received federal funds. The Voting Rights Act of 1965 ended disenfranchisement by means of the literacy test and other "devices." The Twenty-Fourth Amendment, ratified in 1964, ended the use of the poll tax in federal (congressional and presidential) elections, and in 1966, in the case of *Harper v. Virginia Board of Elections,* the Supreme Court declared state poll tax requirements for voting in state elections to be unconstitutional as well. The Fair Housing Act of 1968 forbade discrimination on the basis of race in the sale, rental, and financing of housing.

Yet even as the traditional interracial civil rights movement was coming to its peak between 1965 and 1968, the black "ghettos" exploded and burned. The discourse of "integration," which sought to erase consciousness of difference, was challenged by the vocabulary of black nationalism and black pride. This discourse demanded consciousness of difference, pride in difference, and respect for difference. It rejected assimilation and the goal of eradicating consciousness of difference. In 1964, Malcolm X formed the Organization of Afro-American Unity and (re)articulated the philosophy of black nationalism. He called for a "cultural revolution" as a necessary step toward black liberation."[5] In June 1966, Kwame Ture (Stokely Carmichael) and Willie Ricks enunciated the phrase "Black Power," and Ture and Charles V. Hamilton published the book *Black Power* in 1967. In October 1966 the Black Panthers were formed.

In Newark, New Jersey, in the late 1960s, Amiri Baraka carried the message of the Black Arts movement to the masses. Baraka also sought to join cultural awareness with political power in an effort to elect a black mayor in Newark. In 1968 Don L. Lee (Haki Madhubuti) published a book entitled *Black Pride*. Hoyt Fuller edited *The Black World,* and in 1972 Addison Gayle and Hoyt Fuller proclaimed the "Black Aesthetic." Meanwhile James Brown proclaimed "I'm black and I'm proud," and a younger generation of "Negroes" declared that they were now "black" and "black is beautiful." These developments signaled a cultural and psychological revolution taking place in the hearts and minds of a younger generation of African Americans.[6] Above all else, this "revolution" rejected the earlier sense of shame and stigma attached to blackness and to African ancestry, and it involved a rejection of the goal of assimilation (into the melting pot of Anglo-conformity).[7] It also involved a rejection of the goal of "color-blindness" or eradication of the consciousness of difference, in favor of pride in difference and positive consciousness of difference (hence the terms "black consciousness" and "race consciousness"). The black cultural revolution was a profound shift (or about-face) in attitudes.

The development of Black Power, black nationalism, black consciousness, the Black Arts movement, and the Black Aesthetic in the 1960s and 1970s has been well told by authors such as Clayborne Carson, Manning Marable, Rodney Carlisle, Robert L. Allen, Raymond Hall, and William Van Deburg, among others, and there is little need to recapitulate it in detail here.[8] Likewise, I assume that readers are sufficiently familiar with the concept of black nationalism that I do not need to define it exhaustively.[9] It may be sufficient to say that one of the foremost authorities on the subject of black nationalism is Nigerian scholar E. U. Essien-Udom. In 1964 he offered a concise definition:

The concept of nationalism . . . may be thought of as the belief of a group that it possesses, or *ought to possess,* a country; that it shares, or *ought* to share, a common heritage of language, culture and religion; and that its heritage, way of life, and ethnic identity are distinct from those of other groups. Nationalists believe that they *ought* to rule themselves and shape their own destinies, and that they *should* therefore be in control of their social, economic, and political institutions. Such beliefs among American Negroes . . . are here called black nationalism [emphasis added].[10]

This definition captures much of the black nationalist idea and of the aspiration of black people to achieve self-determination and control over their own destiny—to be free of white domination and control. The flowering of black nationalism in the 1960s was reminiscent of a similar upwelling of black nationalism and black pride in the 1920s, most closely associated with the mass movement of Marcus Garvey, except that Garvey was an emigrationist who advocated a return to Africa. Few nationalists in the 1960s proposed this. The black nationalist resurgence of the 1960s was represented by organizations such as the Nation of Islam, Organization of Afro-American Unity, Congress of Racial Equality (CORE), Student Nonviolent Coordinating Committee (SNCC), Republic of New Africa (RNA), Revolutionary Action Movement (RAM), the Black Panthers, and Dodge Revolutionary Union Movement (DRUM), among others.

The prominent nationalist (or near-nationalist) activists of the 1960s and early 1970s included the Honorable Elijah Muhammad, Malcolm X, Kwame Ture, Floyd McKissick, Roy Innis, H. Rap Brown, James Forman, Courtland Cox, Richard Henry (Imari Abubakari Obadele), Milton Henry (Gaidi Obadele), Bobby Seale, Huey Newton, Eldridge Cleaver, Bobby Hutton, David Hilliard, Cleveland Sellers, Fred Hampton, Mark Clark, Angela Davis, Elaine Brown, and Maulana Karenga, among many others. The black nationalist organizations and ideologies included a multiplicity of ideas, including territorial, revolutionary, and cultural nationalism. For example, Elijah Muhammad, an advocate of territorial nationalism, argued that the descendants of the slaves must be separated from the descendents of the slavemasters, "in a state or territory of our own—either on this continent or elsewhere."[11] The most fully developed territorial nationalist idea was embodied in the Republic of New Africa, which was more specific about its goals and sought to create a sovereign, independent African American nation–state consisting of South Carolina, Georgia, Alabama, Mississippi, and Louisiana. This was true, full-blown, literal separatism, and it would entail a partition of the United States into a white nation and a black nation.[12] Avowed "revolutionary nationalists" such as the Black Panthers combined black nationalism with socialism and the desire for the overthrow of American capitalism and imperialism. According to Huey Newton and George Jackson, the attainment of these goals might require "revolutionary suicide" and urban guerrilla warfare.[13]

Historically, black nationalism has expressed itself in an almost infinite number of varieties. Martin Delany, writing in 1852, said of black people in America: "We are a nation within a nation; as the Poles in Russia, the Hungarians in Austria; the Welsh, Irish and Scotch in the British Dominions."[14] For others, in the 1960s, African Americans comprised a colonized nation or an abducted, captive, submerged, imprisoned, or projected nation. For still others, African Americans were a chosen people or covenant community for whom Jesus had been a black messiah, and they would be sustained by black religious nationalism or liberation theology.[15] These ideas were articulated by men such as Albert Cleage, who established the Shrine of the Black Madonna in Detroit, and James Cone, the author of *Black Theology and Black Power* (1969), *A Black Theology of Liberation* (1970), and *God of the Oppressed* (1975). Throughout black America the paintings of a white Jesus were taken down and replaced by pictures of a black Jesus. The Honorable Elijah Muhammad, in his version of the idea of a chosen people, said, "Furthermore, we believe we are the people of God's choice, as it is written, that God would choose the rejected and the despised. We can find no other persons fitting this description in these last days more than the so-called Negroes in America."[16]

Maulana Karenga, founder of the African American cultural holiday of Kwanzaa, emphasized that African people in the United States were a *cultural* nation. He said that a cultural revolution and psychological rehabilitation with a "cultural revolution," and a change of consciousness and identity among oppressed people must precede the conquest of state power or any political revolution.[17] He concluded that "the need is for a cultural revolution which would break the monopoly the oppressor has on Black minds and begin to rescue and reconstruct Black history and humanity in their own image and interests."[18] Karenga was one of the foremost proponents of black cultural nationalism. Hereafter, when I use the term "black nationalism," I am referring to all of these strands of thought *collectively* and the manifold variations and permutations upon the theme of a black nation in some form or sense of that word.

Kwame Ture insisted that black people in the United States were members of an internal or domestic colony and that their greatest need was to achieve power over the circumstances of their own lives. The Black Power movement (and black nationalism) emphasized the desire of African American people to achieve group self-determination and freedom from control and domination by whites. In their wish to control their own destiny, black Americans wanted control over their own neighborhoods and communities, and the institutions (schools, fire and police departments, businesses, political structures) within their communities. Ture insisted that where black people were the majority, they wanted to use that power to exercise control. Where they were not the majority, they wanted proper representation and a proportional share of political and economic power.[19] A corollary of this would be black capitalism, with blacks creating businesses and generating employment for their own people within their own neighborhoods. It would also imply group solidarity in voting, with blacks voting for black candidates. In *Black Power,* Ture declared "Black Power recognizes . . . the ethnic basis of American politics as well as the power-oriented nature of American politics."[20] Further, he and Hamilton said that "before a group can enter the open society, it must first close ranks."[21] Moreover, they asserted that "the American pot has not melted. Italians vote for Rubino over O'Brien; Irish for Murphy over Goldberg, etc. This phenomenon may seem distasteful to some, but it has been and remains today a central fact of the American political system."[22]

Ture also stressed the need for African Americans to create, lead, and control their own communal organizations and associations. However, the demand that black people should establish their own racially (or ethnically) exclusive in-group clubs, caucuses, and associations was perceived as racial "separatism" and exclusion of whites.

It was also possible to view African Americans as a national minority, whose distinctive sense of identity was analogous in some ways to that of regional or national minorities such as Alsatians, Corsicans, Bretons, Basques, or Frisians in Western Europe; or Sikhs in Pubjab in India; or Slovenes in the former Yugoslavia, Slovaks in the former Czechoslovakia, or "Ruthenians" in pre–World War I Hungary. The identities of Eritreans in Ethiopia or of the Dinka in Sudan might offer African parallels. Frequently, people in peripheral areas (such as the American South) that have functioned as "internal colonies" and experienced delayed or uneven development in the process of industrialization come to perceive themselves as "national minorities." African Americans might be thought of as an historically subordinated group, with the ghettos as internal colonies in the North. Because the South was for so long the semicolonial "periphery" relative to the Northern industrial "core," and an American internal colony, African Americans in the South were the colony within the colony. The mass migration of Southern blacks to the North in the twentieth century brought a distinctive racial and regional group (and national minority) into the core as a superexploited proletariat.[23] Racial and ethnic identity were reinforced by economic stratification and residential discrimination. Walker Connor points out that Western scholars have repeatedly confused the terms "nation" and "state," and referred to "nationalism" as devotion to the state, when nationalism correctly refers to the sense of loyalty that one feels to the ethnic group into which one is born (*nasci*). Black nationalism is a sense of identity based on birth and membership within the black American ethnic group, and is a form of ethnonationalism. As such, however, it stands in contrast to the sense of allegiance to the country or state (the United States), the *patrie*.[24]

Cumulatively, the spread of the race-conscious philosophy of Black Power ideology, the idea of community control, and various forms of black nationalism represented a generational break with an older understanding of "integration." The older conception had emphasized individuals (rather than groups) and sought to obliterate or minimize consciousness of race, ethnicity, religion, and group identity in the melting pot of America. It believed that "equality" required the erasure of difference.

The Battleground of Culture

Furthermore, reaching beyond the boundaries of Black Power and black nationalism, a substantial portion of the younger generation of the 1960s shared the belief in a distinctive African American culture with roots in the African ancestral past and slavery. This belief gave rise to the celebration of "soul" and was reflected in the Black Arts movement, most closely associated with Amiri Baraka and novelists, playwrights, and poets such as John Oliver Killens, Larry Neal, Don L. Lee (Haki Madhubuti), Joseph Walker, Ed Bullins, Blyden Jackson, Askia Muhammad Toure, Julian Mayfield (in exile in Ghana), Gil Scott-Heron, the "Last Poets," Sonia Sánchez and Nikki Giovanni, and songstress Nina Simone. In 1971 Addison Gayle edited *The Black Aesthetic*, and Hoyt Fuller, Larry Neal, and George Kent also sought to delineate what this "aesthetic" was or ought to be. Indeed, as William Van Deburg has argued, the cultural legacy of the black nationalist–Black Power–Black Aesthetic-Black Arts movements succeeded in producing a cultural and psychological revolution that reached far beyond the domain of political doctrine and organizational membership.[25] Many African Americans who might have been skeptical of the ideology of black nationalism nevertheless absorbed the messages of black consciousness, black pride, and belief in a distinctive black American culture. Precisely as Van Deburg has suggested, millions of African Americans embraced the distinctive black music of jazz, blues, black gospel, rhythm and blues, and the "Motown" sound. Southern "soul" food cuisine became enormously popular, and the "Afro" hair style became another symbol of black distinctiveness.[26]

Despite personality conflicts, factional infighting, and differences of ideological emphasis, the proponents of Black Power, black nationalism, and the Black Arts movement shared at least two things in common. First, they all rejected Martin Luther King's tactic of unconditional nonviolence in favor of Malcolm X's dictum that black people had a *human* right to defend themselves against attack, and that black people would only be nonviolent with people who were nonviolent with them.

Second, the black nationalists, the Black Arts activists, and the proponents of Black Power, all rejected the then-prevailing notion that black Americans had no culture of their own. Until his death in 1962, E. Franklin Frazier had promoted this idea. In the mid-1960s, Nathan Glazer, Daniel Patrick Moynihan, Norman Podhoretz, and Bennett Berger reiterated this concept. Bristling with indignation, the ideologists of Black Power, black nationalism, and the Black Arts movement insisted that African Americans *did* have a distinctive culture, ethos, or aesthetic of their own that was different from that of white, European Americans. This difference was difficult to define: intangible, but rooted in the mysteries of the sorrow songs, the "Negro" spirituals, jazz, blues, gospel, and the oral tradition. Sometimes it was called "soul." In this context, Raymond Hall has argued that, "cultural nationalism asserts that black people have distinctive culture, life-styles, values, philosophy, etc. which are essentially different from those of white people."[27] Some authors have attempted to explain this ethos in philosophical terms, as a contrast between the (supposed) collective, communal, humanistic values of ancestral Africa and the individualistic, competitive, materialistic values of the capitalist West. Others attribute the difference to essentialist biological causes (such as the ability of the body to produce melanin as opposed to albinism) or the impact of climate (evolving in a warm, abundant region as opposed to the harsh Arctic wastes of Ice-Age Eurasia).[28] Nevertheless, whatever the origin and nature of this elusive quality or ethos, the advocates of Black Power, black nationalism, and the Black Arts movement regarded this distinctive culture as positive, valuable, and worthy of preservation.[29]

Accordingly, these groups rejected the goal of assimilation (acculturation) into the melting pot of Anglo-conformity.[30] Quite the contrary, they heaped scorn on the notion of the "superiority" and "universality" of Western, white, European-centered culture. They criticized the dominant white culture as sterile, materialistic, exploitative, and imperialistic. Consequently, the Black Power movement and black nationalism were oppositional to assimilation and can be characterized as counter-assimilationist.[31] Whereas some of the proponents of the civil rights movement advocated assimilation and the *obliteration of consciousness of difference* as the road to "equality," Black Power insisted upon pride in difference and identity, and hence the *continued consciousness of difference.*

In the late 1960s the adherents of Black Power, black nationalism, and black cultural distinctiveness also came to reject older notions of a society composed of atomistic individuals detached from race, ethnicity, and other "particularistic" group attributes and characteristics. Instead, they perceived America as a society of racial and ethnic *groups,* and (often competing) interest groups, who possessed differing degrees of power, privilege, and advantage. This recognition of group pluralism and cultural pluralism, articulated quite forcefully by Kwame Ture, convinced a generation of young African Americans that black people in the United States needed to perceive themselves as, and needed to act and organize themselves as, a self-conscious interest group. In other words, there was a realization that African Americans did not constitute simply a group-*in*-itself but needed to become a group-*for*-itself.[32]

The challenge of integration, then, became that of ameliorating inequities among groups. This in turn implied nothing less than a new social contract and the question of power sharing. Many African Americans who were not self-described nationalists or advocates of Black Power shared this perspective of group and cultural pluralism. The crucial divide, therefore, became that between black pluralists and nationalists on the one side and black assimilationists (Anglo-conformists) on the other.[33] The perception of group interest was at odds with the underlying assumption of the traditional civil rights movement that America was a society in which rights inhere in individuals only.

Cumulatively, Black Power, black nationalism, and the Black Arts movement created a black cultural and psychological revolution, and a profound "paradigm-shift." This revolution was the total of Black Power, black nationalism, black consciousness, black pride, the Black Aesthetic, the Black Arts movement, black Christian nationalism, liberation theology, and religious nationalism. These developments should be understood as a cluster or constellation, as a gestalt, rather than as random, even contradictory strands without an underlying reason or unifying logic. Fundamentally, it was an expression of the desire for "group self-determination,"[34] and it constituted a revolt against assimilation and white supremacy. In a sense, then, the group pluralist and counterassimilationist assumptions of Black Power and the black cultural revolution of the 1960s collided head-on with the individualistic and assimilationist assumptions of the older civil rights movement. The Black Power revolution assumed a posture of race consciousness. The civil rights movement traditionally had articulated a nonracial vision of a society of individuals, without races or beyond race. This seemed to be a vision of the *erasure* of difference and the *consciousness* of difference. These two very different visions of "integration" were incompatible, and when advocates of Black Power and advocates of nonracial integration spoke the language of "integration," they simply talked past each other. Their conceptions of American society after the dismantling of de jure segregation were very different.

The Impact of Black Power Ideology on Black Students

Thus far I have described the contours of the black cultural revolution at an ideological and national level. But the paradigm-shift taking place nationally was reflected in parallel developments among African Americans and especially African American college students at the local level. In particular, for the discussion at hand, Black Power, black nationalism, and the cultural revolution influenced African American students at the University of Pennsylvania. Not only did they read the literature of Black Power–black nationalism and the Black Aesthetic and Black Arts movement, and not only did they hear about if secondhand, but four prominent expositors of the "revolution" actually came to Penn between 1967 and 1969 and transmitted their message personally. These four individuals were Dick Gregory, Floyd McKissick, Muhammad Ali, and Amiri Baraka. On later occasions Kwame Ture spoke at Penn, and Sonia Sánchez and Askia Muhammad Toure read their poetry on campus. Therefore, the link or mode of transmission between black nationalism and black students at Penn need not be a matter of speculation and conjecture. It was quite direct.

After 1967 black students at Penn demanded that race and disadvantage be taken into consideration in admissions decisions and that a certain percentage of black students be admitted to each freshman class. They formed a student organization, initially called the Society of African and Afro-American Students (SAAS) and later called the Black Student League (BSL) that, in practice, seemed to permit full voting membership only to African Americans while also providing for a (rarely if ever used) category of nonvoting associate membership (presumably for non–African Americans).

African American students also initiated a pattern of "dual organization," with parallel black organizations alongside "white" (nominally desegregated) campus organizations. They formed numerous undergraduate black clubs, caucuses, and preprofessional organizations, such as the Black Wharton[35] Undergraduate Association, Society of Black Engineers, Black Pre-Law Society, and Black Pre-Health Society. They formed campus or local chapters of historically black Greek-letter fraternities and sororities, such as Alpha Phi Alpha, Omega Psi Phi, Kappa Alpha Psi, Alpha Kappa Alpha (AKA), Delta Sigma Theta, and Zeta Phi Beta. They also formed a chapter of Groove Phi Groove Social Fellowship. Eventually there would be a black Bible study group and a gospel choir. By 1978–79, Ralph Murray and other black students were attempting to establish their own newspaper on campus, and ultimately there was a minority newspaper called *The Voice*, succeeded later by *The Vision*.[36]

At the graduate and professional level, a Black M.B.A. Association, Black Law Students Association, Black Medical Students Association, a local chapter of the Alliance of Black Social Work Students, and the campuswide Black Graduate and Professional Student Association emerged. In time, Mexican American, Puerto Rican, Japanese American, Chinese American, Korean American, Caribbean American, and other "racial minority" students formed similar ethnic or cultural organizations. This pattern of "dual organization" is striking because the individuals involved certainly were seeking to achieve upward mobility and had not rejected the American system. Indeed, they were striving to compete and participate successfully within it.

As some might expect, critics of this pattern of "dual organization" asked, "Why had black students elected to come to Penn if they were not willing to integrate with whites and assimilate?" If African American students wanted a black environment, why hadn't they chosen to attend Howard or Fisk or Morehouse or Spelman? As for Du Bois College House, critics asked how black students could insist on attending a predominantly white school and then recoil from close association with whites (such as living with them as roommates) by demanding a separate black residence hall on that very campus? Weren't they trying to have it both ways? Wasn't a separate "black" dormitory simply a matter of "voluntary segregation"?

Although some might decry this pervasive pattern of "dual organization" as "separatism," I will argue that it is better understood as group and cultural pluralism and reflects the desire of African American students to achieve a measure of autonomy.[37] Van Deburg has argued, most persuasively, that African Americans tend to fall into three groups: These are assimilationists, pluralists, and nationalists.[38] The African American students at Penn who participated in these organizations certainly were not assimilationists, but neither were they most often really separatists. Rather, informed by the perspective of Black Power, black nationalism, and the Black Aesthetic, these students were *pluralists*. They were *bicultural.* They were not seeking to withdraw from American society into permanent isolationist sects or enclaves such as the Amish or Hutterites. They were not actively seeking to secede from the United States and partition the country into a white country and an independent black nation–state (which is what territorial nationalists and genuine separatists did seek and still do seek). Nor were they seeking the overthrow of capitalism through revolutionary suicide or urban guerrilla warfare, as described by Huey Newton or George Jackson.

Rather, they were seeking to create their own in-group communal associations, similar to ethnic group associations, while also participating in the life of the larger campus and society. The purpose of their (ethnically or racially) homogeneous organizations was not to withdraw from society altogether but to organize a power base from which to enter the mainstream as a self-conscious *group-for-itself* and compete from a position of group strength. In effect, they wanted *both* a communal space of their own and participation in the larger campus. Again, this is not separatism, but rather biculturalism and group pluralism.

Nor was this remarkably different from what white students at Penn were doing. In the 1990s, for example, the Student Activities Council at Penn also listed numerous student organizations whose membership was based on ethnicity or some other aspect of identity. They included the German Club, Irish Club, *Jewish Quarterly*, Lesbian, Gay and Bisexual Alliance, Muslim Students Association, Penn Christian Fellowship, Scottish Society, Society of Women Engineers, Wharton Asian Association, and Penn Women's Alliance, among many others, as "recognized" organizations at the University. The existence of these groups reflects the ethnic, religious, cultural, and international diversity that one ought to expect at a world-class institution of higher learning.[39] Essentially, because Penn was such a large, impersonal, bureaucratic campus (by the mid-1970s entering classes were as large as 1,800 students, and there were 7,000 doctoral, medical, law, M.B.A., veterinary, dental, and engineering graduate students), white students, too, found it necessary *to create their own sense of community and belonging*—hence the proliferation of affinity groups.

Furthermore, even as African American students were vigorously expressing their desire for group self-determination and communal autonomy, they were also participating in the wider life of the predominantly white campus. Hence, black students also participated in the undergraduate student government, called the Undergraduate Assembly, and the Student Activities Council. In 1990 one African American student, Miriam "Duchess" Harris, was elected chairperson of the Undergraduate Assembly. Some black students joined the Philomathean Society (the leading campus literary society), and others wrote for the major campus student newspaper, *The Daily Pennsylvanian*. Viewed in totality, therefore, the prevailing pattern of dual organization reflects not genuine separatism but traditional patterns of group and cultural pluralism and biculturalism.

The "Hidden" Tradition of Self-Determination and Pluralism

It is also crucial to note that this pattern of in-group self-organization by African Americans is not new, but can be documented back as far as 1787, when Richard Allen and Absalom Jones formed the Free African Society in Philadelphia, and Prince Hall established the first black Masonic order in the United States in Boston.[40] In 1794 Richard Allen established the Bethel African Methodist Episcopal Church in Philadelphia, the "mother" church of the separate, independent, black A.M.E. denomination. Separate, independent black Baptist churches preceded even Richard Allen and seem to date back as far as George Liele and David George at Silver Bluff, South Carolina, about 1773.[41] Andrew Bryan established the First African Baptist Church in Savannah, Georgia, in 1788. Although some people might say that the separate black church was formed under conditions of forced segregation and exclusion or discrimination by whites, after two hundred years, "separation" has become the "normal" condition of the black church.

In the 1820s, African Americans such as John Russwurm and Samuel Cornish established their own newspapers, and the independent black press (joined more recently by radio, television, and cable companies) continues to this day. In the 1840s, African Americans held the Negro Conventions. In the 1850s, black nationalists such as Henry Highland Garnet, Martin Delany,[42] and Samuel Ringgold Ward were at the height of their popularity. In the late nineteenth century, African Americans chose to establish separate black towns such as Mound Bayou, Boley, and Langston in Mississippi and Oklahoma.[43]

Since the 1770s and 1780s African Americans have always had dual organization, in the form of their own autonomous churches, newspapers, lodges, and benevolence and mutual aid societies. Even before the Civil War there were Free African schools, and after the Civil War the historically black colleges were created. And W. E. B. Du Bois, while tirelessly condemning legalized segregation, was not an assimilationist. Instead, he held that black Americans had a unique culture of their own and should maintain their own separate in-group schools, churches, and institutions. He was a pluralist.[44] Thus, it can be argued that group self-organization is actually a deep, enduring tradition within the African American community, and that African American students who created dual organizations on college campuses in the 1960s and 1970s were simply rediscovering and reconnecting with the imperatives of their organic folk tradition. This is even clearer if one views African Americans as an ethnic group (as well as part of a transoceanic racial group), or as members of a national minority, in which case African Americans are simply pursuing ethnic (and national minority) group self-determination.

I conclude that African American people are not drawn together only or simply as a "necessary evil" imposed by enforced segregation and exclusion from white institutions. Rather, they are often drawn together by a positive force of attraction called *affinity*, wherein they identify with one another and delight in one another's company simply for the sake and the pleasure of the interaction itself. This group affinity possesses a quality of "given-ness," as "already always *having been*" or "having existed."[45] Unfortunately, some people seem unable to recognize or understand this affinity, and unable or unwilling to distinguish between segregation as *enforced association* imposed on black people by an external group (the dominant white culture) and an association that is voluntary and chosen and based on affinity.

Furthermore, it is crucial to point out that African American students who participated in dual organizations or lived at Du Bois College House were not forced to do so. They voluntarily chose to do so, because they wanted to do so. It is paramount to understand the difference between being compelled to inhabit a world circumscribed by the boundaries of inherited race, ethnicity, or even religion (the religion of one's parents), and inhabiting a domain of race, ethnicity, religion, or class because one has chosen and prefers to do so. Previous generations of European immigrants may have found that the way to achieve upward mobility and "acceptance" in American society was to embrace Anglo-conformity by assimilating into the dominant Anglo-Saxon culture and relinquishing group distinctiveness and differentiating ethnic or religious origins. Under such conditions, communal background was—for some—a shackle from which they wished to have the choice of escaping by "passing" as Anglo-Saxon or as culturally assimilated.

On the other hand, many European immigrants have refused to surrender their distinctiveness, especially in the matter of religion. This is quite evident on the part of Irish, Polish, and Italian Catholics who refused to convert to Protestantism and even created their own parochial schools. It is also notable among observant Jews. I do not wish to convey the misimpression that all immigrants, even among European immigrants, have chosen to "assimilate."

African Americans, thus far, have largely refused to pay the price of assimilation in exchange for "acceptance" and the attainment of upward mobility. In pursuing the pattern of dual organization, African American students at Penn were rediscovering and reconnecting with a deep tradition of independent organization. But it is an open question whether this tradition of communal group self-organization, which might sometimes be a form of *ethnic* group self-organization, should be characterized as "nationalism." Is the quest for ethnic group self-determination equivalent to nationalism? Nevertheless, as Robert Allen has argued, "Black nationalism is an ever-present but usually latent or unarticulated tendency, particularly among blacks who find themselves at the lower rungs of the socio-economic ladder. The members of this class traditionally exhibit a sense of group solidarity because of the open hostility of the surrounding white society."[46] Furthermore, Allen has suggested:

When white society appears to shut the door on integration . . . the black bourgeoisie responds by adopting a nationalist stance. Like a child refused a stick of candy which it knew belonged to it by right, the black bourgeoisie rejects the white world and flouts its blackness. It becomes loudly nationalist and threatens to rain destruction on the offending whites. Conferences are called, manifestos issued, and delegations are dispatched to confer with African leaders.[47]

This might be partially true of African American ethnic identity as well. Historically, then, the black middle class has been ambivalent and has oscillated between assimilation and nationalism. And ethnic or cultural pluralism has been a third path that, implicitly, has been there "all along," although "latent" in the sense that it was little noticed.

Structure of the Book

In the succeeding chapters I apply William Van Deburg's model of a cultural revolution and the "Black Power paradigm-shift" to a study of black student activism at the University of Pennsylvania from 1967 to 1990, with greatest emphasis on the years from 1967 to 1978. Admittedly, the concepts of a black cultural revolution, the Black Power paradigm-shift, and the tripartite distinction among assimilationism, pluralism, and nationalism are not new, and I acknowledge my indebtedness to scholars such as William Van Deburg, Harold Cruse, and Jacqueline Wade.[48] The use and application of these concepts, however, to document and interpret black student activism and the black student "movement" at Penn, longitudinally, from 1967 to 1990, is *new* and is the intended original contribution of this book.

Such a cultural and ideological revolt challenges American society to understand integration as a process that involves the adjustment of relationships among groups and not only detached individuals. The events at Penn were not unique, as similar accounts could come from other universities. In documenting the black cultural revolution at Penn, however, we are looking into a mirror that can provide important insights into the forces at work in the larger American society over the last thirty-five years.

CHAPTER ONE

TO OPEN THE DOORS OF OPPORTUNITY

Men make their own history, but they do not make it just as they please; they do not make it under circumstances chosen by themselves, but under circumstances directly found, given and transmitted from the past.

—Karl Marx, *The Eighteenth Brumaire of Louis Napoleon*, 1852

We make our history ourselves, but, in the first place, under very definite assumptions and conditions.

—Friedrich Engels to Joseph Bloch, 1890

Between 1964 and 1968 the civil rights movement reached its climax. In this period the Civil Rights Act of 1964, the Voting Rights Act of 1965, and the Fair Housing Act of 1968 were passed. African Americans and their progressive white allies demanded "integration" in the North as well as the South. They demanded that nominally integrated institutions in the North, too, "must do more" to bring about greater inclusion and participation of black people in such heretofore overwhelmingly white institutions as universities, faculties, unions, corporations, neighborhoods, police and fire departments, and newsrooms. Penn had not been officially segregated, inasmuch as it had admitted its first African American students in 1879, but in the early 1960s fewer than forty African Americans matriculated each year. Thus, it was still an overwhelmingly white institution.

Amid the growing clamor for a greater degree of integration in the "unsegregated" North, and greater equality as an outcome and not simply as a theoretical opportunity, in the mid-1960s Penn took two steps in that direction. First, it entered into a cooperative relationship with Morgan State University.

This cooperative relationship was known as the Morgan State College–University of Pennsylvania Project and began as an exchange of faculty. In 1968 it was broadened to include the exchange of students. Next, more dramatically, in 1967–68 Penn revised its undergraduate admissions policies to recognize "diversity" in the composition of the freshman class as an explicit goal of the admissions process. Henceforth, in the regular admissions process, the "subjective" factor of diversity would be balanced with and against "objective" (quantifiable) factors such as performance on standardized tests. Between 1967 and 1968 the number of African American undergraduates rose from forty to sixty-two, and for the class entering in September 1969 the number of black undergraduate matriculants had *doubled* from sixty-two the previous year to one hundred and fifty, an historic and unprecedented increase.

The First Generations of African American Students

The beginnings of the African American "presence" or community at Penn date back to 1879, when the first African American students at the University of Pennsylvania were enrolled. Of the four students, the first to graduate was James Brister, who received a degree in dentistry (D.D.S.) in 1881. Other schools and disciplines at the university graduated their first black students soon thereafter: for example, Medicine in 1882, the College in 1883, Engineering in 1887, Wharton in 1887, and Law in 1888.[1] From 1900 to 1920 only seven African Americans appear in Penn yearbooks as seniors.[2] Another of the early African American graduates of Penn was Julian Abele, the first black graduate of the Department of Architecture (1902). He helped to design Irvine Auditorium and Eisenlohr Hall on the Penn campus, but the most famous building he participated in designing is the Philadelphia Museum of Art. Sadly to say, however, tens of thousands of people from all over the world come to view the museum each year, and most of them never realize that an African American architect collaborated in its design.

Still another of the early black graduates from Penn was Sadie Tanner Mossell Alexander, niece of the famous black artist, Henry O. Tanner. She received her B.S. in education in 1918, a Ph.D. in economics in 1921, and a law degree (LL.B.) in 1927. She was the first black woman to receive a law degree at Penn. Her husband, Raymond Pace Alexander, was a 1920 graduate of the Wharton School, who had attended Harvard Law School. This generation of African American students often experienced prejudice and discrimination. They could not enter the cafeteria with white students, and local establishments did not serve blacks. Provost Edgar Fahs Smith insisted he was powerless to force local businesses to serve blacks, or to make them "off limits" to Penn students because of their discrimination. Nor had he the budget to provide an alternative campus setting that would serve or accommodate blacks and other students. Therefore, Sadie Mossell and Virginia Alexander (sister of Raymond Pace Alexander) ate their lunch at a long table under the stairs of the library in the historic Furness Building.[3]

Furthermore, some of the racism that African American students experienced in the early decades of the nineteenth century seems to have been institutional. As Marvin Lyon Jr. has shown, a prime example is the experience of Willis D. Cummings. Cummings was an alumnus of Fisk, who graduated from Penn with a D.D.S. in 1919 and ran track and cross-country for Penn from 1918 to 1920. He was the first black team captain at Penn and in the Ivy League. In the "lily-white" photograph of the cross-country team in the Yearbook of 1918, however, team captain Cummings and the other black members did not appear. Supposedly, this "white-out" was due to the "war."[4]

Moreover, Cummings earned a second letter for cross-country while doing graduate work at Penn in 1920. Mysteriously, it was "lost in the records" until 1935. In addition, when Dr. Cummings graduated from the Dental School, sixth in a class of 259, and became the first black member of a national dental society in 1919, he was not even invited to the dinner at which membership certificates were distributed. This "oversight" was not corrected until 1972.[5] Belatedly, in 1980, as Penn celebrated the centennial of the admission of African American students to the University, Dean of the Dental School D. Walter Cohen honored Dr. Willis Cummings at an annual dinner for faculty, alumni, and students.[6]

The number of African American students at Penn remained small until the late sixties. Earlier, Rhodes scholar John Edgar Wideman was a student at Penn (Class of 1963), and he has written about the sense of isolation and alienation that came from being one of a handful of blacks at a white university.[7] Black students in general found themselves in an environment that was often indifferent and sometimes hostile to them.

Although it is not well known, Penn has a connection to the careers of two other famous African Americans. One was W. E. B. Du Bois, the other Martin Luther King Jr. In 1896, Susan P. Wharton and members of the settlement movement in Philadelphia thought a study of African Americans in the City of Philadelphia would be of help to them. She sought the aid of Provost Charles C. Harrison and Samuel McCune Lindsay of the Sociology

Department. Lindsay asked W. E. B. Du Bois to conduct the survey, and in 1896, as an "assistant in sociology" at Penn, he interviewed African Americans in the Seventh Ward of the city. His work is often regarded as the first sociological study conducted in the United States, and it was published by the University of Pennsylvania in 1899 as *The Philadelphia Negro*.[8] While Martin Luther King Jr. was a student at the Crozer Theological Seminary in Chester, Pennsylvania, he audited three graduate classes in philosophy at Penn, including a class on the philosophy of history, taught by Professor Elizabeth Flower, in 1949–50. The course covered such thinkers as Giambattista Vico, Johann Herder, Karl Marx, Herbert Spencer, Georg Hegel, Oswald Spengler, Karl Mannheim, and Max Weber. In fall 1950, King took a course on Immanuel Kant, taught by Professor Paul Schrecker, and "Problems of Esthetics," taught by Professor John S. Adams. The class taught by Professor Flower met in Bennett Hall, and, accordingly, a plaque in King's honor is to be found in that building today. King received his bachelor's degree in divinity from Crozer Theological Seminary in 1951.

The civil rights movement emphasized the need to dismantle the artificial barriers of race in public life, and in 1965 the administration at Penn made an effort to add diversity to the curriculum and the faculty. As Penn had practically no black faculty members in the School of Arts and Sciences at that time, one way to bring black faculty to the campus to be accessible to undergraduate students would be to "borrow" them from an institution that did have black faculty. A cooperative relationship between Penn and Morgan State College in Baltimore, Maryland, was formalized in May 1965 with an agreement between President Gaylord Harnwell of Penn and President Martin Jenkins of Morgan. The Cooperative Program was funded through a grant from the Department of Health, Education and Welfare (HEW), under Title III of the 1965 Higher Education Act, and also grants from the 1907 Fund of the Ford Foundation.[9] Initially, the director of the exchange program on the Morgan end was Professor Willie T. Howard Jr., while the director of the program for Penn was Dr. Edward Cahill. Working with the directors in an advisory capacity was a committee of the members of both faculties, originally cochaired by Dr. Frank DeCosta, professor of education and dean of the graduate school at Morgan, and Dr. E. Digby Baltzell, professor of sociology at Penn.[10]

Under the Exchange Program, faculty members taught classes at the sister-school. Eventually, in 1968, the exchange was broadened to include students. Penn was certainly aware of the rising civil rights movements and pressures to increase the number of African American students at predominantly white universities—especially those receiving federal funds. Penn was a private university, but, as a leading world-class research institution, Penn received millions in federal money for medical and scientific research. In the 1960s it had conducted research for the military. It had navy and air force Reserve Officer Training Corps (ROTC) programs. And it received federal money for student financial aid. Thus, it was not immune to the implications of the Civil Rights Act of 1964.

The McGill Report on Undergraduate Admissions

During 1966–67 Penn reexamined its admissions policies, and on August 1, 1967, the Committee on Undergraduate Admissions, chaired by Dr. Daniel McGill, issued a set of recommendations that explicitly embraced "diversity" in the student body and the "mingling of cultures" as goals of the admissions process. It recommended that 90 percent of the freshman class be selected under a regular admissions process, but that a portion of those so selected might be chosen on the basis of a combination of subjective factors (such as diversity) *and* objective factors (such as performance on standardized tests). It also recommended that 10 percent of the freshman class be set aside for "special admissions," with given percentages to accommodate athletes, applicants from economically and culturally deprived backgrounds, and children of Penn faculty, alumni, and staff members. The report has since come to be known as the McGill Report.[11] This new policy opened the doors to a greater diversification of the student body, which had previously been mostly white, affluent, male, and from the Northeast. Critics of the "liberalization" of admissions policy, however would complain that this diversification occurred at the cost of declining academic standards and falling Scholastic Aptitude Test (SAT) scores.

The McGill Committee Report was not an administrative coup, nor was it a palace revolt. Most of the members of the committee were faculty members, and in addition to Chairman McGill, the members were E. Digby Baltzell, Sidney Bludman, Douglas Dickson, Robert Eilers, John Free (University Counseling Service), Peter Freyd, Provost David Goddard, David Lavin, Nancy Leach, A. Leo Levin, John McCoubray, Jacob Nachmais, Dean of Admissions William Owen, Richard Schwartz, and Douglas Vickers.

The McGill Report observed that, at the time, the number of applicants seeking admission to colleges and universities far exceeded the number of available spaces. At Penn, for the academic year 1967–68, there were almost five applicants for every space available (p. 2). For the class selected to enter in

September 1967, 7,702 applications had been received, 3,103 of these had been approved, and of that number 1,700 matriculated. The "yield," or "the percentage of approved candidates who actually matriculate[d]," was about 55 percent (p. 20). The committee began with the premise that "admission policy must be dynamic, fluid, and responsive to the challenges of its time" and should be subject to continual review and scrutiny (p. 2). The committee explicitly rejected the view that the goal of the admissions process should be to recruit a student population of "well-rounded" individuals (p. 5). Instead, it asserted that "the quality that should be sought above all others in a student body is intellectual power. A university exists to nurture the intellect and all other goals are subservient to this fundamental premise" (p. 6).

The committee felt, however, that this needed to be balanced with or against another set of considerations. The committee suggested:

A major part of the total educational experience of a university student is found in the interchange of ideas with other students and the mingling of cultures represented within the student body. Thus *it* [the Committee] *believes that diversity of student background is a positive educational value and should be positively pursued, even at the expense of other desirable attributes* (emphasis added). The admission policy of the University should be designed to produce a student population having the highest possible diversification as to (1) intellectual interests, (2) special talents, (3) social and economic background, and (4) cultural characteristics. The social, economic, and cultural homogeneity of the present student body is a source of some concern to the Committee, and some of the subsequent recommendations of this Report reflect this concern (p. 5).

The committee believed that diversity would "enrich" the educational environment (p. 12). At the same time, the committee rejected "as an instrument of policy, discrimination against any applicant purely on the basis of race, religion, national origin, geographic location, political persuasion, or other similar characteristic" (p. 6).

The committee also felt that "the correlation between predicted and actual performance, based on indices such as scores on standardized tests, class rank in secondary school, and grades, was not high enough to justify sole reliance on them" (p. 9). It took cognizance of exceptional artistic, literary, dramatic, musical, scientific, and athletic talent (p. 10), and noted that "a highly motivated person will outperform a more indolent person of equal or even greater ability" (p. 10). It also felt that leadership ability should be rewarded (p. 11).

To achieve the goal of excellence *with diversity*, the McGill Report recommended that 90 percent of each entering undergraduate class be selected under a "regular admission" process (p. 20). Within this 90 percent, the committee recommended three components. The first component, of 25 percent for each undergraduate school (arts and sciences for men, arts and sciences for women, nursing, allied medical professions, business, and engineering), was to be admitted "*solely on the basis of objective evidence of intellectual ability.*" "Objective evidence" referred to factors such as standardized test scores (Scholastic Aptitude Tests, achievement tests), secondary school class rank and grades, and assessment of the standards of the school attended (p. 21). Within the regular admissions process, 5 percent (of the 90 percent) should be selected on the basis of *subjective and diversity factors* (pp. 22–23; emphasis added). Within the regular admission process, 60 percent (of the 90) should be "selected on the basis of a *combination* of objective, subjective and extrinsic factors" (p. 23).

Subjective factors referred to character, emotional stability, creativity and special talents, motivation and commitment, leadership and activities (pp. 9–10), and could be assessed by the recommendations of high school counselors, principals, coaches, the University glee club or band director, and similar "expert" specialists. It could also be detected in the interview with the admissions staff. Extrinsic factors referred to "background" (diversity) and "institutional considerations." The euphemism "institutional considerations" actually referred to the children of faculty members and university employees (pp. 24–26). The McGill Report recommended that the children of faculty members and other university employees be assured of admission, *if* they applied under the Early Admission process. This gave a preference to individuals—in the absence of any "indications of failure"—who pledged to attend Pennsylvania, in return for an early offer of admission (pp. 25–26).

In addition to the 90 percent of the entering undergraduate class to be selected under the regular admission process, the McGill Report recommended that the remaining 10 percent of the class be selected under a "special admission" process (pp. 26–27). This 10 percent was to be divided into three categories. Of the special admissions seats 5 percent were allocated to athletes (p. 27), 3 percent were to be "reserved for applicants from economically and culturally deprived backgrounds" (p. 28), and 2 percent were to be made available to children of faculty, staff, alumni, and a "special interest group" (p. 29). "Special interest" here referred to residents of the Commonwealth of Pennsylvania (which gave Penn an annual appropriation of nearly $13 million at that time), and "applicants endorsed by trustees, political figures, important alumni, and other persons closely identified with the welfare of the University" (p. 26).

The "special interest" category took cognizance of the political reality that, "the University's welfare is heavily dependent upon harmonious relationships with the Federal government, the Commonwealth of Pennsylvania, and the City of Philadelphia. A substantial percentage of the University's funds for physical plant construction, research, and operating costs is derived from governmental sources" (p. 15). For the entering class of 1967, there were thirty-one special-interest cases and forty children of faculty, staff, and alumni who were admitted outside the regular admission procedure (p. 29).

The committee reaffirmed the traditional Ivy League ideal that admission should be offered to academically qualified candidates without regard to their need for financial assistance (p. 39). The McGill Report also recommended an elaborate "point" system that attempted to quantify how much weight should be assigned to particular factors such as special talent, motivation and commitment, leadership and activities, personality, background, and institutional considerations (p. 24). The report also sought to limit the number of academically "at risk" students in the "special admissions" category. It stated: "For this category as a whole, no more than half of the approved candidates can represent academic risks" (p. 29).

This document became the "blueprint" for the deliberate and conscious pursuit of a policy of excellence with diversity, which would attempt to balance "sheer intellectual power" with an enriching cross-section of talent from different cultures and class backgrounds. At no time, however, did Penn construe the McGill Report to require rigid numerical quotas. Nor did the report establish preferences *solely* on the basis of race. Penn did not set aside a specific subpool or a fixed number of slots for which only racial minority students could compete. (In contrast, the medical school at the University of California at Davis reserved sixteen seats for racial minority students exclusively.) Admissions "goals" at Penn would be met through reliance on letters of recommendation from high school teachers and counselors, the student's essay, and the interview—in addition to consideration of grades and scores and standardized tests.

The socioeconomic disadvantage category was *not* a race-specific category. Whites from low-income or disadvantaged backgrounds would fall into this category as well. White students from small towns and rural areas, in particular, might be included here. Race and socioeconomic disadvantage were simply two factors taken into account along with many other factors in the pursuit of diversity. In the *Bakke* case of 1978, the Supreme Court subsequently ruled that race and other factors (such as socioeconomic disadvantage) could be taken into consideration in an admissions process as part of a university's interest in promoting a "diverse student body."[12]

In April 1968 the outgoing Dean of Admissions William G. Owen reported that, in the class that had entered in September 1966, Penn had accepted 98 blacks; for the class entering in September 1967, it had accepted 85; and for September 1968, it had accepted 125 of 175 black applicants.[13] However SAAS Chairman Michael Williams suggested that "about" 40 black students (of the 85 who were accepted) had actually matriculated in September 1967. The figures given by Dean Owen were not matriculation figures, and therefore tended to overstate the number of actual enrollments by African American students. Penn has maintained for many years that, before 1968, it did not keep statistics by race. Its best estimate, therefore, is that in September 1966 and September 1967, 40 black students entered as freshmen.[14] There is strong evidence, however, that a significant increase in acceptances occurred in the cycle for the class of 1972 (those admitted in September 1968). Of the 125 black students accepted for September 1968, 62 seem to have actually matriculated.

Based on the McGill Report, and the increase in black matriculants from 40 in September 1967 to 62 in September 1968, it appears that a policy decision had been made in 1967 to begin increasing the number of black students, and this policy began to be implemented in 1968. It was possible, however, that this increase in black admissions would have unforeseen consequences. For even as the university moved toward greater diversity, the Black Power movement was already erupting onto the national scene. Feelings of remorse over the assassination of Martin Luther King Jr., on April 4, 1968, may have provided an additional impetus to accept more black students. Together, these influences would contribute to the increase in black acceptances for the class entering in September 1968, and the doubling of the number of matriculants for the class entering in September 1969 to 150. Although probably no one realized it at the time, Penn soon would have its own rendezvous with destiny.

CHAPTER TWO

YEARS OF DISCORD, 1967 AND 1968

Racism is not merely exclusion on the basis of race but exclusion for the purpose of subjugating or maintaining subjugation. The goal of the racists is to keep black people on the bottom, arbitrarily and dictatorily, as they have done in this country for over three hundred years. The goal of black self-determination and black self-identity—Black Power—is full participation in the decision-making processes affecting the lives of black people, and recognition of the virtues in themselves as black people.

—Kwame Ture and Charles V. Hamilton, *Black Power*, 1967

The number of black students at Penn remained small until the late 1960s. Forty may have matriculated in 1967. During the academic year 1967–68, Penn made a conscious decision to pursue greater diversity in its student body. This was in keeping with the goal of desegregation that blacks demanded and liberal white elites had embraced or acceded to by the mid-1960s. Penn, however, could no more escape the turbulence of the 1960s than could Harvard, Columbia, or other universities. In 1966, the Black Power–black nationalist–black pride movements emerged as equal and opposite reactions to conservative white resistance to the biracial civil rights movement. The civil rights movement had been advancing along a path of erasing consciousness of racial difference, but the Black Power movement deflected the civil rights movement from its course. The effect was to push the African American movement into a more militant, radical direction of race consciousness.

Thus, even as Penn "liberalized" its admission policies in 1967 and began to move in the direction of "greater diversity and integration" in the undergraduate population, the Black Power movement was erupting around it. Already, in June 1966, Kwame Ture and Willie Ricks had enunciated the doctrine of "Black Power." In October 1966, in Oakland, California, Bobby Seale and Huey Newton formed the Black Panthers. In 1967 Kwame Ture and

Charles V. Hamilton published *Black Power.* As the movement spread nation-wide, Penn, too, was affected. In 1967 Dick Gregory, Floyd McKissick, and Muhammad Ali spoke at Penn. Ali spoke to the Society of African and Afro-American Students (SAAS), which excluded white students and reporters who tried to get into the meeting. Later, in 1969, Amiri Baraka (Leroi James) spoke at Penn. Following the public lecture, there was a closed-door session with SAAS, from which whites again were excluded. In short, as early as 1967, within a year after Kwame Ture uttered the words "Black Power," the ideology had been rapidly transmitted to black students at Penn directly, by leading advocates of Black Power—in person.

This chapter explores this direct transmission of the ideology of Black Power to black students (persons of African extraction) at Penn, by leading Black Power advocates, in the period from 1967 to 1969. I examine evidence of the impact of the philosophy of black self-determination on SAAS. I conclude that, as early as 1967, the philosophy of Black Power influenced at least a segment of black students at Penn, and certainly those in SAAS, and that at least some of the black students at Penn (and SAAS as an organization) had adopted the Black Power perspective in 1967 and 1968, even before the historic doubling of the number of black freshmen matriculants (from 62 in September 1968 to 150 in September 1969). The assassination of Martin Luther King Jr. on April 4, 1968, further estranged black students at Penn from the dominant white culture and prompted marches, vigils, and petitions. This combination of the heightened, impatient militancy of Black Power and the tragic assassination contributed to a profound alienation and "radicalization" of (some) black students at Penn, as elsewhere. It was in this highly charged climate that Penn began receiving the substantially larger cohorts of African American students mandated by the 1967 McGill Report.

A word is necessary, however, about why some black students at this time sought admission to predominantly white universities rather than to the historically black colleges, as they had since the late 1860s. Most African Americans who attended college over that century had gone to historically black colleges and universities such as Howard, Fisk, Hampton, Morehouse, Spelman, Atlanta, Lincoln, and Cheyney. By the 1960s many African Americans from the North turned to colleges and universities in their own part of the country, and those with professional aspirations in medicine, law, business, or engineering saw a degree from a "good" school with a reputation for academic rigor as a stepping stone to upward mobility. Hence, in the North, more African Americans were choosing to attend integrated universities rather than the historically black colleges of the South or even Lincoln University in Pennsylvania. Black students were not choosing to attend predominantly white colleges rather than the historically black institutions, for their enrollments did not decline. Rather, the increase in black enrollments at predominantly white colleges reflected expanded opportunities at these institutions.

The "Black Power" Awakening Reaches Penn

Following the emergence of the Black Power movement in June 1966, it was not long before the new mood of assertiveness and pride in blackness made itself felt and heard at Penn. Evidence of this can be found in some of the nationalists who spoke at Penn after Ture enunciated the phrase "Black Power." On March 29, 1967, Dick Gregory spoke at Irvine Auditorium on the topic of "black power." The invitation had been extended by Connaissance (a student organization that invites speakers to campus) and the International Affairs Association.[1]

In the fall of 1967 SAAS invited Muhammad Ali to campus. Ali, formerly the heavyweight boxing champion of the world Cassius Clay, was also a follower of the Nation of Islam. In April 1967 he had refused induction into the armed forces of the United States. Ali claimed conscientious objector status on the grounds that he was a Muslim. Ali said, "The real enemies of my people are right here, not in Vietnam." Ali was convicted of draft evasion and sentenced to five years in prison, which he appealed (and, subsequently, in June 1971, the Supreme Court ruled in his favor). The boxing commission also stripped him of his boxing title, which he regained in 1974 after a fight with George Forman in Zaire (now Congo, Kin'shasa).[2]

On October 31, 1967, Ali spoke to a group of approximately one hundred black students in the auditorium of the Christian Association Building. This is itself was not controversial, but SAAS closed the meeting to whites and, according to the *Daily Pennsylvanian,* turned away three white students who persisted in trying to get into the auditorium as well as a white reporter from the *Philadelphia Inquirer.*[3] This version of events is corroborated by the *Philadelphia Inquirer,* which reported, "White students were barred from his talk, and a white reporter was 'asked to leave' when he tried to cover the meeting."[4] During the speech, Muhammad Ali said, "There's no sense in Negroes wanting to integrate with whites," and that the "only hope" of African Americans "was to unite and separate from the whites."[5]

This episode generated a small furor on the campus. On November 3,

Penn's student newspaper *The Daily Pennsylvanian* (hereafter *DP*) ran an editorial condemning SAAS because it "barred whites at the door."[6] The editorial asserted that "blacks-only gatherings are the latest manifestation of militant black power thinking," and condemned the actions of SAAS as "flagrantly totalitarian behavior."[7] The editorial continued, "One wonders whether students here would have taken as lightly a meeting of Nazis barring Jews at the door," and referred to Christian Association Director the Reverend Jack Russell as an "Uncle Tom White." It concluded, "This is everybody's place. We all want to do our thing here. No little islands of exclusivity. It makes no sense."[8]

Billy Riley, chairman pro tempore of SAAS, responded in a letter, which appeared on November 7. He wrote, "Historically . . . this idea of exclusiveness has worked two ways; it had in the past been used against us and in that respect it was wholly sanctioned: we now use it for ourselves to help ourselves."[9] He said the notion of a supposedly free interplay of ideas that the *Daily Pennsylvanian* championed was in reality "a systemized process to acculturate the Black student into a generally indifferent and unresponsive white society." And, he insisted, "Equating Black societies in America with Nazism is a poorly constructed analogy. Primarily because the Nazis were oppressors, and we as Blacks are the oppressed."[10]

In a letter published on November 9, Drake Turrentine defended the Christian Association Director, the Reverend Jack Russell: "I oppose the black militants who preach racism, but I think that it is hypocritical for whites to condemn the blacks for doing what we have done for hundreds of years. They have learned exclusivism from us, and they now use it for themselves as we used it against them. Should we preach ideals to them when we can't even keep our own society in order?"[11] Turrentine concluded: "For many of us raised to believe in civil rights and integration, it is sad to watch a society polarizing into opposing black and white factions. It is even sadder to watch attacks such as yours [the *Daily Pennsylvanian* editorial] driving the wedge deeper."[12]

Soon thereafter Mary Lovett, probably an African American student, wrote a letter defending SAAS. She wrote in part: "It should be remembered that SAAS stands for the Society of African and Afro-American Students: it is by definition exclusive; its membership is obviously limited to that segment of the population which is African and Afro-American. Also, its purpose is to afford blacks the opportunity to identify with blacks."[13] Lovett also pointed out that "for the meeting of October 31 Muhammad Ali was invited *by* SAAS to speak *to* SAAS."[14]

Finally, Joel Aber of the Young Socialist Alliance wrote a letter defending

SAAS, which appeared on November 13. He wrote that the *Daily Pennsylvanian* editorial accused a group of Afro-Americans of flagrantly totalitarian behavior "simply because they had a private meeting."[15] He asked if private fraternity parties, meetings of the Faculty Senate, and closed meetings of the *Daily Pennsylvanian* editorial board, therefore, were also flagrantly totalitarian.[16]

This episode reveals several things. First, it suggests that SAAS was already influenced by the Black Power movement at least as early as 1967. Second, SAAS had embraced a position of organizational "separatism" or exclusivity, based on in-group homogeneity. Full membership in the organization was limited to persons of African extraction only. This, of course, was in keeping with what Malcolm X and Kwame Ture had advocated. The ideas of black nationalism and Black Power were known in some form to various segments of the Penn community. And even the *Daily Pennsylvanian* editorial of November 3 and the article of November 6 had characterized the actions of SAAS in terms of "Black Power." It also should be noted that, following the controversy over Ali's speech to SAAS in October 1967, the Christian Association and Connaissance invited Muhammad Ali to campus for a *public* speech. As a result Ali spoke at Irvine Auditorium on March 6, 1968. The audience was estimated at twenty-five hundred people, mostly white. It was an "open" event. Coverage of the event by the *Daily Pennsylvanian* stressed that Ali favored separation of the races rather than integration, as illustrated by a four-column headline, which read "ALI URGES SEPARATION OF RACES."[17]

On Thursday, November 16, 1967, just two weeks after Ali spoke to SAAS, Floyd McKissick, national director of CORE, spoke at Irvine Auditorium, at the invitation of Connaissance. His topic was "The Black Revolution."[18] In view of the invitations extended to Gregory and McKissick, the topic of Black Power was of interest to members of the Penn community, both black and white. McKissick's speech emphasized self-determination and the need to develop black political power and "consumer power." He also rejected King's philosophy of nonviolence.[19] Furthermore, the topic of Black Power was of sufficient interest that, on January 18, 1968, the *Daily Pennsylvanian* printed a favorable three-page review of Kwame Ture's *Black Power* by Cecil Burnett, a faculty member from the Political Science Department.[20]

In November 1968 Julian Bond (who is *not* an avowed black nationalist) spoke at Penn on the topic of "Black Political Power."[21] Subsequently Connaissance sponsored speeches by Ralph Abernathy on January 31, 1969, and by Amiri Baraka (Leroi Jones) on February 17, 1969.[22] Baraka said, "The black man must control his own space—the schools, hospitals, police departments—all the institutions that directly affect him."[23] He continued, "At present, we are a nation of people—a cultural nation. What we do not have is the power to be a political nation. We are a nation without power—a nation that is controlled by another nation."[24] Following the speech to nearly two thousand at Irvine, Amiri Baraka spoke at a closed meeting of SAAS, to an audience of about sixty black students. It was reported that three white students "were threatened with forcible eviction when they attempted to sit in on the meeting."[25] Once again SAAS seemed to be practicing in-group exclusivism and separatism.

The Ideological Influence of Black Nationalism

The question arises, where did this ideological orientation and perspective come from? The most proximate answer would be, from Kwame Ture (formerly Stokely Carmichael) and the philosophy of Black Power, which in turn had been derived from and influenced by the black nationalism of Malcolm X. The self-determinationist philosophy of Malcolm X was in turn inspired by Elijah Muhammad and Marcus Garvey.

On the subject of group self-determination (so-called separatism), Malcolm X believed that sometimes blacks should form homogeneous or all-black organizations. On April 12, 1964, he said: "Whites can help us, but they can't join us. There can be no black–white unity until there is first some black unity. There can be no workers' solidarity until there is first some racial solidarity. We cannot think of uniting with others, until first we have united among ourselves."[26]

Following directly in the footsteps of Malcolm X, Kwame Ture and Charles V. Hamilton said black people must "lead their own organizations and support those organizations."[27] Furthermore, blacks must choose their own leaders and hold those leaders accountable to the black community.[28] They insisted that only black people leading and running their own organizations could "convey the revolutionary idea . . . that black people are able to do things for themselves."[29]

Ture and Hamilton were concerned to combat the psychology of dependency and self-doubt among blacks that reinforced, in the minds of both whites and blacks, the stereotypical view that blacks were children who were unable to manage their own affairs. They also were anxious to combat the "paternalism" of well-meaning Euro-Americans who seemed to feel they were doing blacks a favor by "helping" them and that the hapless blacks ought to be appropriately "grateful."

Young African Americans reacted against the perception of paternalism by asserting their right to self-determination and their right to control their own destiny. This meant the right to make their own decisions for themselves and to make their own mistakes and learn from them. Ture and Hamilton were also wary of white paternalism because of the danger of reinforcing the historic relationship of inequality (white superiority and black inferiority). They felt that it was exceedingly difficult for whites, however well-meaning, to free themselves entirely from the "tug of superior group-position." They also felt that it was difficult for blacks to overcome their own conditioned reactions of deference to whites. They believed, however, that there could be coalitions among self-determined groups of blacks (African Americans) under black leadership and groups of whites, so long as these coalitions were based on mutual gain rather than inequality and "sentimentality." Otherwise there was the danger that blacks would continue to enter coalitions from positions of weakness and find themselves in the role of junior partner. Under these circumstances they would be vulnerable to manipulation and to outside pressure, influence, and funding. They might then be forced to compromise to accommodate the stronger, wealthier "ally."[30]

Group Self-Determination Not Segregation

The emphasis of black nationalism and the Black Power movement on self-determination, black control of black organizations and communities, and exclusion of whites from black organizations seemed to many whites to be little more than self-segregation and reverse racism and discrimination. This compelled black nationalists and self-determinationists to explain how black self-determination or exclusivism was different from the old-fashioned segregation of the Jim Crow South. This idea is critically important because self-determination has become axiomatic among black nationalists, pluralists, and other segments of the African American community.

Malcolm X, like Elijah Muhammad before him, distinguished between segregation and separation. In the *Autobiography of Malcolm X,* he argued that segregation is something that is imposed on a community of people externally, by someone else, in an effort to control those who are segregated or kept apart. Segregation was a relationship between a person or group ascribed as superior and a person or group ascribed as inferior. In contrast, separation was not imposed on a group from without, by another. Separation was voluntary and chosen. It was also a relationship between equals.[31] Malcolm X also wrote of the process of affinity, which he observed in his pilgrimage to Mecca in 1964. He wrote:

Being from America made me intensely sensitive to matters of color. I saw that people who looked alike drew together and most of the time stayed together. This was entirely voluntary; there being no other reason for it. But Africans were with Africans, Pakistanis were with Pakistanis. And so on . . . where true brotherhood existed among all colors, where no one felt segregated, where there was no "superiority" complex, no "inferiority" complex—then voluntarily, naturally, people of the same kind felt drawn together by that which they had in common.[32]

Along similar lines, in 1967, Kwame Ture and Charles Hamilton suggested in *Black Power* that separation in itself was not necessarily or always bad. Rather, the *purpose* for the separation was crucial. Some separation was for the purpose of dominating, subjugating, and exploiting another group, and excluding them from access to educational and economic opportunity, as in the case of white supremacy under the Jim Crow system. Other separation was merely voluntary association, where people who shared something in common such as religion or ethnicity or culture chose to come together. The goal of Black Power, they said, was "not domination or exploitation of other groups," but attainment of an "effective share in the total power of the society."[33] Under the legalized system of Jim Crow segregation, it was not separation in and of itself that had been objectionable, but rather the imputation of black inferiority as the rationale for the imposed separation.

Responding further to those who condemned the black desire for both organizational and community self-determination as black "exclusivism" and "separatism" and "supremacy," Ture and Hamilton wrote, "No other group would submit to being led by others. Italians do not run the Anti-Defamation League of B'nai B'rith. Irish do not chair Christopher Columbus Societies. Yet when black people call for black-run and all-black organizations, they are immediately classed in a category with the Ku Klux Klan."[34] Ture and Hamilton also insisted that in building black-run and all-black organizations, blacks would only be emulating what other ethnic groups had done.[35] Ture and Hamilton compared "blacks" with European ethnic groups such as the Irish, Jews, Italians, and Poles. This illustrates that even though they used the term "black," in some respects (though obviously not all) they were thinking of

African Americans as an ethnic group (as well as a racial group) along with other ethnic groups in American society. They believed African Americans must become an organized and self-conscious interest group in the American process of interest-group competition. Many Euro-Americans, however, did not see African Americans as an ethnic group but simply as a racial group. Thus, they saw African American *ethnic* homogeneity as *racial* exclusion against whites.

In addition, Ture urged whites to understand that the black man wanted "to build something of his own, something that he builds with his own hands. And that it is *not* anti-white. When you build your own house, it doesn't mean you tear down the house across the street."[36] Yet despite these disclaimers, the media and whites generally perceived "Black Power" and black nationalism as antiwhite hatred, as separatism, and as advocacy of violence.

It was also misleading to call the desire for organizational self-determination "separatism." Genuine separatism is territorial nationalism, which manifested itself in groups such as the Republic of New Africa (RNA). The RNA sought a partition of the United States so that five states in the South could form a separate, independent, sovereign African American nation–state on the soil of North America. Neither Kwame Ture nor SAAS advocated this. There is a fundamental difference between trying to separate from white America by forming a black nation, and pursuing autonomy as a means to the end of sharing power with Euro-Americans within American society. Race consciousness need not make one a "separatist."

Alliance with Antiracist White Liberals

Many black nationalists and self-determinationists believe that African American self-determination requires racial or ethnic exclusivity in the membership of independent black institutions and organizations. Of course, this stance then raises the question of the role of progressive European Americans who believe sincerely in the struggle against white supremacy and institutional racism. A premise of Black Power since 1966 has been the belief that a crucial role for progressive whites is to confront the racism and prejudice of the white community in the white community. This would enlist progressive whites as allies in a united front against white supremacy. Black Power also suggests that, because people of African extraction in the United States do not control the institutions of society and do not possess the institutional power or means to subjugate and dominate other groups, there is no black "supremacy" over Euro-Americans to be combated.

The idea that progressive whites have a critical role to play in the white community derives from Malcolm X. After the *hajj* to Mecca in spring 1964, Malcolm X suggested that racism was learned as a matter of socialization, indoctrination, and conditioning. Therefore, whites needed to "unlearn" their racism. White liberals could play a critical role in this reeducative process. On January 18, 1965, barely a month before his assassination, Malcolm X acknowledged that, when he was a member of the Nation of Islam and had spoken on college campuses in 1961 and 1962, he had noticed that the younger generation was different from the older and its members were "more sincere in their analysis of the problem and their desire to see the problem solved."[37]

Malcolm X felt that African Americans had to work on solving their own problems first, and then could join with others. He insisted that "blacks must take the lead in their own fight."[38] Nevertheless, he insisted that he was open to alliance with progressive individuals and groups sharing similar objectives. On May 29, 1964, Malcolm X said:

We will work with anyone, with any group, no matter what their color is, as long as they are genuinely interested in taking the types of steps necessary to bring an end to the injustices that black people in this country are afflicted by. No matter what their color is, no matter what their political, economic or social philosophy is, as long as their aims and objectives are in the direction of destroying this vulturistic system that has been sucking the blood of black people in this country, they're all right with us.[39]

Much like Malcolm X, Ture and Hamilton wrote, "Let black people organize themselves *first,* define their interests and goals, and then see what kinds of allies are available" (emphasis in original).[40] They, too, suggested that the best role for progressive whites who wished to contribute to the movement was to reeducate the white community in unlearning its racism. Ture said that whites could play an important role by going "into the white communities and developing those moderate bases that people talk about [but] that do not now exist."[41] The insistence on ethnic homogeneity within African-American organizations did not preclude alliances between self-determined groups of African Americans with progressive, self-determined groups of whites. Thus, the Black Panthers sought to work with whites in the Students for a Democratic Society (SDS) to their mutual advantage.

Self-Determination and Self-Organization

Historically, black nationalists such as Marcus Garvey, Elijah Muhammad, Malcolm X, and Kwame Ture insisted upon the need for black organizational self-determination. Essentially this meant that people of African extraction should control their own destiny, develop their own institutions, and lead and control those institutions. They should set their own goals and choose their own methods for attaining those goals. For black nationalists, self-determination meant that black people should become a self-conscious, organized interest group. In 1966 SNCC, CORE, and the Black Panthers embraced this position. Black self-determination pointed to the need for group self-organization and independent institutions of one's own.[42]

Absent a statistical survey, it is impossible to say to what degree Billy Riley and Mary Lovett were "representative" of black students at Penn in 1967–68. It would seem, however, that many if not most African American students felt that SAAS should be for Africans and African Americans exclusively. These same students would have said it was likewise perfectly okay for a campus chapter of the Sons of St. Patrick to admit only Irish American students, for the Knights of Columbus to admit only Italian Americans, or for other ethnic associations to limit membership to persons of a given ethnicity. African American students saw the BSU as parallel in some ways to ethnic associations, or even the Hillel Foundation (a Jewish organization). Although the latter organization might be construed as a religious rather than "ethnic" organization, the similarity with ethnic associations is that membership within it is based upon an aspect of identity.

In any case, the black "separatism" that was manifesting itself on college campuses such as Penn in 1968 was a microcosm of the larger society. As the ideological children of Malcolm X and Kwame Ture, many African American students had moved to an ideological position of group and cultural pluralism, self-determination, ethnic solidarity, and race and color consciousness rather than seeking the eradication of consciousness of difference.

Together, the black nationalists who spoke at Penn, the emergence of SAAS (which excluded whites from full membership), and the closed meetings with Muhammad Ali in 1967 and Amiri Baraka in 1969 demonstrate the diffusion and dissemination of black nationalist ideas on the Penn campus from 1967 to 1969. The campus discussions of the philosophy of Black Power and the letter of Mary Lovett are further evidence of this. It is fair to infer that by 1967 and 1968 the black student movement at Penn was definitely influenced by Black

Power and black nationalism. Furthermore, there must have been influences even before 1967, or the students would not have known whom to invite.

The Impact of the King Assassination

The assassination of Martin Luther King on April 4, 1968, further alienated, polarized, and radicalized African Americans. On the day that King died, some gave up their last shred of hope that white Americans could be purged of their pervasive white racism. The assassination had an immediate impact on the black students at Penn. On Thursday, April 4, Philadelphia Mayor James Tate issued a declaration of limited emergency that banned gatherings of more than twelve persons, supposedly in an effort to prevent riots and disorders. On Thursday evening SAAS called on black students not to attend classes on Friday, April 5. On the same evening, Provost David Goddard and University Chaplain the Reverend Stanley Johnson, announced that all one o'clock classes would be canceled on Friday, April 5, and a memorial service would be held at Irvine Auditorium.[43]

Prior to the 1 P.M. memorial service, SAAS organized a vigil at Houston Hall Plaza. Sixty black students then briefly violated Mayor Tate's order by marching up the middle of Walnut Street from Van Pelt Library (at 34th Street) to 37th Street, south to Spruce Street, and east to Irvine Auditorium at 34th and Spruce Streets. At the memorial service, attended by twenty-five hundred university students, faculty members, and administrators, King was eulogized by President Gaylord Harnwell, Chaplain Stanley Johnson, members of SAAS, and others.[44]

Over the weekend another group of students announced they would conduct a meeting on Monday, April 8, at the Fine Arts Building (now Meyerson Hall) at 34th and Walnut Streets, where they would gather more than twelve people on the sidewalk. This group of students (most of whom were white) was led by Daniel Finnerty, Larry Simon, and Martin Goldensohn.[45] Subsequently at 2 P.M. on April 8 a group gathered at the Fine Arts Building. Finnerty, Simon, and Goldensohn spoke, and Lieutenant George Fencl of the Philadelphia Police Civil Disobedience Squad read the mayor's proclamation over a bullhorn and ordered the group to disperse peacefully. Goldensohn continued reading the First Amendment, and Fencl shouted that he was under arrest. The demonstrators linked arms and began to sing "We Shall Overcome." Reportedly, one hundred fifty police officers and fifty mounted Fairmount Park guards surrounded and arrested the demonstrators. They did not resist, and fifty-four students and two faculty members were arrested for violating the mayor's limited emergency proclamation. Bail was set at $500, and Dr. Robert Rutman, a professor of biochemistry in the Veterinary School, and others began raising a bail fund for those students who could not post bail.[46]

Also in response to the assassination of Martin Luther King, on Tuesday, April 9, the Reverend Stanley Johnson sponsored a "town meeting." It was attended by two hundred whites and twenty-five blacks. E. Max Paulin, an African American and assistant dean of admissions, urged whites to know the prejudice within themselves.[47]

The assassination of King seems to have galvanized SAAS. The society collected 2,148 signatures on a petition urging the House of Representatives to approve the civil rights legislation already passed by the Senate, which included provisions for open housing. The *Daily Pennsylvanian* and the student newspapers of Dartmouth, Yale, Princeton, Columbia, Brown, and Cornell sent telegrams urging passage of the civil rights bill as well.[48] Here again, the actions of black and white students overlapped. SAAS then declared April 15–20 "Black Week," beginning with a rally at Houston Hall Plaza on April 15. Other events included poetry reading and music, and SAAS stated, "The Society of African and Afro-American Students Black Week is a means of stimulating this sense of Black awareness and Black pride." The week was also dedicated to the memory of Malcolm X, Medgar Evers, Dr. Charles Drew, and Lemuel Penn.[49]

The Demonstration of April 29, 1968

Two weeks later, on Monday, April 29, SAAS held a demonstration at 133 S. 36th Street (also called the "bank building," at 36th and Walnut Streets), where a branch of Girard Bank (since acquired by Mellon–PSFS) was located. Here SAAS charged the owners of the building with racial discrimination because there were no black employees.[50] At 8:30 A.M. on April 29, members of SAAS, carrying placards, blocked the front and side doorways of the building and picketed in front of both entrances. Some workers in the building were "trapped inside" and could not get out, while others could not get into the building. Among the SAAS demonstrators were freshman Jon Flenyol, juniors James Winston and Samuel Cooper, and freshman Barbara Grant. The Philadelphia Police arrived at 8:45, and Winston said, "The building is closed." At 9:30 Lieutenant George Fencl of the Philadelphia Police Civil Disobedience Squad arrived. Winston gave Fencl a statement from SAAS that made demands of the Penn administration. Reportedly two black students from the Law School, Harry Jackson and Harvey Johnson, persuaded the members of SAAS to stop the demonstration and urged them instead to take legal action against the corporation that owned the building.[51]

At 9:45 A.M. SAAS stopped blocking the doorways, and soon thereafter thirty-five members marched to the office of President Gaylord Harnwell at College Hall. President Harnwell and Vice Provost for Student Affairs Leo Levin met with three representatives of SAAS while the other members maintained a presence in the hallway. Following the meeting, Harnwell and other high officials in the administration met with the full delegation from SAAS.[52]

The firm of Richard J. Seltzer, Inc., was the rental agent for the building. The head of the corporation was Dr. Harry Fields, who also happened to be Assistant to President Harnwell for Athletic Affairs. The spokespersons for SAAS maintained that it had tried to work privately with the administration for two months prior to this event, to resolve the complaint of discrimination at the bank building, and had achieved nothing. SAAS then demanded that Fields be fired and carried placards stating this.[53]

After a meeting with President Harnwell and high officials of the administration, Fields denied any personal knowledge of discrimination at the building but promised that two blacks would be hired to fill two existing vacancies and that SAAS would be notified of any future job openings in the building.[54] One informant also indicates that SAAS had gotten blacks to apply for jobs at the bank, but they had been told that there were no vacancies. Then SAAS got a white student to make an inquiry, and he was offered a job.[55] This suggested to SAAS that racial discrimination was in fact taking place, and it also shows that there were progressive whites of conscience who did work with SAAS even though it was ordinarily an all-black, racially (ethnically) homogeneous organization.

Subsequently African Americans were hired at the bank building, and SAAS may be said to have "proven its point" and won the essence of what it really wanted. This incident is revealing in several ways. First, SAAS maintained it had tried reasoned dialogue, persuasion, private negotiation, and cooperation for two months, with no results. But when it resorted to mass direct action and a public demonstration that disrupted "business as usual," it achieved results within hours. For SAAS there was a lesson in this: The university administration did not take black student demands seriously, or respond to them, unless it was confronted with pressure and the threats of public controversy, negative publicity, civil disobedience, and disruption. This kind of perception inevitably leads to an escalation of such tactics, and it is a perception the black student movement at Penn reached many times over the years.

Second, it is worth noting that the issue that precipitated the demonstration was not one that related directly to the conditions of the students themselves on campus, but a broader issue of "racial discrimination" in hiring. It most directly affected workers and the larger black community seeking employment at the bank building. This illustrates that students were concerned about more than their own narrow interests as students and felt a wider sense of identification with the black community beyond the campus.

Third, the SAAS demonstration of April 1968 was one of the very first recorded protests by black students at the University of Pennsylvania. Fourth, it occurred at a time when about forty black students had matriculated in the freshman class the previous September. The April 1968 demonstration was a harbinger of things to come. Consistent with the goals of diversity and a greater degree of integration (racial), in the late 1960s Penn was moving in the direction of increasing its admission of black students. Yet, already in 1967–68, some African American students and their student organization (SAAS) had a self-determinationist, "Black Power" orientation. This can be plainly seen in the fact that SAAS limited membership to African Americans and sometimes closed its meetings to nonblacks. These students sought autonomy and the creation of a space that reflected their ethnic culture, not assimilation into the status quo. They did not simply accept the campus as they found it; rather they sought to transform it. If the demonstration at the bank building and this degree of group self-consciousness could occur with an incoming class of only about forty black students (in September 1967), what would happen when that number doubled, tripled, and nearly quadrupled within two years? The likely result would be a "radicalization" of black students with an eruption of Black Power and self-determination among them. As the succeeding chapters reveal, that is exactly what happened.

CHAPTER THREE

THE SIT-IN OF 1969

Power concedes nothing without a demand. It never did and it never will. Find out just what people will submit to, and you have found out the exact amount of injustice and wrong which will be imposed upon them; and these will continue till they are resisted with either words or blows, or with both. The limits of tyrants are prescribed by the endurance of those whom they oppress.

—Frederick Douglass, "No Progress without Struggle," 1849

After the adoption of the McGill Committee Report in 1967–68, the admission of black students at Penn increased significantly, from 40 matriculants in September 1967 to 62 in September 1968. Black admission at Penn was on an ascending curve, and, at a constant rate of increase of about 22 a year, one might have expected 84 African-American matriculants for the class entering in September 1968. But in 1969 a number of issues came together in an explosive way. Penn found itself confronted by the acute tensions of "urban renewal," the black awakening of the 1960s, intense opposition to the Vietnam War, and the need of the university to expand into the surrounding black community. In the process of expanding, more than twenty-six hundred people, over half of whom were black, were traumatized by the demolition of their homes. In protest, in February 1969 there was a massive sit-in at College Hall. The circumstances of the sit-in placed intense pressure on Penn to admit more black students, especially from the inner-city public schools of Philadelphia. The sit-in accelerated the process of admitting more black students. When the smoke from the sit-in cleared, the number of black matriculants doubled, from 62 in September 1968 to 150 in September 1969. Without the sit-in of February 1969, it is highly doubtful that the increase would have been so large. This doubling of the black enrollment, *in a single year* (although starting from a small base to begin with), marked a turning point in the admission of black students at Penn. The sit-in would have the effect of reinforcing assertiveness and a Black Power orientation among African American students at Penn.

Before proceeding, a word of caution is in order. Admissions statistics can be imprecise. They are sometimes difficult to follow because of the differences between the number of students who apply, who are "accepted" (offered admission), and who actually matriculate. Furthermore, on occasion there are students who apply, are admitted, send in their deposits indicating acceptance of the offer of admission, but may not actually show up when school opens. Moreover, there are students who arrive but for some reason change their minds and leave within days of their arrival. Therefore, the number of matriculants may vary from moment to moment, and one can notice inconsistency in the numbers cited from one instance to the next. With this caveat in mind, the discussion that follows gives the best estimate that can be derived on the basis of the shifting and imperfect evidence available thus far. The narrative given here might be modified by the future revelation of information which is as yet "classified."

In April 16, 1968, the outgoing Dean of Admissions, William G. Owen, reported that in the class which had entered in September 1966 Penn had accepted 98 blacks; in the class entering in September 1967, it had accepted 85; and for September 1968, it had accepted 125 of 175 black applicants.[1] However SAAS Chairman Michael Williams and SAAS member Vivian Vix suggested that "about forty" black students (of the 85 who were accepted) had actually matriculated in September 1967. The figures given by Dean Owen were not matriculation figures, and therefore tended to overstate the number of actual enrollments by African American students. On the other hand, the figures cited by the dean indicate Penn's willingness to make offers of admission. The university has maintained for many years that before 1968 it did not keep statistics by race. Its best estimate, therefore, is that in September 1966 and September 1967 40 black students entered as freshmen.[2] There is evidence that a significant increase in acceptances occurred in the cycle for the class of 1972 (those admitted in September 1968). Of the one hundred twenty-five black students accepted for September 1968, 62 seem to have actually matriculated. According to journalist James Cass, from academic year 1968–69 to 1969–70 Penn's enrollment (matriculation) of black students more than doubled, from 62 to 150. In spring 1969 the Ivy League schools and the so-called Seven Sister colleges jointly announced the admission of a record number of African-American students.[3]

Table 1. Black freshman enrollment at Ivy League and Seven Sister universities, academic years 1968–69 and 1969–70

Institution	1968–69		1969–70	
	Accepted	Enrolled	Accepted	Enrolled
Brown	56	22	165	76
Columbia	58	29	115	51
Cornell	115	60	157	67
Dartmouth	58	28	130	90
Harvard	55	51	109	95
U. of Pennsylvania	125	62	251	150
Princeton	76	44	126	68
Yale	70	45	150	100
Barnard	33	20	81	40
Bryn Mawr	22	10	31	15
Mount Holyoke	46	18	61	31
Radcliffe	17	14	51	37
Smith	34	19	86	46
Vassar	24	24	43	22
Wellesley	19	9	104	57

Source: James Cass, "Can the University Survive the Black Challenge?" *Saturday Review* 52, no. 25 (21 June 1969): 83.

As table 1 shows, the quantum leap in the number of black students matriculating at Penn dates from September 1969. It is important, however, to note that these students would have been recruited in the fall and winter of 1968–69. I have argued that the decision to substantially increase the number of African American students was made *before* 1969 and can be traced to the McGill Report of 1967.

Penn hired an African American, William R. Adams, to recruit minority students in the spring of 1968 (the exact month cannot be confirmed). In October 1968 George Schlekat assumed duties as the dean of admissions and strengthened the commitment to recruit a more diverse student body.[4] With the hiring of Adams, Penn clearly was moving in the direction of increasing its admission and enrollment of black students. This movement would be institutionalized further in 1972 with the creation of the Minority Recruitment Program (MRP).

Seismic Activity: The Sit-in of 1969

In 1968 and 1969 Penn and the other Ivy League universities were moving in concert in the direction of increasing the number of their black students. At the same time, the overall size of the incoming classes was also rising, and Penn found itself facing an acute housing shortage. The solution to this problem was to expand the physical boundaries of the university into the surrounding neighborhood. That neighborhood happened to be predominantly African American. In these years, the housing and space problem set Penn on a collision course with the surrounding black community of Mantua, which would culminate in a massive six-day sit-in by more than eight hundred people at College Hall, beginning on February 18, 1969. The McGill Report had already begun to move Penn in the direction of increasing the number of African American students. The repercussions of the sit-in of February 1969 would propel Penn to accelerate greatly this process and also the acceptance of far more students from inner-city, public school backgrounds than ever before.

The Already Existing Climate of Protest

The sit-in of February 1969 was not an entirely isolated event. The late 1960s was a period of turmoil at the university, related to opposition to the war in Vietnam and the role of the university in scientific research for the military. There was also opposition to the presence of recruiters from Dow Chemical Company, which produced napalm for the Defense Department (after it had been developed in a laboratory by scientists at Harvard University). In addition, some students objected to class rankings that were used by the military to determine eligibility for the draft. In 1967, the military had also discontinued deferments for graduate students. At Penn, Professor Philip Pochoda of the Sociology Department was actively involved in the antiwar effort, and draft counseling was a focus of activity at the Christian Association.

The opposition on campus to classified research for the military was especially heated over research for chemical and biological warfare. In 1966 and 1967, the focus of controversy was two projects for the military called "Spice Rack" and "Summit." Penn had become involved with a project called "Big Ben" in December 1951, and in 1963 signed contracts with the Air Force for Summit and Spice Rack as a continuation of Big Ben. In October 1965 there was a demonstration against the projects. In November 1965, the Faculty Senate had already asked for an end to nonpublishable research at the university, and during 1966 and 1967 faculty opposition intensified.[5] The Harnwell administration responded by seeking to transfer the unpopular and controversial contracts to an independent entity, the University City Science Center.[6]

Therefore, Penn could deny that it was involved in the research, because ostensibly the Science Center (UCSC) was independent of the University.

On April 26, 1967, more than two hundred students began a sit-in at the Office of the President and in College Hall. The sit-in lasted for fifty-one hours. In May the trustees directed President Harnwell to divest the university of the troublesome contracts "as soon as practical," and ultimately the Air Force allowed the contract to lapse on September 1, 1967.[7]

This episode was followed by a sit-in on the third floor of Logan Hall on November 1 and 2, 1967. Recruiters from Dow Chemical Company and the Central Intelligence Agency were interviewing students at the Office of Career Planning and Placement. About sixty protesters sat in, while another twenty blocked doorways. The protest was aimed at the "complicity" of the university in the Vietnam War in allowing Dow Chemical Company and the CIA to recruit on campus. This "sit-in" consisted of disruptions lasting for a few hours on both days, followed by another "action" on November 8.[8] Ultimately the university felt constrained to conduct recruiting activities and interviews by controversial agencies in satellite facilities off-campus.

The sit-ins against secret military research in April 1967 and against on-campus recruiting by Dow Chemical Company in November 1967 were successful. They also demonstrate that by 1967 Penn was no stranger to protests and sit-ins. In retrospect, these two incidents seem like minor rehearsals for the sit-in that erupted in February 1969 to protest the expansion of the University City Science Center and the University of Pennsylvania into the adjoining, predominantly black, neighborhood of Mantua.

Plans for Expansion

By 1968 Penn was faced with a housing shortage. In 1968 the campus extended to parts of Chestnut and Walnut Streets on the north and to 38th Street on the west. Penn and the Philadelphia Redevelopment Authority initiated a plan to "redevelop" a plot of land north of the campus. This area, called "University City Area III," was bounded by Chestnut and Ludlow Streets on the south, and Lancaster and Powelton Avenues on the north, and ran from 34th to 40th Streets. Today it is the site of such facilities as the expanded University City Science Center, the Monell Center for the Chemical Senses, the Institute for Scientific Investigation, and the University City High School. In 1968, however, the vast majority of this area consisted of rowhouses, which by conservative estimates, housed more than 2,653 people, of whom 1,780 were "non-white."[9] On the "street," this section of Mantua was called the "Black Bottom." In 1966 a tract of land in this region had been condemned by the City of Philadelphia, by right of "eminent domain," on behalf of the Board of Education, for the construction of a new high school to concentrate on science and math (the current University City High School). This tract was located on Market Street between 36th and 38th Streets.[10]

Penn also wanted a tract west of 38th Street, to 40th, between Spruce and Walnut Streets, for the construction of several high- and low-rise student residences, collectively called the "Superblock." This would include three massive high-rise towers, more than twenty stories high. This expansion of Penn for dormitories, the expansion of the Science Center, and the School Board's construction of the University City High School would entail the massive removal of several thousand people and the demolition of their homes. Not surprisingly, this effort produced intense opposition from the surrounding black community, which the university regarded as a slum.

On December 6, 1967, Governor Raymond P. Shafer signed a bill creating the Pennsylvania Higher Education Facilities Authority. Its purpose was to assist Commonwealth colleges and universities in providing housing for students.[11] In January, Penn Trustees agreed to proceed with plans for construction of the new housing units. Then, on January 20, 1969, as the trustees gathered for their customary quarterly meeting, President Harnwell announced his intention to retire.[12]

At that same meeting, a new force, the Students for a Democratic Society (SDS), made its presence felt on campus by holding a rally outside the Furness Building, where the trustees were meeting, which attracted over a hundred students. The focus of their protest was the expansion of the University City Science Center, with a demand that corporations provide financing for the construction of housing in West Philadelphia, especially for the residents displaced as a result of the expansion of the Science Center. They also demanded full disclosure of all university documents relating to the Science Center.[13]

On Saturday, January 25, 1969, the Reverend Edward Sims, an African American minister and the director of a group called the Volunteer Community Resources Council (VCRC), announced that the residents of West Philadelphia would mobilize to stop the destruction of the Walnut Street Center. The center was an experimental elementary school, located at 3944 Walnut Street, near the Philadelphia Free Library branch at the corner of 40th and Walnut Streets. The center was directly in the way of the university's demolition plans and was scheduled to be demolished in July 1969. In fact, the building was owned by Penn. Sims, however, also asserted that the expansion of the University City Science Center was displacing five thousand persons from their homes. The fight over the Walnut Center was but a symptom of the wider resentment in the black community of the expansion of Penn and the Science Center and the destruction of their homes and neighborhood.[14]

Meanwhile, within the university itself, students became angry over the refusal of President Harnwell to release to them a report on the Science Center, which he had given to the trustees in May 1967. Students became convinced that Harnwell was hiding something, and that "dirty" research would go on in secret at the Science Center. On January 27 and 29, the *Daily Pennsylvanian* ran editorials essentially calling for full disclosure from Harnwell about Penn's relationship to the Science Center and the kind of research that would go on there, and also warning of the growing anger simmering in the surrounding black community about the expansion of Penn and the Science Center. The second editorial even invoked the image of the uprising at Columbia University the previous year.[15] As the *Daily Pennsylvanian* predicted, three weeks later, the issues of alleged secret research for the military at the Science Center and the expansion of the Science Center and the university into the black neighborhood of Mantua converged to produce a "blow up."

The "Science Center" Sit-in

sds had scheduled a rally for Tuesday, February 18, 1969, and invited supporters from Swarthmore, Temple, Bryn Mawr, Haverford, and other local colleges and universities. The rally was organized by Joe Mikuliak, who spoke at the 11 A.M. rally, as did the Reverend Sims, who condemned the way the university had taken land from the black community. At noon a group of four hundred protesters gathered at the construction site at 36th and Market and Filbert Streets. There they watched "guerrilla theatre," and destroyed a mock "science center." At approximately 12:20 P.M. they marched to College Hall to present a list of demands to President Harnwell. When President Harnwell returned from lunch at 1 P.M., protesters went into his office. Before television cameras, Mikuliak and others confronted Harnwell, and then the protesters retired to Room 200 College Hall at 1:20 P.M. to decide what to do next.[16]

The hundreds there assembled decided to hold a sit-in. Ira Harkavy, a junior in the College and cochair of the Community Involvement Council, argued that the demonstrators were in a position to force Harnwell to stop evading the issues and urged that the group ask for a meeting with the trustees. A Steering Committee was constituted, which at 4:30 P.M. issued a statement demanding that "the trustees . . . be called within the next 24 hours to discuss the demands about the University City Science Center and the role of the University of Pennsylvania in the community." As the evening progressed some six hundred students began what would become a six-day sit-in. The sit-in was unrestricting. College Hall remained open and classes continued to be held.[17]

A mass meeting of students on the first night approved three demands. They were that the UCSC return land to the community,[18] that low-income housing be built on the land, and that the charter of the UCSC be changed so that it could no longer do classified or military research.[19] Meanwhile seven of the fifteen members of the Faculty Senate Advisory Committee met in an emergency meeting and opted to support the student demand for a meeting with the trustees. The Faculty Senate had previously proposed similar measures to prevent the Science Center from conducting classified research. On Tuesday night, too, SAAS met in a closed meeting in 200 College Hall, but had not yet issued a statement about its position on the sit-in. This would soon change, however, as the black student movement intersected with the white student movement.[20]

On Wednesday, February 19, the Faculty Senate Advisory Committee helped to arrange a meeting of the Student Steering Committee with the eight-member Student Affairs Committee of the Trustees at the Christian Association Building. This group included Trustees William Day, Robert Trescher, Robert Dechert and Bernard Segal. On Wednesday, also, SAAS voted to support the basic demands of the sit-in concerning the return of land from UCSC to the community.[21]

Black Mantua Awakes

On Thursday, February 20, the volcano called Mantua awoke and made its voice heard. Herman Wrice, president of the Young Great Society, Forrest Adams of Renewal Housing, the Reverend Edward Sims of the Volunteer Community Resource Council, and John Segody of Mantua Community Planners appeared at College Hall to announce that black leaders in Mantua had met earlier in the day and decided to present a united front with the students and faculty. The self-proclaimed spokesmen of black Mantua demanded the cessation of all construction in predominantly black areas of Philadelphia without the prior consent of black residents. They also demanded that the

UCSC return the disputed land to the West Philadelphia community; that the trustees provide funds to build housing for the displaced residents; and that a halt be made in expansion by Penn and nearby Drexel University without authorization from the black community.[22] Then, SAAS took a position firmly in support of the activists from Mantua.

Resolution of the Sit-in

On Sunday, February 23, the trustees agreed to accept a "Quadripartite Commission" and six resolutions. The Quadripartite Commission would include representatives of the community, students, faculty, and the administration. The most significant demands were that the commission be empowered to review all existing plans for future land acquisition or development of currently owned land contiguous to existing residential neighborhoods. Furthermore, the commission was to operate on the principle that where future expansion involved the demolition of existing housing units, the university would "undertake to guarantee the provision of an equivalent number of housing units, at equitable cost or rental."[23]

The plenary session approved this document, and thereafter decided to elect four students to the Quadripartite Commission, and empower those four to elect the fifth member. The body elected Ira Harkavy, Joseph Mikuliak of Penn SDS, Jules Benjamin, and Robert Fried. These four then unanimously voted to name Cathy Barlow, of SAAS, as the fifth student member of the commission.[24] Herman Wrice, the Reverend Sims, and the Mantua activists also approved the draft agreement. The Penn Trustees agreed to raise $10 million for community development and committed themselves to rebuilding equivalent housing for those displaced by university expansion.[25]

For cynics, however, the "loophole" was that although Penn might encourage banks and others to provide the additional $10 million—in the form of loans—the applicants still had to qualify for the loans. Penn pledged to "make available" $10 million. True to its word, it asked institutions in the city of Philadelphia to "make available" $10 million. William Day, chairman of the Board of Trustees at Penn, was a director of the First Pennsylvania Bank and therefore in a good position to make such a request. Acceding to his request, commercial banks in Philadelphia pledged $5 million for a revolving fund, and savings and loan associations pledged $5 million. Thus, the letter of the promise was fulfilled. Penn did use its "good offices" to provide "access" to these sources, in that individuals could apply for or request the funds, but Penn had not committed to generate (give) $10 million of its *own* money, nor could it guarantee that banks would lend money to displaced low-income residents in Mantua who requested it. In many cases, the amount of money needed to qualify as being "credit-worthy," or needed in order to be accepted for the housing that was being constructed, exceeded the annual income of many Mantua residents.[26] It would be more than a decade before low-income "townhouses" finally were built in the immediate vicinity of Penn.[27] Fortunately, the sit-in was resolved peacefully, without the Harnwell administration resorting to calling in Frank Rizzo, the chief of police and his Philadelphia force.[28]

Penn had been forced at least to pay "lip-service" to the principle that, if it took something away from the community, it had an obligation to provide compensation for the loss. Of equal importance was that the constituency that experienced the loss had sufficient political clout to wrest or extract the compensation from the university. In June 1969, at the request of President Harnwell, the trustees established the Urban Affairs Committee to coordinate its relationship with the city and community. This committee was subsequently renamed the External Affairs Committee.

Retrospective: The University as Contested Terrain

The Columbia University sit-in of April 1968 began with Mark Rudd and SDS raising concerns about Columbia's involvement with military research and the Institute for Defense Analysis (IDA). Black students took the opportunity to mobilize around the issue of the construction of a gym in Morningside Heights, which then became the focal point of the uprising. The Harvard sit-in of April 1969 began with SDS challenging ROTC, but black students used the opportunity to promote the issue of the Black Studies Department. They inserted themselves into the process, and the sit-in ended as a referendum on Black Studies.

The events at Penn followed the same pattern as those at Columbia and Harvard. The sit-in at Penn of February 1969 began with SDS raising the long-simmering issue of secret military research at the Science Center. Black activists from Mantua (such as Herman Wrice and the Reverend Edward Sims) and SAAS then capitalized on this opportunity to focus more attention on the issue of university expansion into the black community.[29] In effect, they brought pressure upon Penn to give something back to the African American community as compensation for the loss the community was sustaining in the demolition of the homes of more than two thousand six hundred people. In the sit-in of February 1969, SAAS and the black student movement at Penn, and the Mantua activists, intersected with SDS and white student activists. It was a successful interracial coalition of the sort that the Black Panthers had practiced with SDS.

The sit-in of 1969 was also a powerful reminder to the university that sometimes geography is destiny. Penn was not a splendidly isolated island. It was situated in the very midst of an overwhelmingly African American community in a major metropolitan area. The university, in decades past, had received land from the City of Philadelphia in exchange for a promise to admit a number of students from the city and provide them with scholarships. In time that land was utilized by the Penn Medical School and the Hospital of the University of Pennsylvania. It grew into some of the most lucrative real estate in Philadelphia. Penn received an annual appropriation from the Commonwealth of Pennsylvania. By 1967 this amounted to $13 million, and by 1977 it had risen to $17 million. The university's immediate neighbors to the north and west consisted of members of the black working class. These geographic realities constrained and even "politicized" Penn's decision-making process. Penn was accountable to a variety of constituencies and publics, both internal and external. It had to balance traditional considerations of academic merit, qualification, and "standards," and the concerns of the heretofore mostly white faculty, students, and alumni with the political pressures emanating from its social and political environment and its geographic location.

One of the most sensitive zones of contention in this interplay was the area of admissions—especially the admission of African American students to the elite Ivy League university located in predominantly black West Philadelphia. The African American community complained that the university expanded into its neighborhoods, uprooted its people, and demolished their homes— thereby taking all that they had—and that they received next to nothing in return. In effect, poor and working-class black people were asked to "pay the price" and "bear the burden" of "progress" to benefit wealthy, privileged whites who already had the best of everything, anyway. But few African American students could even attend Penn. In general, people from the community could not even play basketball in the Penn gymnasia or borrow books from the libraries, which were normally reserved for Penn students, faculty, and staff only. Members of the African-American community insisted that Penn owed them something, collectively, in return for what it was taking from them. One way that Penn could address this debt and mend fences with its neighbors was to admit more African Americans to the university, especially African

Americans from Philadelphia and from socioeconomically disadvantaged backgrounds. This would mean admitting students who were from inner-city, public high schools, who might not have "good" standardized test scores and might be considered academically "at risk."

But here the institution would find itself caught between the political pressures of an aroused African American community and the concerns of (white) faculty, students, and alumni who invoked the mantle of maintaining "academic standards based on merit and qualification." Traditionally, Penn had conceived itself as an Ivy League school and a world-class institution of higher learning for the "best and the brightest" only. As an elite institution competing with Harvard, Princeton, and Yale, its mission was to educate the privileged few on the basis of academic merit.[30] Now, in the political climate of the late 1960s, it was under pressure to amend and expand its academic mission. Penn discovered that it was accountable not only to its traditional constituencies but to the aroused, surrounding black community. The black community, too, was in a position to exert force and punish Penn if the university did not meet its demands. The Harnwell administration (and its successors), then, like those of Columbia University and the University of Chicago, was caught in the middle and would have to reconcile these competing pressures as best it could.

The sit-in of 1969 created a political climate in which Penn was under intense, excruciating pressure to admit more African American students and to give an opportunity even to students who might be academically at risk or "not qualified" by traditional admissions standards. From September 1968 (before the sit-in) to September 1969 (after the sit-in), the number of African American matriculants more than doubled, from 62 to 150. One may infer that Penn yielded to the political pressure. The sudden increase in the numbers cannot be explained without taking into account the circumstances of February 1969. Indeed, this author would hazard the conjecture that in the absence of the sit-in of February 1969, the dramatic increase in the number of African American admits and matriculants simply would not have been so great—it would have been inconceivable. Although local events probably were decisive, similar increases in black student enrollments were taking place nationwide. King's assassination and the subsequent riots were also factors in this rapid change.

The sit-in of February 1969 and the awakening of black Mantua was like an earthquake. Its aftershocks were felt most forcibly in the area of African American admissions. In the absence of the sit-in, the number of African American matriculants in September 1969 probably would have been closer to 62 than

150. Had the increase from 1968 to 1969 been on the same order as the previous increase from 1967 to 1968 (of approximately 22 students, from 40 to 62), the figure for the entering class of 1969 would have been 84 African Americans. A similar rate of increase would have produced an entering class of 106 African Americans in 1970 and 128 in 1971.

The number of African American matriculants would increase to 170 in 1970, and remain in the range of a 150 to 160 through the first half of the 1970s, before a precipitous decline to 104 in 1978. The figures for the years 1970 to 1975 are given in table 2. Dean Schlekat left the Admissions Office in June 1971, and Peter Seely served as its dean from 1971 to 1974, and Chaplain Stanley Johnson from 1975 to 1977. Carol Black, wife of Bill Adams, worked in the Minority Admissions Program (MRP) from its inception in 1972 until 1976. She was the director of the MRP from 1974 to 1976. More than any other persons, Adams and Black were responsible for the recruitment of rising numbers of African American and other "racial" minority students at Penn in the early 1970s.

For the Penn administration, there was a price to be paid for "giving in" and acceding to the demands of African Americans. White students complained that "less qualified" black students, who had lower scores on standardized tests and who had attended less rigorous high schools, were admitted unfairly while more qualified white students (with higher standardized test scores) had been denied admission. To them, this looked like reverse discrimination and a form of favoritism. There was also much hand-wringing over a decline in SAT scores. At the same time, the size of incoming classes rose (to 1,850 freshmen by 1975). Even worse, as Penn faced financial hardship, the size of the incoming classes had to rise in order for Penn to generate sufficient revenues.

Table 2. Black undergraduate admissions, 1970–1975

Entering class of September	Black applicants	Black acceptances	Black matriculants	Percentage of class
1970	815	330	170	8.8
1971	654	319	153	7.7
1972	771	358	168	9.1
1973	740	365	155	8.0
1974	704	342	150	7.3
1975	752	322	143	7.1

Source: Adapted from the Report of the Task Force on Black Presence, Section II.C, presented to the Trustees of the University of Pennsylvania, June 9, 1977. Published in *Almanac* 24, no. 24 (21 March 1978): 13.

Against this background, some Euro-American students seemed to resent the presence of African American students who they automatically assumed to be unqualified. Some white students openly expressed hostility and labeled black students as people who had been admitted only to fill an "affirmative action" quota. Some of the "remedial" students were also from socioeconomically disadvantaged, inner-city backgrounds. Some white students felt that, whereas they had "earned" entry into Penn and "deserved" to be there, "remedial" black students had not earned a place there and did not deserve to be there. It is also possible that (some) white students from middle-class, affluent, privileged backgrounds felt that Penn and other Ivy League schools "belonged" to members of their class, and the presumably working-class African Americans did not have the same "right" to be there. Indeed, some white students whose parents and grandparents had attended Penn acted as though they thought they had a hereditary right to attend the university. Some of these same white students who were indignant about "preferences" based on race or disadvantage had no such qualms about preference based on unearned privilege as the children or relatives of alumni, or on letters of recommendation from influential donors or politicians.[31]

Under these circumstances, issues of race, class, and academic preparation became conflated. This tug-of-war and contest of wills would make the issue of minority admissions a minefield. It would incite conflict among the administration, deans of admissions, and the faculty over control of admissions policy. It would also cause many black students to perceive the campus and their white fellow students (and sometimes their professors) as hostile and condescending. Also since (some) white students assumed that all black students were "remedial" or "ghetto blacks," African American students from affluent, suburban, or private preparatory school backgrounds found themselves "lumped in" with blacks from inner-city or public school backgrounds, and they resented the tendency of white students to view all blacks as "alike." The result of this volatile mix was mutual alienation and polarization between African American and Euro-American students.

But, again, this campus warfare was not unique to Penn. It was a reflection of a bitter controversy taking place across the country as a whole. It was into this welcoming environment that the substantially increased cohorts of African American students arrived in 1968, 1969, and thereafter. Under these circumstances black students would come to realize that the campus was not always an ivory tower insulated from the ugly pressures of the wider world. Sometimes the campus, too, could be a contested terrain.

The Impact of Increased Black Admissions

The process of admitting more black students sprang from good intentions and political pressures from the black community in Philadelphia. This, however, had unforeseen consequences. The passage of the entering class of 1969 through the university, with an unprecedented number of students from public high schools in Philadelphia, was anything but smooth. It was estimated that half of this class was academically "at risk." The experiences of some of these students revealed the need for an expanded system of academic support services. In fact, the experience of black students at Penn, and their pattern of adjustment to the university, was very like those of other universities at that time.

In a study of thirteen colleges and universities, Marvin Peterson and his colleagues described some of the patterns of adjustment that accompanied the admission of increased numbers of black students between 1969 and 1971. Their observations are revealing. They suggested that white college and university leaders expected that change would occur smoothly and without conflict, while white students assumed that black students would want to be integrated with whites.[32] In many cases, however, the new students were less well-prepared academically and more economically disadvantaged than the white students or earlier cohorts of black students.[33]

As the Peterson study described, for some students the experience of failure produced frustration and alienation. They reacted with anger and resorted to protests and other expressions of discontent. In many instances, black students felt alienated from an overwhelmingly white or Eurocentric academic and social environment and responded with demands for courses in African American history and Black Studies, or demands for black dances, social events, dormitories, and living arrangements.

Universities had also assumed the new cohort of black students would want to "integrate," "assimilate," and "fit in." They discovered that black students wanted to preserve their own culture and have their own (exclusively black) organizations, social activities, and events. The outcome, according to the Peterson study, was a pattern of "mutual indifference" and race relations characterized by "voluntary segregation or by indifference thinly covering interracial conflicts and feelings of mistrust."[34] Numerous other studies support the findings of the Peterson study.

The research of Patricia Gurin and Edgar Epps, however, cautions us not to reduce student interest in black nationalism to a matter of academic deficiencies. Instead, Gurin and Epps found that students who participated in the black student movement and expressed support for black nationalist positions on surveys were those who believed that "racism is not an institutional anomaly but the very essence of the system." They believed that African American "are exploited and subjugated *as a group,* not [merely] as individuals" (emphasis added).[35] Although these students were confident of their own abilities, they believed that their opportunities for achievement were blocked by racism and they blamed the system (social structure) for this inequity. As a solution, "they had dropped the notion that the individual alone could make a difference; they came to believe in the theme of nationalism, that only a group determined to act together could alter injustice."[36] Black students combined individual aspirations for achievement and professional success with a commitment to collective action and uplift.[37] In addition, Gurin and Epps suggest that identification with black nationalism was not correlated with precollege family and social backgrounds, family income, or parental educational attainments.[38]

The patterns described by Peterson et al. in their study of black students at thirteen colleges and universities, and by Gurin and Epps, offer useful models for assessing the interaction between the suddenly increased numbers of black students and the universities in the late 1960s. After 1968 black students at Penn agitated for a School of Afro-American Studies, a black student dormitory, a prefreshmen summer program and tutoring center, and black faculty and administrators to serve the needs of black students. Their vehicle for the expression of discontent and their demands was the Society of African and Afro-American Students (SAAS), subsequently renamed the Black Student League in 1971.

The bank building demonstration of April 1968 and the march on College Hall to demand a meeting with President Harnwell were the first signs of conflict between SAAS and the Penn administration. This was followed, however, by a letter to the *Daily Pennsylvanian* published on October 31, 1968. It was a classic statement of discontent and alienation. In it the author, George Royal, described a twofold problem faced by African American students in adjusting at Penn. These two problems were "adjusting . . . to the academic pace of the University and adjusting as a Black to the University as a white community."[39] Poignantly, Royal wrote:

How does one make the transition from studying eight hours a week to do well in high school to studying five and six hours a day in college? Our confusion was intensified by a lack of meaningful counseling on the part of the University. No one paid any particular attention to us until each found himself on probation. A successful student was one whose grades kept him off probation despite failure in any one course. The only people we felt free to ask for advice were in the same predicament. Upperclassmen, graduate students and faculty might as well have been part of another university.

The problem of academic adjustment is not limited to Black students but the difficulty of transition is amplified for us by a sudden immersion in a white community. School is no longer a six hour-a-day association with whites. There is suddenly a tremendous almost overwhelming self-consciousness about being Black. We are no longer individuals, but representatives of our race. This self-consciousness distorts everyday life in a manner that it is impossible to fully explain.

It is this double transition from high school to college and from living in a Black community to existing in a white community that hinders the Black student.[40]

Royal went on to list seven demands: (1) to provide extension courses for black businessmen and technicians in the College of General Studies, with financial aid; (2) to substantially increase the numbers of black administrators, faculty, staff, and students, reflecting no less than the percentage of black people in Philadelphia; (3) to establish both an African Studies Institute and an Urban Affairs Institute on graduate and undergraduate levels; (4) to correct inconsistencies in the policies of the Office of Student Financial Aid; (5) to adequately counsel and integrate all students into a meaningful educational experience; (6) to include in the decision-making process those who will be affected by the decision; and (7) to redefine vital education at an urban university as a dynamic radical arm of the community, rather than a stagnant reactionary string-puller of the community.[41]

This letter clearly articulates the double problem of making the academic transition from high school to a highly competitive university and the social transition from a predominantly black environment to an overwhelmingly white one. The first problem may be a situation that all freshmen encounter, but the second was one that presumably members of the white majority did not face. One may infer that some (but not all) of the African American students then being admitted to Penn were from public high schools and inner-city backgrounds ("living in a Black community"), and they were being thrust into a predominantly white environment for the first time. The letter pointed out the lack of an "early warning system" to identify students who were academically "at risk." Instead, students only came to the attention of the academic advising system at the end of their first semester, after they had already failed courses and were on academic probation with their continuation at the university in jeopardy. Black students felt that their ability to achieve was hampered and blocked by an insensitive, indifferent, unsupportive campus environment.

In the years following the publication of this letter, SAAS would launch a campaign of demonstrations and other forms of direct action to demand a nationalistically oriented prefreshman summer program, academic support services, a separate dormitory for black students, and a school of Black Studies. George Royal's letter was a manifesto of the concerns of black students at Penn in the late 1960s and a blueprint for what was to come. It is also a symbol of the transition from the raceless and colorless "integration" demanded by the civil rights movement to the race- and color-conscious pluralism and group self-determination demanded by the black cultural revolution and the Black Power paradigm-shift of the late 1960s.

CHAPTER FOUR

REFLECTIONS IN THE MIRROR,
REFLECTIONS IN THE CURRICULUM

The South earnestly submits that over a period of thousands of years, the Negro race, as a race, has failed to contribute significantly to the higher and nobler achievements of civilization as the West defines that term. . . . In terms of enduring values—the kind of values respected wherever scholars gather, in the East no less than in the West—in terms of values that mean something and excite universal admiration and respect, what has man gained from the history of the Negro race? The answer, alas, is "virtually nothing." From the dawn of civilization to the middle of the twentieth century, the Negro race, as a race, has contributed no more than a few grains of sand to the enduring monuments of mankind.

—James Kilpatrick, *The Southern Case for School Segregation*, 1962

I n 1967 the McGill Report had recommended that Penn increase its admission of African American students. As the number of black students rose, however, so did their discontent. Some of the first signs of this disaffection took the form of complaints about the Eurocentric content of their courses. African American students found themselves immersed in an overwhelmingly white environment socially, but they also felt invisible in the curriculum. Their history, literature, and experience were missing, because there were not yet any courses at Penn devoted to these topics. Black students did not see their own image reflected in the mirror of the curriculum, but rather it was always the image of someone else—and "someone else" was always white and male. The absence of the black experience in coursework alienated many black students. Thus, at Penn, as elsewhere across the nation in the late 1960s, black students arriving on predominantly white campuses demanded that the curriculum be enlarged to include their history, literature, and experience, too. They were not content to integrate into "whiteness" culturally, by assimilating. Instead, they rejected assimilation and demanded cultural pluralism and courses in and a department of Black Studies.

It cannot be emphasized too strongly that the demand to make the curriculum more inclusive came from the agitation and "pressure from below" of black students themselves. They "raised hell" about their desire for courses in African American history and literature, and it was partly to placate their unrelenting pressure that the university attempted to diversify its course offerings and its faculty. At Penn one effort in this direction was an exchange program with Morgan State University, with faculty visiting between the two sister institutions and later student exchanges as well. The Penn–Morgan Program was a precursor to the eventual emergence of an Afro-American Studies Program at Penn.

Culture and Discontent

As early as February 1968, African American students from the Society of African and Afro-American Students (saas) urged the History Department to establish a course in Afro-American history. It is worthwhile to note that this initial request actually preceded the significant increase in the number of black matriculants, which occurred in September 1968, and the leap in black admissions of September 1969. For this reason I examine dissatisfaction with the curriculum—and the central role of culture—before turning to the issues of academic support services and student life, which were also questions of immediate concern to African American students in 1969. In fall 1968, a course in Afro-American History was inaugurated, but no sooner had the History Department done so than (in November 1968) African American students escalated and modified their original demand to insist that the instructor should be an African American as well. Only a month after the sit-in of February 1969, Provost David Goddard would charge a committee to study creation of an academic program in Afro-American Studies. The establishment of an Afro-American Studies program at Penn, however, was a long and circuitous process that took place over several years.

The demand for courses in African and Afro-American history, literature, music, and the Afro-American experience grew out of the conviction that African Americans had a culture of their own, which included music, dance, literature, folklore, an oral tradition, anthropology, and history. In the classroom, however, African Americans were fed a curricular diet exalting the glories of Greece, Rome, the Renaissance, the Enlightenment, and American exceptionalism. Prominence of place was given to Alexander the Great, Julius and Augustus Caesar, Charlemagne, Henry VIII, Louis XIV, Napoleon Bonaparte, Otto von Bismarck, Woodrow Wilson, Winston Churchill, and Franklin Roosevelt—to the almost complete exclusion of any mention of the contributions of Africa, China, India, or of any people of color, to human or Western civilization. Somehow, in this grand epic, Egypt, Nubia, Axum, Ghana, Mali, Songhay, Benin, Ife, and Zimbabwe were left out, and Piankhi (Piye), Taharqa, Shabaka, Ezana, Sundiata, Mansa Musa, Sunni Ali Ber, Askia Muhammad Toure, and Shaka were nowhere to be found. Plato, Aristotle, Socrates, Cicero, Beowulf, Chaucer, Shakespeare, Milton, Twain, Hemingway, and Mailer were required reading, but Frederick Douglass, Paul Lawrence Dunbar, Langston Hughes, Gwendolyn Brooks, Richard Wright, Zora Neale Hurston, Ralph Ellison, James Baldwin, and Chinua Achebe were not.

In American history and textbooks in the 1960s, Phillis Wheatley, Peter Salem, Benjamin Banneker, David Walker, the Massachusetts 54th, Charles Drew, Lewis Latimer, Garrett Morgan, Granville T. Woods, and Dorie Miller were missing, for all that was European and Euro-American embodied the "universal," and whatever was African or Afro-American (or Mexican, Puerto Rican, or Chinese) was narrow and "particular." African American students at Penn, as elsewhere, revolted against these assumptions of "superiority" and "universality." And they revolted against the doctrine that Afro-Americans had no ethnic culture of their own.

Black Power, black pride, and the Black Arts movement engendered an aroused sense of group identity among African Americans and an intense interest in their history and culture. By the mid-1960s, African-descended Americans insisted that African Americans do have a culture of their own, which is different from the culture of European-descended Americans, and insisted that they value that culture, perceive it as worthy, and wish to preserve it. Consequently, since that time, many African Americans have come to reject the goal of cultural assimilation into the melting pot of Anglo-conformity.

The prevailing social science view in the early 1960s, however, was still that black Americans had no particular culture of their own, and that any vestige of the African ancestral cultures had been wiped out by the experience of the transatlantic slave trade. Therefore, social scientists such as E. Franklin Frazier, Nathan Glazer, and Daniel Patrick Moynihan assumed that "Negroes" had no culture to protect or preserve, and their language, religion, and political values were identical to those of the white majority or merely imitative variations of them. E. Franklin Frazier had written:

Consequently, when one speaks of Negro culture in the United States, one can only refer to the folk culture of the rural Southern Negro or the traditional forms of behavior and values which have grown out of the Negro's social and mental isolation. . . . Since the institutions, the social stratification, and the culture of the Negro minority are essentially the same as those of the larger community, it is not strange that the Negro minority belongs among the assimilationist rather than the pluralist, secessionist or militant minorities. *It is seldom that one finds Negroes who think of themselves as possessing a different culture from whites and that their peculiar culture should be preserved* [emphasis added].[1]

Echoing this sentiment, Nathan Glazer had written, in *Beyond the Melting Pot* in 1963, "It is not possible for Negroes to view themselves as other ethnic groups viewed themselves because—and this is the key to much of the Negro world—*the Negro is only an American and nothing else. He has no values and culture to guard and protect*" (emphasis added).[2] In the second, revised edition of the book, in 1970, Glazer attempted to clarify what he had meant, by revising the original statement to read: "But more important, it is not possible for Negroes to view themselves as other ethnic groups did because the Negro is so much an American, the distinctive product of America. He bears no foreign values and culture that he feels he needs to guard from the surrounding environment."[3]

Norman Podhoretz also seemed to believe that black Americans had no distinctive culture or identity of their own that they valued and wished to preserve. In 1963 he wrote:

I think I know why the Jews once wished to survive (though I am less certain as to why they still do): they not only believed that God had given them no choice, but they were tied to a memory of past glory and a dream of imminent redemption. What does the American Negro have that might correspond to this? His past is a stigma, his color is a stigma, and his vision of the future is the hope of erasing the stigma by making color irrelevant, by making it disappear as a fact of consciousness.[4]

Expressions such as these reflected a view, perhaps subconscious, that African Americans had no *positive* sense of group identity or peoplehood, no past apart from New World slavery, no customs or heritage they cherished.

As Robert Blauner has described, these authors simply found it inconceivable that African Americans might have produced a culture of their own that was more than an imitation of Europe.[5] This tendency to ignore, dismiss, and devalue African American culture was a reflection of Eurocentric cultural imperialism. In that spirit, in 1967 Bennett Berger wrote:

For stripped of its mystique, black culture is basically an American Negro version of *lower class culture,* and, race prejudice aside, it can expect *on this ground alone* to meet strong resistance from the overwhelming majority of the American population which will see in the attempt to legitimate it an attempt to strike at the heart of the ethic of success and mobility, which is as close as this country comes to having any really sacred values [emphasis in original].[6]

Berger's peroration to assimilation read: "No lower class culture has ever been fully legitimated in the United States because the basic right of members of the lower class has been to rise out of it but not to celebrate its style of life!"[7]

At the same time, American social scientists in the 1950s and early 1960s used the term "ethnic group" in a way that recognized European immigrants as "ethnic groups" because they had foreign languages and customs to "lose," but regarded American "Negroes" as a race only and not as an ethnic group. Evidently the privilege of being an ethnic group was reserved "for whites only." With penetrating insight, Robert Blauner wrote in 1972:

Many of the ambiguities of American race relations stem from the fact that two principles of social division, race and ethnicity, were compressed into one. With their own internal ethnic differences eliminated, people of African descent became a race in objective terms, especially in the view of the white majority. Afro-Americans *became an ethnic group also,* one of the many cultural segments of the nation. The ethnicity of Afro-America, however, is either overlooked, denied, or distorted by white Americans, in part because of the historic decision to focus on the racial definition, in part because of the racist tendency to gainsay culture to people of color beyond what they may have assimilated directly from the European tradition. This merging of ethnicity with race, in the eyes of people of color as well as of whites, made it inevitable that racial consciousness among blacks would play a central part in their historic project of culture building, and that their institutions, politics and social character would be misinterpreted in a restricted racial paradigm [emphasis added].[8]

Revealingly, social scientists of that era did not regard American Anglo-Saxons as an ethnic group, because ostensibly they were the dominant group and were "native born" and not "foreign." The British American culture, consciously or unconsciously, was regarded as normative and as the "foundation" culture of U.S. society.[9] This blindness was, of course, an extension of white supremacist ideology and propaganda. It illustrates, however, the "invisibility" of the ethnicity and culture of British Americans, given that historically their culture has been the dominant culture, into which everyone else has been constrained to assimilate.[10]

During the 1960s Americans of African extraction rejected the doctrine that they had no distinctive culture of their own. With indignation, they asserted that they *did* have a culture of their own, which was derived from fragments of the African ancestral past. Furthermore, they proclaimed that the assorted Ibo, Bakongo, Mende, Wolof, Bini, and other African-descended people in the United States had developed a new culture in the New World. Over time, this innovative, syncretized African American culture had given rise to the shouts, work songs, spirituals, and riddles of the slaves. The African American culture had produced jazz, blues, gospel music, and rhythm and blues. Animated by the ethos of black pride and black consciousness, African Americans in the 1960s began to celebrate their own cultural heritage.

Whereas previous appeals to African American culture often had been confined to elite intellectuals such as W. E. B. Du Bois and Carter G. Woodson, the new cultural movement was transmitted to a mass audience by literary figures such as John O. Killens, Askia Muhammad Toure, Hoyt Fuller, Addison Gayle, George Kent, Amiri Baraka, Nikki Giovanni, and Sonia Sánchez. And the new mood was captured by James Brown in "I'm Black and I'm Proud," which became the anthem of an entire new generation. The Motown musical explosion was proof positive that African-descended people in the United States had a music and culture of their own. The electronic media and the music industry disseminated these new cultural products to everyone who had a radio or a phonograph. Consequently the cultural renaissance of the 1960s was imbibed by a mass constituency, especially young people, that included all segments of the working and lower classes as well as the elite. This facilitated a "vertical integration" of African Americans among class lines, and this cultural revolution reigned among most African Americans as popular culture.

The new African American cultural revolution rejected traditional images of the African background as primitive and heathen. It rejected the legacy of shame toward African origins, and rediscovered the Pan-Africanism of Alexander Crummell, Martin Delany, Edward Blyden, Henry McNeal Turner, and W. E. B. Du Bois; the black cultural pride and chauvinism of Garvey; and the positive sense of group identity espoused by Monroe Work, Benjamin Brawley, and Carter G. Woodson. This transvaluation of blackness (physical and phenotypical features) and Africa (lineage, ancestry) "reversed the polarity" of how African-descended people felt about being black in color and originating in Africa. The revitalized sense of pride came in large part with the inspiring heroism of the civil rights activists. In this way the black pride psychological revolution became an important part of an awakened, assertive (even aggressive and chauvinistic) form of African American identity.[11]

Cultural nationalists were prepared, when necessary, to invent new traditions and mythologies. In this spirit, Maulana Karenga, one of the "fathers" of the black cultural nationalism of the 1960s, emulated the West African harvest festival and other traditions to create Kwanzaa, which is now an African American cultural holiday that celebrates African heritage. The cultural nationalism of the 1960s and the companion black pride–black consciousness movement can be regarded as a revitalization movement.[12] It was not the "revitalization" of a subjugated nation on its own ancestral territory, but the revitalization of the consciousness and identity of African-descended people in the United States. In this cultural revival, Africa becomes a symbol of the glories of an ancient past, whether real or imagined. Indeed, the virtue and utility of the mythical Africa was precisely that it was not European, and so offered an alternative to the vaunted "superiority" and "universality" of Western, European, white culture. After all, this same Europe had given the world five centuries of colonialism and genocide in Africa, Asia, and Latin America, the transatlantic slave trade, two world wars in the twentieth century alone, and the Nazi Holocaust. And the hands of American exceptionalism were drenched with the blood of millions of black slaves and of more than three thousand African Americans who had been lynched. Some had even been burned alive. In these crimes against humanity, there was little for African American students to recognize as "superior."

By the late 1960s, the premise of a distinctive and valuable African American aesthetic, sensibility, and culture had become accepted among the younger generation. For many African Americans it became a closed matter, no longer subject to debate. Some African Americans who were proud of their culture became intolerant of any contrary view and regarded those who professed not to be able to recognize this culture as uninformed and blind. Black students arriving at Penn in the late 1960s brought these beliefs with them and fought the assumption that the purpose of the university was to transmit the Western white Eurocentric canon. In this climate, in 1968, with the demand for a course in black history, the "culture wars" at Penn began in earnest.

The Morgan State–Penn Exchange Program

Penn was not unaware of the "black awakening" of the 1960s. As early as 1965 the administration at Penn made an effort to add diversity to the curriculum and the faculty. As Penn had practically no black faculty members in the School of Arts and Sciences at that time, one way to make black faculty accessible to undergraduate students on campus would be through an exchange program with a black college. A cooperative relationship between Penn and Morgan State College in Baltimore, Maryland, was formalized in May 1965 with an agreement between President Gaylord Harnwell of Penn and President Martin Jenkins of Morgan. The Cooperative Project was funded through a grant from the Department of Health, Education and Welfare (HEW), under Title III of the 1965 Higher Education Act, and also grants from the 1907 Fund of the Ford Foundation.[13] Initially, the director of the exchange program on the Morgan end was Professor Willie T. Howard Jr., while the director of the program for Penn was Dr. Edward Cahill.[14]

Under the Cooperative Project, faculty members taught classes at the sister school. Thus, in 1968–69, for example, Dr. Harriet Trader of Morgan State taught a class in the Graduate School of Education at Penn, Dr. G. James Fleming taught in the Fels Institute of Government, and Dr. Ulysses G. Lee taught in the Department of American Civilization. Dr. Thomas Reiner and Dr. Julian Wolpert of Penn taught courses in Urban Geography at Morgan State.[15]

In the academic year 1969–70, the program was expanded to allow for student exchanges. Exchange students spent a semester or more at the sister school. Between 1969 and 1974, twenty-eight undergrads from Morgan State attended Penn (most for one semester), and nine students from Penn spent at least a semester at Morgan.[16] An outstanding success of the Morgan–Penn exchange was in serving as a conduit for black students from Morgan State to graduate study at Penn. In 1971–72 thirty-four Morgan students applied for admission to Penn's graduate programs. Fifteen were accepted.[17] During 1972–73 fifty-three Morgan graduates submitted applications to Penn's graduate programs, and ten were accepted. This brought the enrollment of Morgan graduates in Penn graduate schools to twenty-five.[18]

In the summer of 1972 Justine Rector became director.[19] Also during 1972–73 two students from Morgan attended the Summer Medical Intern Program under Dr. Helen Davies of the Microbiology Department at the Penn Medical School.[20] In December 1972, Dr. Helen Davies became the faculty chair of the Morgan–Penn Project.[21]

In 1974 Penn and Morgan entered into an agreement to continue the cooperative program for another five years. In 1974 twenty-one Morgan State alumni were doing graduate work at Penn.[22] By 1974, however, student interest in the exchange program began to dissipate on the Penn side. In 1973–74 eight Morgan State students attended Penn for the fall semester, and two in the spring. One of them was accepted by Penn as a transfer student. No Penn students attended Morgan during fall 1973, although three attended in the spring of 1974. There were also difficulties, however, because the number of students who could participate was constrained by the limited amount of money available for student housing and stipends. The exchange program provided housing for only one semester per student. In addition, only $10,000 per year was available to provide financial aid to Morgan graduate students entering Penn.[23]

In the late 1960s there were relatively few black students at Penn, and almost no black faculty in the undergraduate schools. There were black faculty members in the Medical School and the School of Social Work. A school such as Penn preferred to hire faculty with doctorates from other Ivy League schools or other elite, white institutions. As yet, there still were few blacks who were "qualified" in this very selective way, and few new black Ph.D.s from these sources. If courses in African American literature, history, politics, art, and music were going to be taught, by African American faculty, those faculty members would have to be "borrowed" from other institutions. The Penn–Morgan Exchange Program was an innovative attempt to make courses and lecturers in African American Studies available at a predominantly white institution such as Penn.

A Course in Afro-American History, Fall 1968

By 1968, however, pressures were beginning to build for a different approach. In February 1968 the *Daily Pennsylvanian* reported that the previous week three representatives of SAAS had suggested to Dr. Alfred Rieber, chairman of the History Department, that a course on black history should be offered.[24] Rieber was receptive to the idea of a course, taught at Penn by Penn faculty, and on March 19 the *Daily Pennsylvanian* ran a story about a forthcoming course on Negro history (History 473) to be taught in fall 1968 by a white professor. In an interview with the *Daily Pennsylvanian,* he was asked about a white teacher's lecturing on black history. He responded, "Penn is an integrated school. Individuals come here by choice. If they wanted a course taught by a Negro they could have gone to other schools, like Howard."[25]

The course was organized as a two-hour lecture with a discussion section, with four hundred students enrolled. The course became the object of controversy, however, precisely over the issue of a white instructor's teaching black history. On November 13, 1968, during the break in the two-hour lecture, a member of SAAS, began circulating a petition asking that the white lecturer be removed. The petition criticized his presentations as "distorted" and referred to his lack of qualifications to lecture on a variety of topics. Reportedly eight students in the class signed the petition.[26] The lecturer was not removed, but members of SAAS had served notice that merely offering a course in black history was not enough. If SAAS were to be satisfied, the instructor also would have to be black. Moreover, African American students wanted to know why there were no courses on black literature, or folklore or jazz or art, and why Penn couldn't find qualified full-time black faculty members to teach them.

A week earlier, black students at San Francisco State College had launched a strike to induce the college to concede to their demand for a Department of Black Studies that would be under black control. Black students at Penn, therefore, were attuned to the emerging national issue of the need for not simply a course here in history or a course there in literature, but a department and discipline of Black Studies. Furthermore, there were the critical questions of who would control the curriculum and the selection criteria for students and faculty in these departments. By the winter of 1968–69, Penn had arrived at a point where African American students were beginning to articulate a demand for a Department of Black Studies at Penn, with resident instructors who held regular appointments and tenure and would be responsive to black students and the black community. Visiting professors from Morgan State would no longer suffice. These (ethnically) assertive and race-conscious students were not content to accept the campus as they found it. They sought to reshape the campus and the curriculum in their own image. The black cultural revolution at Penn was intensifying. It would lead to a series of open conflicts between 1969 and 1972, culminating in the creation of an Afro-American Studies program at Pennsylvania.

CHAPTER FIVE

THE SOJOURN OF THE AFRO-AMERICAN
STUDIES PROGRAM

What library houses the works of a Nubian Thucycides? Who was the Senegalese Cicero? . . . What are the contributions of the Negro culture to enduring art, or music, or literature, or architecture? To law, jurisprudence, government? To science, invention, mathematics, philosophy? Here was a race, if the horrid word may be used (or a culture or subculture or ethnic group), that lived for thousands of years in effective possession of one of the richest continents on earth. Here were a people who lived by the sea, and never conceived the sail; who dwelled in the midst of fantastic mineral deposits, and conceived no more than the crudest smelting of iron and copper. The Negro developed no written language, not even the poorest hieroglyphics; no poetry; no numerals; not even a calendar that has survived. . . . Nothing aroused the Negro from his primitive sleep. He did not adapt. He did not copy. He did not profit.

—James Kilpatrick, *The Southern Case for School Segregation*, 1962

B y the late 1960s a new generation of African American students, aroused by black pride, Black Power, and the cultural revolution, began to arrive on predominantly white college campuses in greater numbers. This was true at Penn in 1968 and 1969, as elsewhere. This generation of students, however, now had the "critical mass" to protest against what they perceived as the absence and exclusion of black people from the curriculum, especially in disciplines such as history, English literature, sociology, and political science. There might not be a black biology or electronics, but African Americans saw no legitimate reason why Daniel Hale Williams and Charles Drew should be omitted from biology, or why Granville T. Woods and Garrett Morgan should be neglected in electrical engineering. Out of this racial and ethnic assertiveness, and of a grievance against the perception of the exclusion of black people from the curriculum, emerged the demand for courses in and a school of Black Studies. The demand for "Black Studies" at Penn, after a protracted process in the critical, formative years of 1969–1972, was met with the establishment of an Afro-American Studies Program in 1972.

In the fall of 1968, a course in Afro-American History had been inaugurated, but, in November 1968, African American students had modified their original demand to insist that the instructor should be an African American as well. They did not believe a white man could know what it is like for black people to be on the receiving end of white prejudice in a society where black people are the numerical minority and white people control the society's institutions. By March 1969, only a month after the sit-in of February 1969, Provost David Goddard charged a committee to study creation of an academic program in Afro-American Studies.

The question of Black Studies was still fraught with conflict. There were faculty members at Penn (as elsewhere) who questioned whether any such thing as "Black Studies" actually existed, doubted that it was a legitimate academic discipline, and opposed a major or department in Black Studies. Therefore Black Studies has always had to "justify its existence." The battle over Black Studies (at Penn, as elsewhere) also raised issues of content and control, as nationalist elements in SAAS sought an autonomous learning center that would be run by blacks, for blacks, and would seek to train black people for the "liberation struggle."

Other advocates of black control proposed a separate school of black studies with its own dean and vice provost, somewhat similar to what black students had demanded at San Francisco State. But how could a separate black school exist within the predominantly white university? And if it did exist, would this be segregation? Furthermore, the creation of schools requires the approval of the trustees. Were the Penn Trustees, most if not all of whom were white, likely to approve a separate School of Black Studies? If the solution was a department of Black Studies, departments could not be created by fiat. Departments exist within schools and must be approved by the faculty members of the school.

It was also not clear how the student demand for black faculty to teach these courses could be reconciled with the traditional elite definitions of qualification and merit and the principle of hiring the most qualified individual regardless of race. What does "qualified" mean? Does it mean holding a degree from Harvard or another Ivy League school but not from a state college? Does it mean that a 3.8 G.P.A. from Howard or Fisk or another historically black college is not regarded as highly as a 3.2 G.P.A. from Swarthmore or Bryn Mawr because of differences in ratings of difficulty or competitiveness by Barron's? Does qualification refer to experience or a credential such as a Ph.D. degree?

Furthermore, there were the critical questions of who would control the curriculum and the selection of students and faculty in these departments, and the criteria by which both would be selected and judged. Moreover, was the purpose of a Black Studies program to provide an academic exercise, for all students regardless of race, or to train black people for the struggle for their own liberation?

In effect, the entire question of how to construct a place for Black Studies was a minefield. Eventually the demands for a program "by blacks, for blacks" and for a separate school of Black Studies were rejected by the faculty and administration, but there was not sufficient support among the faculty in the School (College) of Arts and Sciences to establish a department. Therefore, in 1972, after numerous committees had studied the issue, an interdisciplinary Afro-American Studies Program was established. It reported not to the dean of Arts and Sciences, as would usually be the case, but to the Provost. Not until the mid-1990s did Afro-American Studies become a program within Arts and Sciences.

The 1969 Sit-in as Accelerator

On March 10, 1969, barely two weeks after the sit-in of February 1969, Provost David Goddard appointed the Afro-American Studies Committee, chaired by Dr. Alfred Rieber of the History Department. In the letter to members of the committee stating its charge, Provost Goddard indicated that several different proposals had been made. One was for a joint Afro-American Institute with Morgan State College, in which courses on African and Afro-American life and culture would be centered. A second group of Penn faculty had urged a Black Studies major, while yet a third suggested an independent major or specialty within a major. The charge of the committee was "to study all possible avenues and approaches and to determine recommendations regarding establishment of an academic program as well as the establishment of a black social center." The letter also stated, "We are not committed [in advance] to any one idea" and "We should be open to all suggestions and possibilities."[1]

In addition to Dr. Rieber, members of the committee included Assistant

Dean of Admissions William Adams, Dr. Igor Kopytoff, Dr. F. Hilary Conroy, Dr. Samuel Klausner, Dr. Herbert Wilf, Dr. Robert Rutman, Dr. Herbert Spiro, Dr. Philip Rieff, Philip Pochoda, and the Reverend Allen Happe of the Christian Association. Student members of the committee included Cathy Barlow (who was then a sophomore in the College for Women), Frederick Chandler, Gaynell Oubre, and Clayton Ramey of SAAS, Ira Harkavy, and Barbara Perman.[2] Another student, Mercedes Sherrod, was also named to the committee, as she was a signatory to the final report.[3]

Provost Goddard denied that the appointment of the committee had grown out of the recent Science Center sit-in. Instead, he asserted the initiative had emerged from "a dinner with representatives of Morgan State College, to discuss a cooperative institute for Afro-American studies between the two schools, held Feb. 6, before the sit-in."[4] Black Studies seems to have been on the agenda of the central administration even before the Science Center sit-in of February 1969. It is reasonable, however, to suggest that the sit-in added urgency to the matter and accelerated the process. After the sit-in, Black Studies was no longer an issue that the administration could ignore or address "when it got around to it."

Early in the process some African American students expressed objections to sharing professors with Morgan State College.[5] They wanted to build an African American Studies Institute at Penn, with African American faculty, who would eventually have tenure. Visiting faculty would not have the same permanence, stability, and influence as tenured faculty. At worst, visiting faculty would be simply a "revolving door." Many African American students did not see the Penn–Morgan Project or exchange faculty with other universities as an optimal solution.

The Rieber Committee Report: A School of Black Studies

On April 28, 1969, the Rieber Committee recommended the creation of a separate four-year School of Black Studies. This proposed school would grant both graduate and undergraduate degrees, and have its own vice provost as well. As a separate school, it would have greater control over its own admission criteria and the hiring of faculty members. Students in the School of Black Studies could elect courses in all other undergraduate schools of the university, and courses in the new school would be open to students in other schools of the university. There was no assumption that all black students would be enrolled in the School of Black Studies, nor was there any exclusion of non–African Americans. The "Integrity Statement" on the first page of the report announced that the central focus of the school would be the "culture and cultural heritage of Afro-Americans," and that "such an educational program means a comprehensive and global view of man's battle for freedom and integrity. Such a focus means the rejection of many of the social values, aesthetics and philosophies which are basic to white America." The school was to have five departments, each with its own dean. The five departments were to be: language–linguistics–literature; Afro-American history and culture; Afro-American arts; "studies in freedom: a comprehensive approach to ideologies and philosophies (emphasis upon the struggles of oppressed peoples)"; and "social structure–institutional racism and social change–urban studies."[6]

There were three written dissents, by Dr. Igor Kopytoff, Dr. Herbert Wilf, and Dr. Samuel Klausner. They did not object to Afro-American studies in some form, but disapproved of a separate school. Kopytoff urged that the "University encourage appointments by the various departments of faculty specializing, within their respective disciplines, in Afro-American Studies," and "that these appointments follow the same criteria of excellence or promise that are ideally expected in all such appointments in those departments." Once a core of such faculty members existed, the faculty should then form a committee to consider the creation of an Afro-American major program.[7] Wilf objected to *any* additional separate colleges at the undergraduate level and regretted that the undergraduate student body was already fragmented and divided between the Arts and Sciences, the Wharton School, Nursing School, and Engineering School. He suggested that a separate school raised the specter of "segregation on the ground of color."[8] Dr. Klausner argued:

It is true that . . . American education has provided a "white, western cultural model." However, to establish a model focusing on the "cultural heritage of Afro-Americans," implying the "rejection of many of the social values . . . basic to white America," is not the appropriate response. The University is the one social institution competent in and committed to the scholarly analysis of values. This task is incompatible with the promotion of and propagation of ideologies and with an effort to strengthen black, white, Jewish or Christian "consciousness."

He insisted that a program of Black Studies should "be established within the regular University framework with faculty appointments and admissions based on scholarly merits without regard to race." Furthermore, he felt that "the curricular separation of students on other grounds than disciplinary interests would be retrogressive."[9]

The Phillips Committee, Summer 1969

After receiving the Report of the Rieber Committee, Provost Goddard consulted with the Steering Committee of the University Council. The University Council at Penn is an advisory body to the president and provost. It consists of a given number of faculty members elected by their peers from constituency seats (across the entire university), undergraduates (nominated by the Undergraduate Assembly), and graduate students (named by the Graduate and Professional Student Assembly). The president appoints a handful of administrators and deans, and staff employees and librarians are represented on the council as well. In all, this council has about ninety members, and it is the closest thing at Penn to a parliament or constituent assembly. It is not, however, a legislative body. It is purely advisory and consultative. The Steering Committee of the council consists of the president, provost, chairs of the Faculty Senate (past, present, and elect), the chair of the Undergraduate Assembly, the chair of the Graduate Assembly, and four faculty members, with one graduate student and one undergraduate student elected by the full council. Thus, it numbers only about thirteen members.

In April 1969 the Steering Committee urged that the University Council, as a consultative body to the administration, be asked to appoint a special ad hoc committee to evaluate the Rieber majority report, the three dissenting minority reports, and any alternative methods or approaches to academic programs in African and Afro-American studies. Provost Goddard heeded this "advice" and disseminated the reports and dissents to members of the University Council with a cover letter dated 30 April 1969.[10] The Rieber Committee Report was not well received at the special meeting of the University Council on May 8, 1969. On that date the University Council voted to establish a new ad hoc committee on Black Studies to review the recommendations of the Rieber Committee.[11] Reading between the lines indicates that the decision to review the Rieber Committee Report represented a rejection of its findings.

The new ad hoc committee (of the University Council) on Afro-American Studies was chaired by Dr. Almarin Phillips of the Economics Department.

In May rumors circulated that SAAS believed more weight should have been given to the Rieber Committee Report and that both the Rieber Committee and SAAS should have been consulted on the composition of the Phillips Committee.[12]

Black undergraduates participated in a preliminary discussion with the Phillips Committee in June, but thereafter declined to continue as part of the committee. Black students boycotted the committee meeting of June 23. An "open meeting" to which all interested parties were invited (but not a meeting of the committee members per se) was scheduled for June 30.[13] No black students attended, and it thus appears that SAAS was refusing to participate in the Phillips Committee. One may infer that SAAS had demanded a School of Black Studies and was not retreating from that position. Perhaps SAAS reasoned that, if it could not have the school it had asked for, it would not advance the goals of SAAS to participate in a review committee that was likely to formulate a diluted alternative.

On July 1, 1969, the Phillips Committee discussed whether to continue without participation by African American students, dissolve itself, or hold the existing committee together until the fall and recommend a general commitment to (the concept and principle of) Black Studies by the University Council. The Phillips Committee voted to "dissolve the existing Committee with the recommendation to the Steering Committee that a new committee be established in such a manner [that] the Blacks and the Rieber Committee would cooperate [with the new committee]."[14] The Phillips Committee urged the Steering Committee of the council to reconstitute the *Ad Hoc* Committee on Black Studies in close consultation with SAAS, the Rieber Committee, and other interested persons, in such a way that the newly constituted committee might function with the constructive participation of the major parties concerned.[15] The Phillips Committee seems to have concluded that it was pointless to pursue the design of a program on Black Studies that black people refused to participate in. Any proposal that such a process generated would lack even the appearance of authenticity or legitimacy.

Phillips and the Steering Committee agreed that research on the structure of a Black Studies program should continue during the summer.[16] In September 1969 Cathy Barlow issued a report, which described the essentials needed for a school of Black Studies. These included a core faculty, a separate budget guaranteed by the university, and the freedom to establish its own courses, set policy, and hire faculty.[17] On July 7, following the demise of the Phillips

Committee, the Steering Committee met with Phillips, Rieber, and Cathy Barlow. After this meeting, the Steering Committee decided that in early September it would reconstitute the *Ad Hoc* Committee, and would consult with SAAS and other interested parties in selecting its members.[18]

The Gundersheimer Committee, 1969–70

In September 1969 the University Council Steering Committee appointed yet another ad hoc committee, chaired by Dr. Werner Gundersheimer (History Department). The Steering Committee did "consult" with SAAS and members of the Rieber and Phillips Committees in making its selections.[19] The new committee also reviewed a research report by graduate students Andrew Reshovsky and John Kwoka and another by undergraduate Judith Teller. The former urged a departmental structure for black studies within the College. It also urged that part of the function of a black studies program should be to correct historical neglect of black studies, to educate white America in the history, culture, and ethos of black America, to promote research into areas transcending white Western culture, to make education more relevant to the needs of all students, and to recognize the special obligation the university has to black urban centers.[20] The Teller report suggested the educational and curricular program of a school of Black Studies was only marginally different from what existed in the two liberal arts schools (the College for Men and the College for Women), and "the addition of another School unit is not needed if it will merely duplicate existing services on a racial basis."[21]

The Teller report also examined the structure of the Afro-American Studies programs at Harvard, Yale, Stanford, Princeton, the University of Minnesota, and Wayne State University (Detroit). It explored the question of a separate school versus a department of Afro-American studies versus an interdisciplinary major, without endorsing any one model. The Teller report did state, however: "An Afro-American studies major could be funded, possibly through the Office of the Provost, and still retain its non-departmental nature. Although no appointments could be made to Afro-American studies, per se, a coordinating committee with a budget at its disposal could prod existing departments into making additional appointments, especially if the coordinating committee was willing to assume a large share of the salary burden."[22] Prophetically, Teller outlined the form that Afro-American Studies at Penn would take from 1972 to the mid-1990s.

An Institute by Blacks, for Blacks

However, like the Phillips Committee before it, the Gundersheimer Committee also had difficulty negotiating the unpredictable currents and cross-currents of politics within SAAS. Indeed, it was "broadsided" by new developments within SAAS in the spring semester of 1970. In mid-January 1970, Cathy Barlow, a prominent veteran member of SAAS who served on the Gundersheimer Committee and had served previously on the Rieber Committee, resigned without public explanation. Campus media intimated that a "power shake-up" was taking place within SAAS.[23]

A month later, on Friday, February 20, 1969, a group of students from SAAS led by Olu Hassan-Ali announced that they wished to establish their own autonomous Institute of Black Studies.[24] Olu Hassan-Ali envisioned a type of "free school." He said any black studies program must work to create "black identity, awareness and emancipation—and for all black people, not just students."[25] He felt the learning complex should be set up exclusively by blacks, for blacks. The institute should be run and financed independently of the university, but financial contributions were welcome. Hassan-Ali was concerned that the institute not be an appendage of Penn or "subservient to any white institution."[26]

The institute was intended to be modeled after the Malcolm X Institute in Durham, North Carolina, and the Institute of the Black World in Atlanta, Georgia. It would not be simply an academic environment to enable students to take courses toward a degree. The efforts of Hassan-Ali and the nationalist members of SAAS were closely associated with the House of the Family, located at 3914 Locust Walk. Evidently efforts to establish an academic program in Black Studies within the university setting, whether as a school or department, were at odds with emerging efforts to establish an autonomous, black-run, black-controlled institute. Such an institute would not be constrained by the traditional admissions standards of Penn. Nor would it be hampered by conventional definitions of merit and qualification, such as student performance on standardized tests. The instructors in an institute that was run by blacks and for blacks would not need to be selected simply on the basis of traditional standards of academic merit (completion of a Ph.D. from a highly regarded school with publication credits, for example). Furthermore, this autonomous institute could focus on training individuals for participation in a freedom movement and community organizing, rather than focusing on an academic program. It might even adopt the stance that its major purpose was to train African Americans to lead their own struggle, and only secondarily—if at all— was its purpose to educate whites.

The Gundersheimer Report

In response to the new developments from SAAS, Dr. Gundersheimer was quoted as saying, "I don't see why two black studies programs—one outside the University and one within the regular academic structure—can't coexist and be mutually beneficial." He added, "If we can survive and set up a black studies program that is successful and intellectually viable, it will attract students of both races."[27] Although Cathy Barlow was no longer a member of the committee, and SAAS had declined to name a replacement, there were two black undergraduate students on the committee who were not representatives of SAAS. Barbara Giles and Wilbur Commodore remained as members of the committee despite the change in direction by SAAS.

On the evening of April 22, 1970, the Gundersheimer Committee finalized its report. It recommended that: "Black Studies be instituted at the University of Pennsylvania in the form of a school which admits students after their sophomore year at the University."[28] The proposed School of Black Studies would have its own dean and faculty, and its graduates would receive a Bachelor of Arts in Black Studies from the School of Black Studies of the University of Pennsylvania. Students, who were admitted to the school after their sophomore year, would have to satisfy Penn's admissions criteria that applied to the various undergraduate schools.[29]

The report emphasized that students of any race might enroll in the school, and it was not assumed that only black students would do so or that all, or even a majority of, black students would choose to do so. Although some courses might be restricted to students in the school, other courses would be available to freshmen and sophomores from across the university as electives. The report emphasized that "there is to be no barrier to faculty recruitment on the basis of race, but we anticipate that the School will attract a relatively high percentage of black faculty members."[30]

The report was issued in a period of growing black unrest on campus. A week earlier, on Monday, April 13, 1970, the black associate dean of students had resigned in protest over the failure of the university to accept the political content of a proposed prefreshman summer program. On Thursday, April 16, nearly one hundred black students had marched through the campus to protest the "racism" of the central administration. It is impossible to know what effect, if any, the tensions surrounding the controversy over the pre-freshman summer program may have had on the Gundersheimer Committee. For critics of the report, it probably appeared as if the committee were "caving-in" to pressure and threatening actions from black students.

The Mundheim–Schrieffer Dissent

In any event, two members of the Gundersheimer Committee, Dr. Robert Mundheim (Law) and Dr. Robert Schrieffer (Physics), dissented from some of the majority recommendations and offered their own alternatives in an addendum to the report. Mundheim and Schrieffer urged that implementation of the two-year school be delayed, and that the president instead appoint a universitywide committee of faculty to oversee Black Studies for a few years. On the basis of this experience, a final institutional structure (school, department, two-year program, four-year program) should then be determined. In the report they noted the concern expressed by some members of the university community that the program might be (mis)used in a way counter to academic notions of "objective inquiry," and fears that the Black Studies program might be "pressured into adjusting its standards and requirements so that it could become a safe haven for black (and other) students, admitted under new, experimental standards."[31]

This wording was very similar to an earlier memo of May 1969, from a member of the faculty, suggesting that "what Black students need is Mathematics and English" and that the Penn–Morgan Exchange Program should be expanded to include those course offerings. Furthermore, the author encouraged special courses in math and English for black high school students and warned that, "if well-qualified Black students do not apply [to Penn], then we run the risk of being pressured into admitting poorly qualified ones. These would gravitate into Black Studies for want of the preparation necessary to take advantage of the genuine strength of this University."[32] Others warned that a School of Black Studies would be a "second-class institution, if not worse. It will train black kids who will be distinctly inferior products compared to other students. . . ."[33] In the summer of 1970, Martin Meyerson succeeded Gaylord Harnwell as president of the University of Pennsylvania, and Meyerson inherited the Afro-American Studies controversy and the Gundersheimer Committee Report.

The Gundersheimer Committee had considered the strengths and weaknesses of an interdisciplinary major. But it concluded in its report that such an entity, by having to rely on faculty and course offerings in other departments, would be "extremely vulnerable and fragile." The committee also considered the possibility of a department of Black Studies in the College of Arts and Sciences. However, partisans of the cause of Afro-American Studies objected on the ground that, in the experience of other universities with such departments, there were greater "administrative controls and scrutinies applied to them" than in other, established fields. The other constraint, explicitly cited on page 4 of the Gundersheimer Report, was, "It does not appear likely that the College will establish such a department."[34]

The political reality was that many of the faculty in the School of Arts and Sciences doubted that Afro-American studies was a legitimate field of academic inquiry and opposed the creation of an Afro-American studies department. Furthermore, the creation of a new department would require the allocation of money for faculty "lines," which would compete with already existing departments. Faculty approval is necessary to create an academic department in a school. It cannot be done by presidential or provostial decree. The opposition of the faculty in the School of Arts and Sciences, at that time, placed an obstacle in the path of any proposal for a department of Afro-American studies. But black students demanded Afro-American studies at Penn, to be taught by full-time Penn faculty. By default, then, the only remaining alternative seemed to be a new school. This, however, would require the approval of the trustees.

On October 19, the Committee of Undergraduate Deans unanimously approved a statement indicating that it "finds much to commend in the 'Final Report of the University Council *Ad Hoc* Committee on Black Studies.'" As if to cut the ground out from under proposals for a separate school, the deans added: "The Black Studies major can be put into effect as soon as the faculty of the College and/or College for Women approve it. The Deans of these two schools will take the initial steps to bring this matter before their faculties during the current term." Furthermore, students wishing to engage in such studies "should be encouraged and enabled to begin immediately."[35] Momentum was building for the immediate implementation of black studies, in some form.

On October 20, 1970, the Faculty Senate discussed the Gundersheimer Report. In a straw vote the Faculty Senate rejected the Gundersheimer Committee's concept of a two-year school, but accepted the Mundheim–Schrieffer addendum urging a delay in the final implementation of a structure for Black

Studies. The Mundheim–Schrieffer statement agreed to the importance of a clear-cut statement by the university as to "the goal of creating an organized, academically sound program in Black Studies." The Faculty Senate also approved the statement of the Committee of Undergraduate Deans, of October 19, 1970.[36]

On December 9, 1970, the University Council followed the lead of the Faculty Senate and accepted the essence of the minority Mundheim–Schrieffer Statement.[37] Specifically, it supported the recommended actions of the Steering Committee, "to agree with the desirability of concrete and immediate action, as prescribed in the Mundheim–Schrieffer statement and the statement of the undergraduate deans, and with the wisdom of deferring long-term decisions in institutional arrangements."[38] Cathy Barlow, Conrad Jones, and others expressed disappointment at the defeat of the proposal for a School of Black Studies.[39] Any remaining hopes for a separate School of Black Studies at Penn were now officially dead.

The Walmsley Committee, 1970–71

In November 1970, shortly after the action of the Faculty Senate of October 20, 1970, and even before the formal vote by the University Council on December 9, 1970, President Martin Meyerson began constituting a new presidential committee on Black Studies. The committee had two charges. They were to create an Afro-American Studies Program at Penn and to appoint a director for the program. The committee was finally constituted in May 1971, with Roger Walmsley (Physics Department) as chairman.[40] Robert Engs served as a consultant to the committee. Engs, who was an African American, was a 1965 graduate of Princeton. In 1971 he was completing his graduate studies at Yale, under the direction of the eminent C. Vann Woodward. During 1971–72, Engs served as a visiting lecturer at Princeton.[41]

On Wednesday, December 1, 1971, President Meyerson named twenty-six-year-old John Edgar Wideman as the director of Afro-American Studies. Wideman was a Penn alumnus (1963) and a Rhodes Scholar who received his Ph.D. from Oxford University in 1966.[42] On December 3, 1971 Wideman formally succeeded Walmsley as chair of the Black Studies Committee.[43] His actual first full semester of activity, however, was spring 1972, and for this reason among others, the Afro-American Studies program regards 1972 as the year of its inception. Also in 1972 Dr. Robert Engs arrived at Penn to teach Afro-American History.[44]

While committee after committee studied and analyzed Afro-American Studies, the course in Afro-American History continued. John Wideman had begun teaching creative writing in the English Department in September 1967 and a course in black literature in September 1969. Harry Jones of Morgan State University had begun teaching a course in American Civilization at Penn in September 1969, entitled "The Negro and American Culture." In the Sociology Department, Federal Judge A. Leon Higginbotham began teaching Racial Justice and the Sociology of the Law as an adjunct professor in September 1970. Patrick Cole taught courses on the history of West Africa in the History Department. Non–African Americans were also teaching courses related to Africa and African Americans. For example, John Szwed taught Afro-American Folklore, and Igor Kopytoff taught several courses on Africa in the Anthropology Department.

In March 1972, History Chairman Al Rieber announced that, in fall 1972, Robert F. Engs would begin teaching Afro-American History and a proseminar in comparative slavery. In spring 1973, Engs would teach a course on the Civil War and Reconstruction and a graduate colloquium on the history of the American South. Engs's area of specialization was the Civil War and Reconstruction, and, with degrees from Princeton and Yale, no one could question his qualifications.[45]

A Program with an Advisory Committee of Faculty

In the School of Arts and Sciences there continued to be reservations about establishing a department of Afro-American Studies. Apart from further study of the issue and eventually publishing a major, no concrete action was taken by the school to create a department.[46]

Subsequently, in January 1973, a section of the Development Commission Report dealing with "Black Presence" recommended the establishment of an Institute of Afro-American Studies and that the Afro-American Studies Program be provided with regular funds for its programs and for ten to fifteen full-time or part-time faculty. In September 1973, Louise Stone was appointed as administrative director of the Afro-American Studies Program, and an advisory committee of faculty members was established.[47]

Eventually, in the 1970s, a recognized major in Afro-American studies was established. African American studies at Penn, however, remained an academic program and an interdisciplinary major led by a committee of faculty that reported to the provost until the 1990s.[48] Thus, for two decades, Afro-American Studies became an interdisciplinary program, but not a department.

Some observers have suggested that this arrangement was actually advantageous because it shielded the Afro-American Studies Program from the danger of budget cuts in the School of Arts and Sciences. The most prominent spokesperson for this view is Robert Engs, of the History Department, who has written: "The program survived and grew in those early days because we consciously insisted that it be placed in the Provost's Office—thereby partially insulating it from hostility of some opponents in the various schools and departments, from the competition for perennially scarce resources in the new School of Arts and Sciences, and from the vagaries of the revolving-door deanship in SAS."[49] As a consultant to the Walmsley Committee, Engs had also advised that the advantages and benefits of an interdisciplinary structure outweighed the potential dangers and disadvantages. A program reporting to the Provost was a structural alternative to both the original demands for a separate School of Black Studies (which SAAS had urged, in 1969 but which the administration and University Council had effectively rejected) and a Department of Afro-American Studies (in the cash-starved School of Arts and Sciences).

In October 1973, Provost Eliot Stellar established a committee to identify a pool of black candidates for consideration by various schools and departments as faculty members. Assistant Professor of History Robert Engs chaired the committee and assumed responsibility for recruiting black faculty. Stellar sent a memo to all deans, directors, and department heads stating that the recruitment of black and other minority faculty was "a high priority claim upon University development funds."[50] John Wideman left Penn to go to the University of Wyoming, Laramie, at the end of academic year 1973–74. As part of the effort to recruit black faculty, Professor Engs felt it was a high priority to encourage the hiring of a black faculty person in English to succeed Wideman.[51]

In the summer of 1974 Professor Houston Baker joined the university as a professor in the English Department and as director of the Afro-American Studies Program. Houston Baker received his B.A. magna cum laude at Howard University in 1965, and his M.A. in 1966 and Ph.D. in 1968 from the University of California at Los Angeles. He had been an assistant professor at Yale, and associate professor at the University of Virginia.[52] Baker is known for such studies as *Black Literature in America; A Many-Colored Coat of Dreams: The Poetry of Countee Cullen; No Matter Where You Travel, You Still Be Black;* and *Blues, Ideology, and Afro-American Literature: A Vernacular Theory.*

In the mid-1970s Nell Irvin Painter joined the faculty in the History Department. Her area of specialization is the "nadir," or post-Reconstruction period. She is the author of *The Exodusters, The Narrative of Hosea Hudson,* and a biography of Sojourner Truth. She eventually left Penn for the University of North Carolina and is now teaching at Princeton.

Postscript

In 1997 the Afro-American Studies Program at Penn celebrated its twenty-fifth anniversary. Over that period it has developed under the leadership of such individuals as Houston Baker, Robert Engs, Louise Stone, Joseph Washington, Elijah Anderson, Jacqueline Wade, Ralph Smith, John Roberts, and Herman Beavers. In the 1990s, Afro-American Studies finally became a program in the School of Arts and Sciences. Pressure from African American students in 1968 and 1969 played a crucial role in generating the momentum for an Afro-American Studies Program with an emphasis on courses taught by full-time, tenure-track African American members of the Penn faculty. Without that pressure, it is doubtful a program or department in African American Studies would ever have come into existence.

At Penn, the "nationalists" did not get the lasting institute "by blacks, for blacks" that they wanted. Nor did proponents of Black Power get the separate school of Black Studies that they wanted. This was the significance of the rejection of the Rieber and Gundersheimer Committee Reports. But even after these agendas were rejected, the cultural agenda of disseminating information about black history and the black experience, and pluralizing the curriculum, endures to this day. It is a testament to the tenacity of the cultural revolution.

CHAPTER SIX

THE MOST DIFFICULT YEAR, 1969–70

Black people are legal citizens of the United States with, for the most part, the same *legal* rights as other citizens. Yet they stand as colonial subjects in relation to the white society. This institutional racism has another name: colonialism.

—Kwame Ture and Charles V. Hamilton, *Black Power,* 1967

A cademic year 1969–70 proved to be a difficult and stormy year of transition for both African American students and the university. Just as pressure from African American students was crucial in the formation of a course in African American History and an Afro-American Studies Program at Penn, so, too, it was critical in bringing about an increased commitment to a permanent prefreshman summer program and to tutoring and academic support services for students. Pressure from students was also instrumental in the creation of a black social center, and the appointment of a black assistant to the president (Donald Stewart). All these issues were part of the agenda of SAAS in 1969-70 and were at the center of its engagement with the central administration in that period. Because the issues of social isolation, academic support services, black faculty and staff, as well as Black Studies were combined by the students themselves in this period of agitation, and occurred together in that year, I have woven them together in recounting their development. Before these issues had been resolved, more than a hundred black students would stage a protest march through the campus, and a series of mysterious fires on campus would culminate in the firebombing of two offices in College Hall in April 1970. This was not integration as the architects of the Civil Rights Movement had envisioned it. Rather, perhaps it reflected the influence of the assertive ideology of Black Power and black nationalism, which proclaimed that African Americans must liberate themselves "by any means necessary."

The House of the Family (*Nyumba ya Ujamii*)

As expressed in the previously cited letter of George Royal in October 1968, many black students found themselves confronted with a double transition. For many, who had come from public high schools, they were now confronted with a rigorous, elite university in which they had to go from studying "eight hours a week to do well in high school to studying five and six hours a day to do well in college." At the same time, some black students—from mostly black neighborhoods—went from associating with whites "six hours-a-day" at school to total "immersion" with whites at virtually all times on a residential campus.[1] This situation gave rise to demands that related not only to academic support services (such as tutoring and compensatory education classes) but also to the sense of social isolation and discomfort on campus that black students felt.

Penn responded to the complaints about social isolation in September 1969. At that time the university administration assisted in the formation of a black "social center." On Thursday, September 4, 1969, the *Daily Pennsylvanian* reported that SAAS was negotiating for the creation of an "all black social center." University Counsel John Ballard, however, explained that the university itself would not lease a building for this purpose, as this might violate the Fourteenth Amendment and the Civil Rights Act of 1964. Furthermore, since June 1969, SAAS had been under investigation by the regional office of the Department of Health, Education and Welfare.[2]

In May 1969 the university had purchased the three-story Parish House of St. Mary's Episcopal Church, located at 3914 Locust Walk, for $60,000. On September 11 legal papers were filed whereby a nonprofit corporation was established, called *Nyumba ya Ujamii* (Swahili for House of the Family). The board of directors for this nonprofit corporation included both Penn students and members of the black community. The nonprofit corporation was an independent entity and not a department of the university. The members of the board of directors included Novella Williams of Citizens for Progress, Walter Palmer of the Black Coalition, and students Wendy Butcher (College for Women), Donald Maynard (Engineering), Donald Wallace and Wilbur Commodore (the College), David Wideman (College of General Studies), Patricia

Lane (graduate Linguistics), and Buford Tatum (Law). Many of the students were members of SAAS.

The university rented the house to the Nyumba ya Ujamii Corporation and maintained that its only relationship to the House of the Family was that of landlord. The goals of the House of the Family were "to provide an intellectual and cultural center to promote the exchange of ideas, philosophies and skills relevant to Afro-Americans and Africans, and to extend tutorial services at the university and to members of the community, and to disseminate such information, studies, surveys, plans and programs . . . as it sees fit."[3] By 1972 the House of the Family was publishing its own newspaper, called the *West Philadelphia Black Pages.* It advertised itself as "the black community's political information and news report." Richard Thomas was the editor-in-chief, and Lynwood Ford and Philip Jones were the managing editors.[4] The House of the Family became a center for efforts to build and empower the black community, and became better known simply as the "Black House."[5]

Perhaps not surprisingly, critics contended that leasing a house to the House of the Family Corporation was simply a thinly veiled means for the university to avoid direct responsibility for a racially exclusivist black social center. Whatever interpretation the reader may wish to make, the House of the Family did serve as a headquarters for SAAS. It also came about directly as the result of the initiative of the students themselves.

The Penn administration was very careful as to how it went about responding to the sense of isolation that African American students expressed and their request for a black "social center." Penn had good reason to be careful. In March 1969 Director Ruby Martin, of the Office for Civil Rights in the Department of Health, Education and Welfare (HEW), had sent a memo to the presidents of institutions of higher learning participating in federal assistance programs. The subject of the memo was "separate facilities for minority group students" and compliance with Title VI of the Civil Rights Act of 1964. On the subject of separate housing for students based on race, the memo specified: "All housing which is owned, operated or supported by the institution or a public agency must be available to all students without regard to race, color or national origin and assignment to such housing must be made in a nondiscriminatory manner."[6]

With regard to separate social activity space, the memo read: "Where the institution donates or otherwise makes available institution-owned facilities or land for student use or activities or where it provides funds or other financial assistance to acquire or operate facilities for such activities, it must be assured that the activities are to be operated without discrimination based on race, color or national origin." As for "separate colleges, schools or institutes," the memo stated: "Every service and benefit offered by the institution must be open and available to all students without regard to race, color or national origin."[7]

Reportedly HEW had begun an investigation of SAAS in June 1969. Allegedly a university student had complained to HEW about the university providing funding to a discriminatory organization that excluded whites from its activities.[8] For academic year 1969-70 SAAS had been allocated $4,000 by the undergraduate Student Activities Council, and HEW requested information about SAAS.[9] On September 24, 1969, two HEW investigators met with representatives of the university, the finance committee of the Student Activities Council, and SAAS. According to *Daily Pennsylvanian* reports of the discussions, SAAS member Helen Giles told the investigators that the criterion for membership was "sincere interest as determined by the group." Giles explained that "black students at Penn feel an alien atmosphere. We want to give them the feeling that other people care, provide them with a home basis where they can come with their problems." When one of the investigators asked if she felt these techniques excluded white students, Giles responded, "Black students have a need which is fulfilled by SAAS. No other organization can fulfill that need." When asked if SAAS meetings were open to whites, Ms. Giles reportedly replied, "We've never forced anyone violently to leave." She added that there would be "no interest for them [nonmembers] to stay because the things we do don't concern them."[10]

The HEW investigators also requested information about the House of the Family, and the SAC allocation to SAAS. University Counsel John Ballard took the position that the allocation had been made by the Student Activities Council, and in this sense was an independent action by a branch of student government and not the university administration. A second university lawyer, Henry Hilles Jr., explained that the university had not set up the Nyumba ya Ujamii Corporation, but rather this had been done by black students and community leaders. The university merely leased a building to the corporation.[11]

The establishment of the House of the Family in September 1969 provided African American students with a place they could call their own, hold meetings, and sponsor parties and social events. But it did not satisfy or placate black students. Before the 1969-70 school year had ended, SAAS cum the House of the Family and the central administration would be embroiled in one of the most furious battles ever to take place between black students and the administration at Penn. One source of these controversies was a dispute between saas and the Admissions Office in December 1969.

Squabble over Recruiting, December 1969

A group called the Black Committee on Recruitment (bcr) had been formed by saas. In fall 1969 the group had requested funds for travel to twenty-five cities. The funds were to defray the costs of students who engaged in recruiting activities in their hometowns, especially over the winter vacation. In December 1969, however, Dean Schlekat offered considerably less than saas wanted. Then saas demanded that students be appointed to an advisory committee to the Admissions Committee and also demanded the appointment of a provost for black student affairs. This latter demand was forwarded to the President Harnwell. On December 11, on College Green, about fifty members of saas burned Dean Schlekat in effigy. A placard bearing the name of the University of Pennsylvania was also burned. After this Schlekat and saas agreed to a compromise figure.[12] A fragile compromise over recruiting funds was reached in December, but by April 1970 saas and the Admissions Office were at odds again.

For the incoming class of 1970–71 the university apparently had set a goal (not a target or rigid quota) for at least 9 percent of the entering class to be black. At that time, however, Penn also had a policy whereby 3 percent of "slots" in the entering class were considered for socioeconomically disadvantaged students. Schlekat explained that the 3 percent "socioeconomic" (or se) category had been "instituted years ago to insure that a number of underprivileged high school students with 'marginal academic records' could be granted admission." He insisted this was not a "ghetto category," but was done simply as an attempt to diversify the student body.[13]

The society was angered that a goal of 9 percent black admissions was not *in addition to* the 3 percent "marginal" or se category, but rather was being achieved by admitting black students under the marginal category and converting that category into a proxy or surrogate black admissions channel. Optimally saas seems to have wanted 9 percent of the entering class to be black students admitted under a diversity category, and some blacks admitted under the "marginal" (se) category as well, above and beyond the base of 9 percent, and saas thought Schlekat hoped to achieve the goal of 9 percent by converting the se category of 3 percent into a de facto black category and then increasing black admissions in other categories (such as athletics or diversity) by 6 percent. Whatever the merits of the arguments on both sides, the dispute over admissions policy and the prefreshman summer orientation program lay at the center of the controversy between SAAS and the administration in 1969–70.

The Evolution of a Black Advising Program

The 1967 McGill Report had recommended that 10 percent of the freshman class be admitted under a "special admission" procedure. This 10 percent was in turn to be subdivided to provide for targets (not fixed numerical quotas) of 5 percent for athletes, 3 percent for students from socioeconomically disadvantaged backgrounds, and 2 percent for the children of faculty, staff, and alumni and for "special interest" candidates (generally, those endorsed by public figures or generous donors). The 1969 sit-in, during which the adjoining black neighborhood of Mantua demanded that Penn admit more African American students, accelerated the process of admitting more socioeconomically disadvantaged students. For African Americans, this generally meant students who might have high class rank at an inner-city public high school or be in the top quintile or top tenth of their class, but who had low SAT and achievement test scores. In some instances, the students might not even have taken an SAT or achievement test (this seems to have been so for some athletes).

Penn did realize that the 3 percent of students admitted under the socioeconomic (SE) subcategory of special admissions might be academically "at risk" and would need compensatory education. At that time, a student was considered "marginal" or "at risk" if he or she had three or more indicators of failure. Indicators of failure included low SAT scores, low achievement test scores, low class rank, or lopsided SAT scores (such as high verbal but very low math, and vice versa). Factors such as these would yield a low predictive index or predicted Grade Point Average. In some schools of the university (in 1969), a G.P.A. of 1.4 was cause for a student to be placed on probation. A predicted G.P.A. of 1.8 was cause for concern, and a predicted G.P.A. of 1.4 was cause for deep alarm. These latter students were deemed the most academically deficient. For these reasons, in the summer of 1969, Penn inaugurated a summer program for black prefreshmen. In spring 1969 Penn admitted 150 African American students (for the class of 1973). Some of these students were "late admits" from Philadelphia. It was the judgment of Dean Schlekat and the Admissions Office that approximately half of these students, or 80 of them, "suffered from inadequate educational preparation."[14]

The SAT scores of these students were several hundred points below the mean of the entering class. For this reason, in June 1969, all 80 of the African American freshmen with "inadequate educational preparation" were invited to the campus for a three-day orientation session. For the students most "at risk," special efforts were made to ensure that they could attend the orientation session, and even travel expenses were covered. Eighty African American freshmen attended. They were introduced to upper-class and faculty advisers. "They were tested for reading proficiency to identify those students who would need remedial reading instruction in the Reading Clinic of the Graduate School of Education." Of this group of 80, some 31 with "especially deficient preparation, all from Greater Philadelphia, were enrolled in a six-week summer session." Each student studied in one regular summer session class (in most instances, English or math) and also received tutoring. The summer session was on a nonresidential basis. Many of these students were attending Penn with scholarship assistance.[15]

Costs for the prefreshman summer program included tuition for the course and salaries for tutors. The students also received funds to compensate for the loss of summer earnings (the rationale being that, since they were in school, they lost the opportunity to work full-time). The program of the summer of 1969 was funded in part by the Aron Charitable Foundation and was called "Challenge at Penn." It soon came to be called the "University Advising Program" and was operated out of the Dean of Students Office. The trustees were kept informed of this program as well, as Dean of Students Alice Emerson described its operation in a report to the Trustees' Student Affairs Committee in October 1970.[16]

I am not suggesting that all students from the Philadelphia public schools were deficient. I was a graduate of Overbrook High School, a public high school. Central High School (then for boys) was a college-preparatory public school with an outstanding record of achievement. Girls' High School was a public high school with a fine reputation. Some public high schools, like Overbrook, had a Magnet Program that included (at one time) Advanced Placement courses in history, English, and math. Some of the students recruited by Penn from the Philadelphia public schools often ranked among the top ten students in their class, had the highest SAT scores among the students in their school, and were student leaders with good grades and participation in extracurricular activities. They displayed signs of leadership potential. Few would suggest, however, that West Philadelphia High, South Philadelphia High, Simon Gratz High School, or Benjamin Franklin or University City

High Schools were on par with Central High or Girls' High, or that every student coming out of the Philadelphia public schools had been in a Magnet Program with Advanced Placement courses, four years of science and math, and a foreign language. Far too many students received the "general" curriculum and were consigned to "shop" classes and "home economics." Little wonder, then, that upon graduation they were not adequately prepared for college. Some of the students admitted to Penn from the inner-city high schools did have educational deficiencies, and it is not a libel of all African American students, or the City of Philadelphia, or its public school system to admit this.

During the autumn of 1969 African American students voiced some discontent with the summer program. They resented being labeled and stigmatized as "marginal." The program was so closely identified with "marginal students" that to be associated with it marked a student. Therefore, some students who needed the program were ashamed and reluctant to be involved with it. The students also complained that the program emphasized academic achievement only and neglected areas of social and cultural adjustment. The Society of African and Afro-American Students (SAAS) demanded that the program be modified; urging that the program include all black students, not only those who were "marginal." In this way, the stigma might be diffused. They also demanded greater attention to social and cultural issues and wanted to "insure equally the social, academic and cultural success of Black freshmen. . . ."[17] This view became the genesis of the SAAS Advising Program (sometimes also called the Black Advising Program).

In spring 1970, SAAS demanded university funding for a revised prefreshman and "postfreshman" summer program that would address "social and cultural adjustment" as well as academic achievement. The term "prefreshmen" applied to entering students, while "postfreshmen" referred to students who had completed their freshman year but had failed courses and did not have enough credits to become sophomores.

A dispute developed, however, between SAAS and the administration over the political content of the proposed five-day prefreshmen orientation program, and the summer program for 1970. This dispute escalated into the most serious and destructive clash between black students and the Penn administration in the decade of the 1970s. The formal proposal for the revised program was written by an African American associate dean of students. The stated goals of the proposed program were "to assist the Black freshmen in developing a realistic concept of the Black individual and his relationship to society" and to support "the concept that education should provide students with tools to restructure the black nation now being suppressed by colonial America." A third goal was "investigating and challenging University policy on curriculum, admissions, and other forms of institutionalized racism."[18] Evidently a black nationalist perspective had spread not only to some African American students at Penn, but to some African American administrators as well.

The administration and SAAS disagreed sharply over this proposal. On April 13, Provost David Goddard sent a letter to Dean Alice Emerson, which stated that "no University facilities, funds, or staff shall use this program for the indoctrination of students for a single ideological or political outlook."[19] The same day the author of the proposal resigned in protest over the refusal of the administration to fund the program.[20]

Protest March of April 1970

The tension escalated, and on April 16, nearly one hundred black students marched from the House of the Black Family of the University of Pennsylvania at 3914 Locust Walk to College Hall and Van Pelt Library, and then to the University Museum and back to the Admissions Office at College Hall. The African American associate dean said he had resigned, because "the administration wanted me to compromise the whole concept of self-determination."[21] Dean of Students Alice Emerson, implementing the decision of Provost Goddard, asserted that "a University program could not be so closely tied to one point of view as a basic goal."[22] Apparently the administration regarded the proposed orientation program as a political indoctrination session in black nationalism.

Aside from the dispute over the political content of the orientation program, the proposal also called for prefreshman and postfreshman summer courses that would give black students up to fifteen months to complete the first-year requirements of their school.

At the march Olu Hassan-Ali of SAAS addressed the demonstrators, and SAAS explained that the purpose of the march was to expose to the campus in general, and to black students in particular, the "racist character of this University."[23] The April 16 protest centered around admissions policy and the prefreshman summer program at the same time that the Gundersheimer Committee was considering a proposal for a School of Black Studies. Clearly SAAS and the administration were at odds on a number of issues simultaneously.

The Fires of April

On Thursday, April 23, several acts of vandalism and six mysterious fires erupted on campus. In the predawn hours of April 23, the Franklin Room on the second floor of Houston Hall was gutted by fire, and the neighboring Bishop White Room slightly damaged. Nearby at College Hall, in the Admissions Office, the office of Assistant Dean of Admissions John Cantrell was set on fire. Reportedly these fires had started after 3 A.M. It was reported that two Molotov cocktails were found in the College Hall office. The same night seven windows were smashed at the bookstore. At about 1 P.M. the same day, another fire was discovered in a storage closet outside the Admissions Office. At 3 P.M. residents of the women's dormitory, Hill Hall, were forced to evacuate the building because of a fire in a laundry room on the third floor. At 8 P.M. another evacuation was ordered following yet another fire at Hill. It was reported that phone lines at Hill had also been cut. In the men's dormitory, the Quadrangle, false alarms were sounded.[24]

On Friday, April 24, three anonymous phone calls were made to the university operator warning that bombs were set to go off in Logan Hall, Dietrich Hall, and Walnut Hall. Logan and Walnut Halls were evacuated as the Philadelphia Police and campus guards searched for bombs but found none. Dietrich Hall was searched but not evacuated. All this created an atmosphere of fear and apprehension on the campus.[25]

One informant, who was a student at Penn and a member of SAAS at the time, commented that these events were orchestrated to frighten the university and to pressure the administration into yielding to demands for the pre-freshman summer program. Obviously, no one would wish to admit publicly any responsibility for, or participation in, an unlawful act. Nevertheless, these fires did not start themselves, the bomb scares did not happen by themselves, and it was no accident that these events occurred following the SAAS demonstration of the previous week, in the midst of a confrontation between SAAS and the administration.

On Friday night–Saturday morning, April 24–25, two "firebombs" went off in College Hall. One was thrown into the office of the College of General Studies on the east side of the building in the basement, and the other was thrown into the first-floor office of Francis Betts, assistant to the president for external affairs. This was on the east side of the building, opposite the Furness Building and diagonally across from Irvine Auditorium. At about 1 A.M.

on Saturday morning, April 25, shortly after the fire began, a gray Volkswagon was stopped by the Philadelphia Police on the South Street Bridge, and an individual was arrested. A university student had seen a "bright reflection" in the window of the building opposite the east end of College Hall and then saw a "youth" running away toward Spruce Street. A second student saw three black men running from College Hall to Spruce Street at that time and saw them get into a gray Volkswagon, which then left the scene. A former university employee was charged with arson, carrying explosives, malicious mischief, conspiracy to commit an unlawful act, possession of incendiary devices, and other offenses.[26]

University officials suspected involvement by the House of the Black Family, and therefore a search warrant was obtained. On Saturday afternoon Lieutenant George Fencl of the Philadelphia Police Civil Disobedience Squad served the warrant. Police confiscated several jugs of liquid (kerosene according to the police—floor wax and cleaner according to students). Four black males present at the House were taken in for questioning. Two of the four were Penn students, and all four were released that night and not charged with any offense.[27]

The arrest and the raid on the House of the Black Family outraged SAAS and the members of the House. At a press conference Sunday night, the House of the Black Family issued a statement denouncing the university and protesting the innocence of the accused man. Ultimately, in October, he was *acquitted of all charges by a jury.* None of the witnesses could positively identify him as one of the three black men seen running from College Hall. Verna House and Sylvia Miller, who were collecting tickets at a party at the House of the Black Family between midnight and 1 A.M. on the night of the College Hall firebombing, testified that the accused man was at the party during that time and had not left.[28]

The "mysterious fires" and the firebombing of College Hall may be taken as an indication of the profound frustration, alienation, and anger of a segment of the black community at Penn in the spring of 1970. Simmering discontent over admissions, inadequate financial aid, an ineffective academic support system, and the long-delayed Black Studies program boiled over into destructive acts. In retrospect, it is fair to say that the fires of April 1970 caught the attention of the central administration and convinced it that, if there were to be peace on the campus, it must take steps to address the sources of black discontent.

Compromise over the Freshman Summer Program

On Friday, May 1, in the aftermath of the April 16 demonstration and the fires of April 23–25, SAAS and the administration reached a compromise, when SAAS agreed to allow the university to change the wording of the goals of the prefreshman summer program, in order to secure the funding it would need if there were to be any program at all. The administration agreed in principle that there should be summer courses for black prefreshmen and for "postfreshmen." There should also be a three- or four-day orientation program, and during the regular academic year upperclass-students would serve as advisers to first-year students. Financial aid would be given to the students participating in the prefreshman and postfreshman summer programs on the basis of need. The original SAAS proposal had called for funding regardless of need.[29]

Dean of Students Alice Emerson said the wording of the goals in the statement of purpose (enforcing "the concept that education should provide students with tools to restructure the black nation now being suppressed by colonial America") had been a "barrier of communication." She also insisted the protest march of April 16 had nothing to do with the resolution of the controversy.[30] The revised wording ran:

Success in the University has traditionally been measured in terms of academic achievement alone, but in response to contemporary needs of Black America new concepts of success have evolved encompassing a more realistic view of self-realization and awareness of social responsibility in conjunction with excellence in academic achievement. It is the purpose, then, of S.A.P. [Student Advising Program] (1) to assist the Black freshmen in developing a realistic concept of the Black individual and his relationship to society, (2) to support the concept that education should provide Black students with the knowledge and skills needed to restructure the Black community and overcome the historical and contemporary effects of racism, (3) to provide a broad program of experiences related to main streams of thought in the Black community, *including but not limited to such concepts as Black nationhood and colonial suppression, community control,* etc., so as to encompass the divergent interests of the Black student population, and (4) through the aforementioned goals [to] produce an understanding of the role of academic achievement in the realization of the goals of the Black community [emphasis added].[31]

In the end, then, SAAS did not get the "nationalist" prefreshman summer program it had asked for, but it did get a program designed to assist black students, especially those who were academically "at risk," in adjusting to the university. A nationalist perspective might be included by guest speakers, along with other perspectives, but the program would not be dedicated to one perspective. The academic year of September 1969–May 1970 was probably the most difficult year of transition and adjustment between the enlarged cohort of African American students and Penn. The campaign of arson and vandalism and the firebombing of two offices in College Hall, in April 1970, represented the high-water mark of destructive agitation by black students (and administrators) at Penn. It is probably no accident that the peak of black "nationalist" activity occurred in 1970 and coincided with the near-record enrollment of black students from public school, lower-middle-class, and working-class backgrounds. As John Bracey suggests, traditionally, the black middle class has been inclined toward assimilation, while it is the lower and working classes who have been more nationalistic.[32] I would infer that the tide of nationalism, "separatism," and self-determination among black students at Penn rose in direct proportion to the admission rate of students from this background. The influence of the ideology of Black Power and the black cultural revolution would continue among African American students at Penn long after 1970, but the most acutely damaging and disruptive phase had now passed. The question of how to bring about "integration" of people from different socioeconomic backgrounds, and how to serve those from disadvantaged backgrounds—as well as the privileged and wealthy—still remained.

CHAPTER SEVEN

CONFRONTING CLASS AND DISADVANTAGE

But freedom is not enough. You do not wipe away the scars of centuries by saying: Now you are free to go where you want, and do as you desire, and choose the leaders you please. You do not take a person who, for years, has been hobbled by chains and liberate him, bring him up to the starting line of a race and then say, "you are free to compete with all the others," and still justly believe that you have been completely fair. . . . *We seek . . . not just equality as a right and a theory but equality as a fact and equality as a result* [emphasis added].

—Lyndon B. Johnson, "To Fulfill These Rights,"
Commencement speech at Howard University, June 4, 1965

The most "radical" challenge that black student activists and their allies posed to the university was ideological. But it did not come in the form of the demand for an Afro-American Studies Program or the hiring of black professors or a separate dormitory and social center for black students. Instead, it came in an oppositional challenge to the very definition of merit and qualification; to reliance on standardized tests; and to traditional notions of who deserved to attend an Ivy League university. Black students and (some) black administrators, influenced in part by the ideology of Black Power, argued that black students from academically disadvantaged backgrounds—such as inner-city, public high schools that provided inadequate education—should be given special consideration in the admissions process and compensatory education and academic support services. This demand for compensatory treatment and measures was in direct opposition to prevailing definitions of merit and qualification as determined by performance on standardized tests (such as the Scholastic Aptitude Test and Achievement Tests in given subjects), grades, class rank, and judgments as to the level of rigor of the secondary school.

Furthermore, the demand that the university be cognizant of past historic discrimination by whites against people of color collectively, and that the university take this into account in evaluating the "qualifications" of applicants, directly opposed the discourse of allocating rewards to the most qualified person(s) on the basis of universal standards that should be applied without regard to race, color, ethnicity, religion, or any other distinction. The ideal of "individual meritocracy" itself was contested. Black students and their allies among the black faculty and administrators engaged in a process of ideological struggle to demand cognizance of historic discrimination in evaluating "qualification" in the admissions process and demanded compensatory education for students who needed it, in the period from 1969 to 1976. After 1976, in practice, Penn limited the admission of students with a Predictive Index below 2.0.

Penn was an Ivy League school located in a predominantly African American neighborhood in West Philadelphia, in a city that was approximately 40 percent African American in population. Penn was also a state-aided institution that received, by 1967, an annual appropriation of more than $13 million from the Commonwealth of Pennsylvania. As Penn pursued the laudable goals of desegregation and diversity, it was confronted with the dilemma of how to teach students from inner-city, public school, working-class backgrounds as well as its traditional constituency of affluent white suburbanites from elite, privileged, private preparatory school backgrounds. This proved to be one of the most difficult and painful parts of desegregation.

Many African American students, faculty, and administrators at Penn argued that academic and socioeconomic disadvantage were often the consequences of historic, group, institutionalized discrimination by whites against people of color. Cognizance of group disadvantage and compensatory treatment for it—in the present—was one way to attempt to provide redress for the consequences of that discrimination in the past. From this perspective, black students, and the black community more broadly, challenged "color-blind" notions of quality and merit. This was consistent with the ideology of Black Power, which required a concern for the masses, not only the privileged and the advantaged few. Accordingly, many of those African Americans who were well prepared academically defended the right of those who were not so well prepared to have an opportunity to gain a college education, too.

Again, as a word of caution, not all the black students entering Penn in 1968 or 1969 or the early 1970s were from disadvantaged backgrounds. This chapter simply examines the issues pertaining to *one segment* or subset of the African American student population. In the mid-1970s students such as

Lorene Cary (Class of 1978), author of *Black Ice,* Vickee Jordan (Class of 1979), daughter of Vernon Jordan, Marc Morial (Class of 1980), now the mayor of New Orleans, and Carol Sutton (Class of 1980), niece of Manhattan Borough President Percy Sutton, attended Penn. As did Wilson Goode Jr. (Class of 1986), and Muriel Goode (Class of 1987), son and daughter of the first African American mayor of Philadelphia, and Harold Ford Jr. (Class of 1992), the Tennessee congressman. Black suburbanites from Westchester County, New York, and Long Island also attended Penn. Thus, children of the African American elite and middle class were at Penn, too, rubbing elbows with their soul brothers and sisters from more humble backgrounds.

The Black Advising Program and the Educationally Disadvantaged

A report from the College of Arts and Sciences (for Men) on the academic performance of the African American students who entered in 1969 is highly informative. It suggests that 1969 was the first year in which a significant number of African Americans were admitted, and states that in 1968 only 18 African Americans had matriculated in the College (for Men). In 1969 40 African American males matriculated in the College. The average SAT verbal score for these students was 502, compared to 639 for the entering class in the College as a whole. The average SAT math score was 514 for African Americans as opposed to 669 for the entering class of 1969 in the College as a whole. This indicates an average SAT score of 1016 for blacks in the College as against 1308 for men in the College in the entering class of 1969 overall. Of the African American students, 43 percent were in the first quintile of their high school class, compared to 76 percent for the class in the College as a whole. The average predicted G.P.A. for the African Americans was 1.69. For the class as a whole, it was 2.56.[1] It is crucial to note, however, that if white students with an SAT of about 1300 were among the "cream" of the crop among whites, African Americans with an SAT above 1000 were far above the national average for African Americans as a whole. Even in 1997, the national average SAT score for African Americans on the verbal portion of the SAT was 434, and the national average on the math portion was 423, for a combined total of 857.[2] Thus African Americans with an SAT score of 1000 were in the higher echelons within their own ethnic group ("race").[3]

As of December 1970 (on the basis of three semesters), the average cumulative G.P.A. for the African Americans in the entering class of 1969 in the College (for Men) was 1.9. For the class as a whole (whites as well as blacks) it was

2.8. For the African American students in the entering class of 1969 in the College, the average Achievement Test score was 533, the average of all SAT and Achievement Tests was 507, and the number who had been on general probation was 34 out of 40 (85 percent). Of the 40, 6 had been dropped from the rolls (15 percent), and 3 had withdrawn from the University (7.5 percent). This report also found, however, that for this particular class the "coefficient of correlation between predicted G.P.A. and actual cumulative G.P.A. is -.07, indicating that if there is any correlation between the two values it is negative. However, this value is sufficiently small in magnitude to indicate that there is no correlation at all between predicted G.P.A. and cumulative G.P.A. This implies that, at least for this group, predicted G.P.A. is a very poor indicator of successful academic performance."[4]

To provide students with academic disadvantages an opportunity to learn what they should have learned in high school, Penn had provided the Pre-Freshman Summer Program and a Post-Freshman Summer program for students who had failed courses in their first year and needed to take the failed class again or who wanted to take a summer class so that they could take a reduced load during the regular school year. In May 1970, Conrad Jones was hired as associate dean of students, and his responsibilities included serving as the director of the Black Advising Program.[5] He served until 1972. In the summer of 1970 two six-week programs were offered on a residential basis. Students took two courses for credit. Fifty-one black freshmen in the entering class of 1970 (the Class of 1974) participated in the Pre-Freshman Summer Program, and 51 students from the class that had entered in 1969 participated in the Post-Freshman Summer Program.[6]

The great difficulty that some students faced was passing courses in calculus (a two-semester sequence), biology, chemistry, and physics. Students who ended up on probation and with low G.P.A.s generally had attempted, unsuccessfully, to take these courses. A few examples may illustrate the difficulties that some African American students were having. The data from 1969 and 1970 are fragmentary. They suggest, however, that most African American students were admitted to the College of Arts and Sciences (for Men) or the College for Women, and fewer were admitted in the Wharton School (business), engineering, and nursing schools. Some data for the College and the College for Women are accessible in the archival record. Although the evidence is incomplete, 13 students at risk in the College who entered in 1970 took summer school courses. They had a predictive index of 1.5. In their first "semester," including the prefreshman summer, their average G.P.A. was 2.0. For 23 students at risk in the College who entered in 1970 and did not attend the Pre-Freshman Summer Program, and who had a predictive index of 1.8, their grade point average in the first semester was 1.6. For 17 students at risk in the College for Women, who entered in 1970, with a predictive index of 2.2, and who attended the Pre-Freshman Summer Program, their average G.P.A. was 2.3 in the first semester. For 42 students at risk in the College for Women, with a predictive index of 2.3, who entered in 1970 and did *not* attend the Pre-Freshman Summer Program, their average G.P.A. in the first semester was 2.3. Evidently the Pre-Freshman Summer courses helped students, somewhat, and seemed to help African American males even more than females.[7]

The Black Advising Program continued during the summer of 1971. The format was the same, with freshmen taking two courses and postfreshmen taking one. In 1971 the focus shifted again from African American cultural issues to academic achievement. Thirty-five students attended as postfreshmen in the first summer session. Approximately 65 prefreshmen attended summer session two, living on campus. Most prefreshmen took the English composition course for credit, and they could select noncredit seminars in precalculus and reading-and-study skills. Graduate students lived in residence with the students to maintain order and provide counseling.[8]

Again, data on the performance of students from this period are quite fragmentary. It bears repeating that the majority of African American students were admitted into the College (Men) and the College for Women (arts and sciences). The data from the College and College for Women are the most accessible.

It is estimated that for the entering class of 1969, which included a number of late-admits from West Philadelphia (in the aftermath of the sit-in of 1969), 55 percent of the African American students were classified as "marginal" (with three indicators of failure). By the summer of 1970 (three semesters when the summer is counted as a semester), the African American entering class of 1969 had lost "15–20% of its members."[9] Forty African American men had entered the College in 1969, and as of January 1971, 31 remained (6 had been "dropped from the rolls," and 3 had voluntarily withdrawn). These figures are "soft," however, because students can appeal to be readmitted. The academic preparation for the entering class of African Americans in 1970 was better. It was estimated that in this class 25 percent were "at risk." After three semesters this class had lost only 5 or 6 percent of its members.[10]

In fall 1972, Associate Dean of Students Conrad Jones left Penn to become director of the Office of Minority Affairs in Higher Education, for the Commonwealth of Pennsylvania. At the time of his departure, he noted that the number of black students who still needed academic help after their freshman year had declined from 55 in 1970 to 27 in 1972. Jones also said that the average SAT scores of black students had risen by 75 points over the past two years (since 1970).[11]

One feature of the Black Advising Program was the use of upper-class students as advisers. For example, in 1972 black student Ruth Ann Price served as student coordinator. In November 1972 Price estimated that 60 out of about 130 freshmen were receiving tutoring, and during the freshman year the black freshmen were matched with upper-class advisers who followed their progress.[12]

The establishment of the Black Advising Program raised critical issues. The program was sometimes perceived as a remedial program for black "disadvantaged" students who lacked the same academic background and preparation as other (usually white middle-class and upper-class) students and who therefore arrived at the university with certain weaknesses or deficiencies. Critics asked, if the students in question were "remedial" or "deficient," then, were they really "qualified" to be at Penn? If they were "underqualified," why had they been admitted in the first place? There had been no prefreshman summer programs for "remedial" students of any race in the past (prior to the Black Advising Program), because Penn was an elite Ivy League school and presumably none of its students needed such programs. With the arrival of a significant number of socioeconomically disadvantaged African American students in 1969, Penn apparently became aware of a "special needs" population for the first time. Yet once the prefreshman and tutoring programs were put into place for black students, Penn suddenly "discovered" that it was not only black students who sometimes arrived at the university with academic weaknesses and deficiencies.

For, as soon as it was acknowledged that Penn was going to admit a certain percentage of incoming classes on the basis of "diversity" and 3 percent on the basis of socioeconomic disadvantage rather than purely on the basis of "regular" academic standards, it became evident that there were white students, and Latino and other "minority" students, and some athletes (of any race), who also needed academic support services. Thus pressure began to grow to reformulate the Black Advising Program as an academic support program for *all* students who needed it, regardless of race. Certainly there were small, poor, mostly white, rural communities in Pennsylvania where the quality of education was not much better than in the inner-city "ghettos." But did Penn know *how* to educate students from disadvantaged backgrounds?

It must be added that the purpose of the early Black Advising Program was not to offer a permanent crutch, but rather to bring disadvantaged students "up to speed" with other students by providing the compensatory education that would overcome the gaps and deficiencies in their previous preparation. The theory was that, once this compensatory need had been met, the disadvantaged students would be able (and expected and required) to compete effectively with (and just like) everyone else. The disadvantaged students might need additional tutoring in order to compete effectively and perform at a satisfactory level, but there was never any question of a permanent second "track" or a two-tiered system in which these students would have easier requirements than other students or be exempted from the same expectations as everyone else. Disadvantaged students might receive assistance, and resources might be available to help them to help themselves, but in the end they would have to sink or swim on their own and succeed or fail by their own efforts and merits.

Penn was compelled, by political pressure emanating from the surrounding African American community, to give some "underqualified" students an opportunity to become qualified by attending college. After all, the college applicant is not "qualified." He or she becomes qualified by earning the college degree. The completion and attainment of the degree is what makes one qualified (graduating from the college, not entering it). In allocating admissions slots, one is distributing opportunities to learn and become qualified—one is not giving slots to persons who are already qualified. The same argument could be made about training programs, apprenticeships, and admissions to law, medical, and other professional schools.

Defenders of the policy of cognizance of historic group disadvantage offered a critique of the philosophy of individual merit. They pointed out that if everyone had not had an equal opportunity to attain qualification in the first place, then a reliance upon "merit" only, to the exclusion of all other factors, was unfair. It amounted to perpetuating the calculus of advantage and disadvantage inherited from the past. This policy of being cognizant of historic group disadvantage, however, and making compensations and allowances for it, aroused bitter resentment from those who felt that opportunities for minorities and women were growing at their expense. The admission of a significant number of African American students was a matter of racial or ethnic diversity, which the campus seemed to understand. But the admission of "unqualified" students from inner-city, working-class, public school backgrounds was in some ways a socioeconomic class issue. This the campus did not so readily understand. And some people thought the students in question were not "deserving" of admission.

The ideology of Black Power rejected elitism in favor of sharing opportunity with the disadvantaged and those whom the dominant culture judged "unqualified." Black Power advocates were inclined to argue that standardized tests were culturally biased and did not measure "intelligence." Rather, in their view, the verbal portion of the SAT, and achievement tests in subjects such as history, measured familiarity with white, Eurocentric, middle and upper-class culture. Nor were the tests necessarily reliable predictors of actual performance. Yet another difficult question was how to provide an opportunity for some individuals from educationally disadvantaged backgrounds, as a means of compensating for historic white discrimination, without denying opportunity in the present to someone white who is not personally responsible for the injustices of the past. This balancing act was especially difficult when there were people who felt that they had no responsibility—and denied that the university or society had any responsibility—to make amends for past discrimination by whites against people of color.

Harold Haskins and the Office of Supportive Services

In 1973 Dr. Eliot Stellar became Provost. In fall 1974 the original Black Advising Program was replaced by a new program to provide tutoring and counseling during the regular academic year. This new program was called "Supportive Services," and unlike the Black Advising Program that had been for black students only, the Office of Supportive Services was for all students.[13] In October 1974 Associate Dean of Students Claude Mayberry said about 180 students, mostly black and Mexican American, were participating in the new regular-year advising program.[14]

The new director of the Supportive Services Program in academic year 1974–75 was an African American, Harold Haskins, who began a long career of devoted service to black students and the university.[15] Initially, tutoring concentrated on math, biology, chemistry, and physics. In 1974 a major restructuring of the university also took place. The College and the College for Women, and a number of departments in the Graduate School, were consolidated into the Faculty of Arts and Sciences (FAS), and Dr. Vartan Gregorian became the new dean of FAS. Also the positions of vice provost for undergraduate studies (held by Humphrey Tonkin) and of dean of students were merged into a vice provost for undergraduate studies and university life (VPUSUL).[16] In spring 1975, Dean of Students Dr. Alice Emerson was chosen president of Wheaton College, and Associate Dean of Students Claude Mayberry also made his departure as academic year 1974–75 drew to a close. In September 1975, Dr. Patricia McFate became the new vice provost for undergraduate studies and university life.[17] Dean Jean Brownlee of the (former) College for Women became dean of advising for FAS.[18] In this restructuring, the Office of Supportive Services was shifted from the Vice Provost's Office to FAS Advising.

There was no Pre-Freshman Summer Program in 1974, and a coalition of black student organizations joined with the Mexican American student organization (MEChA, or Movimiento Estudiantil Chicanos de Aztlan) to exert pressure for the restoration of the program. For the summer of 1976 the Pre-Freshman Summer Program was revived, and it has since become a permanent, annual program. Usually, the students are housed on campus for several weeks in July and August and take courses in math and English. The Office of Supportive Services matches students with a tutor and provides funding for the tutors. The office also seeks to employ graduate students as tutors. In 1975 demand for supportive services increased sharply. During 1975–76 about 2,100 students received services. Some 921 students were involved in "instructional workshops" (also known as "reteaching"). At that time, black students accounted for 33 percent of those receiving tutoring.[19]

One of the most important techniques utilized by the Supportive Services Program was the extended courses (or "stretch") program. The advising system was acutely aware of the fact that many African American students had difficulty passing science courses. Some of these students, however, aspired to enter the health professions, for which these courses were prerequisites. Therefore, a program was developed whereby students could take the first semester of introductory calculus, biology, chemistry, or physics in a special "section" of the course over a full year. If the course were a two-semester course, they would then take the second half of the course in the summer, but the second half of such courses would not be extended. After one year of extended instruction, the students would be expected to have developed the same level of competence as their counterparts who took the first-year course in one semester.

One benefit of these extended courses was that they featured diagnostic testing and practice tests, by which the student could practice taking exams without penalty. In general, students were limited to two extended courses in two disciplines, for which they received regular course credit.[20] This alternative method of instruction has proven quite successful at many colleges nationwide. At the end of the process, the students are not necessarily any less competent in the subject matter simply because they took longer to learn it. This underscores the little-examined tendency of the academy to equate intelligence with speed.

Individual schools within the university also took measures to ensure the retention of minority students. Perhaps the most outstanding example of this was the School of Engineering, where Cora Ingrum served as assistant to the dean for minority programs. Dean Joseph Bordogna of the Penn Engineering School also founded a program called PRIME, or the Philadelphia Regional Introduction for Minorities to Engineering. It sought out promising middle school and high school students for summer enrichment classes in science, math, and engineering to give youngsters the skills they would need for entry into collegiate programs in engineering later on. Indeed, it was an enlightened investment in creating a supply or "pipeline" of talented high school students who would become college students in the future.

The Pennsylvania Commonwealth Achievement Program

While Penn developed programs for compensatory education, in 1971–72 the Commonwealth of Pennsylvania established Act 101 (the equivalent of which in New Jersey would be the Educational Opportunity Fund, or EOF). The Act 101 program provided funds for tutoring and academic support for college students who were residents of Pennsylvania and who met certain eligibility criteria with respect to family income and performance on the Scholastic Assessment Test. Penn applied for and received Act 101 funds for academic year 1973–74. An Act 101 program was permanently established there for 1975–76. At Penn it is called PENNCAP (Pennsylvania Commonwealth Achievement Program). In 1975–76 Gilberto Ramón was director of the program. As an example of the eligibility criteria for the program, in 1978 those eligible for participation had to have SAT scores in the range of 750 to 1050. In 1978 Dr. Valarie Swain Cade succeeded Gilberto Ramon as director of PENNCAP.[21]

The PENNCAP symbolized, in part, the fact that Penn received millions of dollars from the Commonwealth, that it was a "state-aided" institution. In particular, Penn's Veterinary School was highly subsidized by the Commonwealth of Pennsylvania. The Commonwealth mandated that Pennsylvania colleges and universities ought to provide compensatory education to students who were residents of the state. This was part of the mission of equal educational opportunity. Politically and financially, this was an obligation the university could not evade.

The Unequal Distribution of Opportunity

The struggle over academic support services for students from socioeconomically disadvantaged backgrounds, and indeed for all students who needed or desired them, challenged basic assumptions about the identity of an elite Ivy League university. The Black Power movement and the black community more widely insisted that institutions such as universities (especially urban ones) must serve the masses, not only the privileged few. Black Power offered a critique of traditional definitions of merit and qualification. Black students at Penn in the early 1970s called for educational opportunity for members of disadvantaged groups, not only for elite individuals. Furthermore, they demanded that even those adjudged to be marginal—through no fault of their own—because of inner-city, public school backgrounds or poor academic preparation and training at inferior schools, be given an opportunity to compete. In their view, black and disadvantaged students (of any race) ought not to be automatically excluded from a chance to compete simply because of low SAT scores or poor prior schooling. To exclude these students automatically was to punish the victim.

Indeed, in May 1976, black students held a (silent) protest demonstration at a meeting of the University Council to oppose plans to limit the admission of students with a Predictive Index (P.I.) below 2.0. Among the "leaders" of this demonstration were outgoing BSL President William "Skip" Knight and President-elect Edward J. McPherson. Evidence showed that three out of ten students with a P.I. below 2.0 achieved a G.P.A. below 2.0 in the freshman year. The BSL contended that if three in ten of those predicted to "fail" did fail, conversely, seven in ten of those predicted to fail exceeded expectations. Furthermore, the data recorded only performance in the freshman year and did not track actual outcomes over four years.[22] This episode may reflect the degree to which ethnic solidarity sometimes overrides class distinctions within the African American community, and the greater sense of accountability to the mass of the ethnic group that is felt by black middle-class elites.

In the agonizing battles over the pre- and post-freshman summer programs, tutoring, and counseling, Penn would discover that it is easy to educate the privileged and advantaged few. It is far more difficult to serve the needs of the many. But critics charged that it was a mistake even to attempt to do so. To their minds, Penn was admitting students who were unqualified, unprepared, and not equipped to compete or succeed at an Ivy League university. These students were "in over their heads" and were being "eaten alive." In the view of the critics, Penn (and the liberals) might have had good intentions, but in their social experimentation and misguided attempts at social engineering they were doing disadvantaged students a profound disservice—and using them as guinea pigs. For some of the students from disadvantaged backgrounds who passed through Penn between 1968 and 1973 the experience was analogous to trial by fire.

On the other hand, there were many examples of excellence. One is Clyde Brogdon, a gifted African American student who graduated from Wharton in 1978, and obtained his M.B.A. from Wharton (1979) with a G.P.A. of 3.9. He went on to work for a major bank, and is now a consultant for Deloitte and Touche. William "Skip" Knight served as president of the Black Student League (1975–76) and yet was not a "militant" political science or sociology major (as the stereotype might suggest), but a student in the Wharton School. Another role model for black Whartonites was Nathaniel James (1977), a president of the Black Wharton Undergraduate Association who went on to establish his own business. Lamont Lee (1980), another president of the Black Wharton Undergraduate Association, held a summer internship at Chase Manhattan Bank and went on to become a development specialist. Linda Shepherd, one of the leading African American female actuaries in the entire country, graduated from Wharton in 1981. She is vice president of an insurance company. African Americans from Penn's engineering school worked as summer interns at Du Pont and Procter & Gamble, and students such as Donald Maynard (1970), Robert Wallace (1978), Ray Wallace (1980), Terrell Partee (1979), William Hoskins (1980), and David Settles (1982) succeeded in graduating from the preeminently difficult engineering school.

From the College for Women, Barbara A. Grant (1971) went on to earn an M.B.A. from the Wharton School (1977), became a news reporter for a local Philadelphia television station, a director of corporate communications, and then spokesperson for the Philadelphia School District. In 2000 she was named director of communications for Philadelphia Mayor John Street. Lawrence Robinson, a graduate of Overbrook High School in Philadelphia (1973), attended Penn as an undergraduate, went on to the Medical School (M 1981), and is now deputy commissioner of health for the City of Philadelphia. Denise Holland (1979), also a graduate of Overbrook High School in Philadelphia, went on from Penn to earn a Ph.D. in clinical psychology.[23] For students in the mid- and late 1970s a great milestone was reached when students such as Edward K. James (Class of 1976), Kim Guishard (Class of 1976), James Ramseur (Class of 1978), and Susan Taylor (Class of 1979) successfully completed the premed curriculum and were accepted to Medical School, and went on to become physicians. Similarly, for the prelaw students, an important milestone was observed when undergraduate students such as Cathy Barlow (1971), Wendella Fox (1973), Malcolm Nelson (Class of 1976), Clay Armbrister (Class of 1979), and Curtis Hilliard (Class of 1979) were accepted at law schools and went on to put an "Esquire" after their names.

The data for 1970 show that only one-quarter of the black admits in that year were "at risk." The African American community is internally stratified, with its own elite, working class, and lower classes. African American students from diverse class backgrounds comingled at Penn, and unfortunately some Euro-Americans assumed that all of them were "remedial" affirmative action cases and grouped them all together. This prejudicial attitude by (some) whites, in turn, served only to anger African Americans from "bourgeois" backgrounds and drive them and African Americans from inner-city backgrounds together in defensive solidarity. If whites stigmatized all African Americans as "remedial" and "ghetto," blacks retorted that whites at Penn were "rejects," for whom Penn was a "safety school" after they had tried but failed to gain admission to Harvard. Obviously, such repartee could create a nasty atmosphere.

Over time Penn became more adept at identifying good "feeder schools," and recruited a greater proportion of its African American students from such sources. In addition, as more African American middle-class parents sent their children to private preparatory schools, the pool of potential students from such schools has grown. By all indications, over the years, more African American students matriculating at Penn have come from middle-class, private school backgrounds. Thus, more of them are better prepared academically to face the rigors of an Ivy League education.

After 1976, Penn limited the number of students admitted with a Predicted Index below 2.0. As the ranks of the black middle class expanded, it became possible to recruit 150 African-American students without having to tap the inner-city public schools. The traumas of the early 1970s would recede into memory, but part of the legacy of the Black Power movement at Penn was the demand for diversity of class as well as race (or ethnicity), and the critique of traditional definitions of merit, qualification, and equality of opportunity. Black Power asked the probing question, "Who has been allowed the privilege and opportunity to become qualified in the first place?"

In the 1960s and 1970s the ideology of Black Power expressed greater concern for equality of outcome and result—not merely the rhetoric of an equal opportunity to compete for unequal outcomes. Black students and activists at Penn asserted that substantive equality would require cognizance of group disadvantage and past historic discrimination by whites against people of color (and by men against women). Attaining greater equality of opportunity for disadvantaged African Americans and people of color would also require special efforts in the present as a remedy—and as partial compensation—for the deleterious consequences of white institutionalized racism against people of color as a group. It would require a policy of race consciousness rather than erasure of consciousness of race, and pluralistic sharing of power and allocation of opportunities among groups—not merely individuals.

It might also mean realizing that white students with SAT scores of 1300 and black students with SATs of 1100 were both in the upper echelons of their groups, and thus both were "deserving." The modest efforts by Penn, however, to accommodate a handful of disadvantaged students (in a given year, 40 or 50 black students out of an entering class of 1,800 or 2,000) incited resentment by those who felt that blacks were being given preferential treatment—which they had not earned—at the expense of better "qualified" and more "deserving" whites with higher SAT scores. This prejudicial perception on the part of whites sometimes poisoned relations between blacks and whites on the campus.

The proponents of a policy of consciousness of race, white privilege, and the historic disadvantage by people of color demanded that Penn (and other institutions) face up to the burden of America's white-supremacist past. These advocates were concerned about diversity as an outcome and as a result. This, however, directly contradicted the "color-blind" ideology of selecting students for admission solely on the basis of the "most qualified individual," as determined by "universalistic" standards, such as performance on standardized tests, without regard to race, color, ethnicity, or other group attributes. This cut to the heart of Penn's identity as an elite institution training students of "superior" intellect, achievement, and qualification as measured by traditional standards.

This challenge was not unique to Penn. It was confronted by almost all universities across the nation. Of course, critics of compensatory education at elite universities regard such measures as one of the "liberal excesses" of the 1960s. It may be, however, part of the price that has to be paid if universities— even elite ones—are to live up to the promise of educational opportunity for all. It is part of the price of accepting—rather than evading—responsibility to make restitution for the institutionalized white racism of our collective past. It is an unmistakable sign of an oppositional discourse that challenges the ideology of "color-blind" individual meritocracy. It also illustrates the process of ideological contest over the meaning of diversity, opportunity, and justice that is still taking place in the "post–civil rights" era.

CHAPTER EIGHT

IS A BLACK DORMITORY
"VOLUNTARY SEGREGATION"?

[Black Power] is a call for black people in this country to unite, to recognize their heritage, to build a sense of community. It is a call for black people to begin to define their own goals, to lead their own organizations and to support those organizations. It is a call to reject the racist institutions and values of this society.

—Kwame Ture and Charles V. Hamilton, *Black Power*, 1967

The advocates of integration in the 1950s and early 1960s seem to have expected that black students would assimilate (acculturate) into white (Anglo-conformed) America. Instead, as black students arrived in large numbers on predominantly white college campuses, they expressed a sense of alienation and isolation. They rejected assimilation and began demanding courses in Black Studies, black social centers, and even black dormitories. This pattern replicated itself at Pennsylvania in 1972, when some black students demanded a separate dormitory. This was a reflection of a growing sense of alienation from white students and a desire to create a comfortable social and ethnic space of their own. In other words, it reflected a desire for autonomy rather than assimilation.[1] This demand would evolve into the W. E. B. Du Bois College House at 3900 Walnut Street. This chapter explores the genesis of that demand and the response of the faculty.

In February 1972, alumna and law school matriculant Cathy Barlow, Percy Helem, Wilbur Commodore, Martin Jeffries, and several other students produced a proposal urging the creation of a residence for black students.[2] Their proposal asserted that for many black students at Penn the college experience was "disappointing and shallow. . . . Rather than developing a sense of belonging, a sense of community with the University, the incoming Black freshmen experience a deep sense of alienation because the University is a white-oriented institution." They contended that many black students did not benefit from residence counselors and resource personnel because these personnel were usually white, and "Black students do not feel that they can understand them or their problems. Many Black students, therefore, do not have the advantage of special counselling services because they do not go to their white residence counselors to discuss problems."[3]

The authors believed it was vital "that Black students, especially in their freshman year, have the alternative of discussing problems and ideas with Black residence counselors and academic advisors." Furthermore, "An alternative residential program primarily for incoming Black freshmen and sophomores could help to maximize the potential benefits of college life both in and out of the classroom." The authors also lamented that "Black students were expected to adjust themselves in whatever manner necessary to function in the white environment into which they had been thrust. They were expected to adapt their thinking, their aspirations, their life style to conform with white middle class values." In addition, "the Black student is dispersed throughout the University residences and is therefore denied the comfort and understanding of his peers."[4]

It was, therefore, proposed that one hundred twenty black students, fifty freshmen, fifty sophomores, and twenty juniors and seniors, would live in the first two floors of Low Rise North with resource persons and advisers, a director, and an assistant director.[5] Moreover, although the House of the Family did exist as a black social center, it was small and could not meet the needs of all black students. The proposed residential program was to be a learning environment with a course taught on-site, a speakers' forum, library, film series, and "independent community study" courses. The program would focus on Afro-American culture and the counseling needs of students. This was very different from a nonresidential social and recreational center.[6]

According to Associate Dean of Students Conrad Jones, the proposal from black students was one of seventeen such proposals for residential programs submitted by faculty and students.[7] An advisory committee of three faculty and three administrators was to review the various proposals and make recommendations to Vice Provost for Undergraduate Education Dr. Humphrey Tonkin. Associate Director of Residence Margo Marshall served as chairperson.[8]

The model or precedent for living–learning programs in which faculty lived in residence with students was Van Pelt College House, the nucleus of which was established in September 1971. The desire to increase student interaction with the faculty became especially pronounced as class size rose in the 1960s, and undergraduates frequently found themselves in huge, impersonal classes with hundreds of students. This was especially true of the introductory classes taken by freshmen, who complained of being taught by teaching assistants.[9]

A particularly poignant episode relating to this issue occurred in February 1972, when a student sent President Meyerson a letter about why he was transferring from Penn. The student wrote that he had entered college looking forward to "the intellectual atmosphere, the 'access to great minds' which is advertised by quality institutions." Instead, as a freshman, he trudged from overcrowded classroom to overcrowded classroom. But he said that he couldn't learn solely through lectures and that "questioning, theorizing, rebutting— these spontaneities are a crucial part of the learning experience and were totally lacking in my first year at Penn." He was told that the "real learning" was in upper-level courses, so he took a 500-level course. But there, despite a superb professor, the "gallant effort" to teach a class of sixty was "not, even in the most flexible sense, quality education." The student regretted that Penn was responding to the financial squeeze by increasing class size. He said that he felt, with "some bitterness" and with "ambiguous, yet genuine affection," that Penn's offerings "too often take the form of unfulfilled promises."[10]

It is painfully clear that this student really wanted a small liberal arts college with a low student-to-faculty ratio, with an opportunity for close interaction between students and faculty. In his letter of reply, President Meyerson acknowledged the problem of large class size, but wondered if the student "would find elsewhere the stimulation . . . lacking at our university." He wrote, "The problem of large size is endemic to higher education generally. . . ." Furthermore, he cautioned that although a "small college can offer intimacy, and an outlet for questions, insights, and mutual learning," it cannot offer many instructors of the caliber of those at Penn. President Meyerson also pointed to efforts to create smaller freshmen seminars for the upcoming year, the College of Thematic Studies, and Van Pelt and Hill Houses, where faculty members lived in the residences alongside students.[11]

The letter cited here is an illustration of how, for all too many students, Penn had become a large, bureaucratic, impersonal machine, an academic "assembly line." Students—both African American and Euro-American—felt little sense of belonging and struggled to create their own sense of community. One way that they would do this was by turning to others with whom they shared something in common, often some aspect of identity (such as religion, ethnicity, region, culture) or mutual interest (sports, art, music). For some other students, the fraternities and sororities provided this sense of community and belonging.

Having faculty members live in-residence with the students was an alternative way to provide faculty–student interaction. In 1971 the Van Pelt project had been organized by Dr. Mark Adams to provide precisely such an environment. The initial housemaster had been Dr. Richard Solomon, and Adams and Dr. Alan Kors were the first faculty members-in-residence.[12] Similarly, a report of the Student Affairs Committee in January 1972 had stressed the need to integrate the academic and residential experience.[13] The college house program was modeled loosely after the residence system at Harvard and Yale.

The Campus Debate Begins

On February 16 a letter from black students Louis Coles and Gary Galloway appeared in the *Daily Pennsylvanian,* criticizing the "refusal to provide a separate all-Black residence" as well as funds for a viable black organization and a relevant communications organ.[14] Campus debate over an "all-black dormitory" set off a firestorm of controversy. Cathy Barlow noted that Barnard College gave freshmen the option of living on an all-black floor, while at Vassar half of one house was reserved for blacks, and at Temple University there were also black floors in the dormitories.[15] The same article, however, quoted Professor Henry Abraham, chairman of the Faculty Senate and the University Council Steering Committee. Abraham asserted that the proposals were "illegal" and would violate the Fourteenth Amendment of the Constitution, the 1954 Brown decision, and the 1964 Civil Rights Act. He expressed the view the proposed black dormitory would be a "step backward" in civil rights.[16]

On February 21 a lengthy letter defending the proposed residence appeared. Law Professor Howard Lesnick pointed out that Low Rise North held 280 students, and the proposed dormitory program would occupy only half of the building. Furthermore, at that time there were 550 black undergraduates at Penn, of whom only 120 would live in the proposed unit, so that three-fourths of the university's black students would not be living in the residence center. Moreover, no black student would be required to live there.[17] The same day the *Daily Pennsylvanian* published a letter from John O'Brien, responding to the previous letter of Coles and Galloway. O'Brien pointed out that the university had also refused to grant "All-White" dorms. Rhetorically, he asked why there should not be an "All-Jewish" dormitory, "so the residents can celebrate their holidays together and keep their food laws? Why not put all Oriental people in their own dorms?"[18]

On February 25, 1972, the *Daily Pennsylvanian* ran an editorial in which it expressed reservations about the proposed "black dormitory," but nonetheless concluded, "We believe that if legal difficulties can be overcome, the University should give its full approval to the proposed black center." The editorial continued, "To date, the University has not dealt with black problems with much success. Ideally, such a black residence program might not be necessary, but since the University must deal with the realities of our situation, we recommend that black students be allowed to create for themselves an environment in which they feel most comfortable."[19]

"Special Needs": Black Student Attrition

In February a new wrinkle in the debate appeared. Over the winter recess, College sophomore Leander McRae and a group of black students had written a report expressing their grievances and frustrations. Among other things, they observed that in the Class of 1973 (those entering in September 1969), after three semesters, some 25 percent of the black students in the College (for Men) were on academic probation. In the College for Women the figure, reportedly, was 15 percent. No figures were available for the other undergraduate schools (nursing, engineering, business). The report also expressed dissatisfaction with financial aid.[20] Partly in response to this grievance report, in late February the university formed (yet another) committee on the concerns of black students. Members of the *Ad Hoc* Committee on Black Student Concerns included Dr. Humphrey Tonkin, vice provost for undergraduate education, the Reverend Jack Russell, vice provost for student affairs, Dean of Students Alice Emerson, Executive Assistant to the President Donald Stewart, Afro-American Studies Director John Wideman, and Conrad Jones, associate dean of students and director of the university advising program. Student members included Percy Helem, Martin Jeffries, Curtis Foster, and Leander McRae. Cathy Barlow was also named to the committee.[21]

On February 29, 1972, Cathy Barlow and McRae met with members of the Committee of Black Faculty and Administrators to discuss both the report that McRae had presented and the black residence proposal. Afterward, on March 1, the Committee of Black Faculty and Administrators issued an open letter to the university community in which it expressed support for the statement issued by the committee of black undergraduates chaired by Leander McRae and for the proposals for a black residence. It also supported the students' request for the hiring of additional black staff within the College of Arts and Sciences, the College for Women, and the Wharton School.[22]

In addition, on February 28, 1972, at an open meeting with a group of members of the university community called the University Forum, and sponsored by President Meyerson, black College junior Richard Rogers had *publicly* condemned the "unresponsiveness" of the university. Rogers declared that blacks were "drowning" at the university. Subsequently, on March 8, 1972, the *Daily Pennsylvanian* carried a letter from Rogers and Arthur Graham that accused the university of ignoring the problems of black students and directly criticized Dean of Students Alice Emerson and Vice Provost for Student Affairs the Reverend John Russell.[23] These public criticisms may be said to have turned up the heat and pressure on the central administration. Only someone who was deaf and blind could have failed to note the rising level of frustration in the black community at Penn.

On March 6, university officials announced that residence proposals had been approved. These included Stouffer College House, an international floor in Harnwell House, a two-floor program in Harnwell House with resource personnel, and a program in Hill House. This news was carried in the *Daily Pennsylvanian* on March 8.[24] In the same issue the *Daily Pennsylvanian* carried a story informing the university community that, at a press conference the previous day, the *Ad Hoc* Committee on Black Student Concerns had endorsed the proposal for a black residence. Furthermore, the University Council would discuss the issue at its meeting on Wednesday, March 8.[25]

In the same article President Meyerson was quoted as saying he felt the university "ought to try it [a black residence center] as a one-year experiment," and "I recognize how very unhappy many of the black students are and I am awfully sad they have not found in the range of choices offered by the University, the satisfactions they want." Also, Meyerson is reported to have said he regretted that some persons felt the black residence center is necessary, "but obviously some do."[26]

The Vice Provosts Signal Tentative Approval

At the meeting of the University Council of March 8, 1972, Vice Provost for Student Affairs Russell announced that he and Vice Provost for Undergraduate Education Humphrey Tonkin had recommended to Provost Curtis Reitz that a modified proposal be approved, subject to certain conditions. First, there must be a minimum of at least one black faculty member in residence, and the search for this faculty member was to be handled through the Black Faculty and Administrators Group. Second, the final number of residents would be determined by the size of the applicant pool, with a cap of forty-five freshmen and forty-five sophomores. Third, a subgroup of the Black Faculty and Administrators organization would screen the applications. Fourth, there would be a preliminary report to evaluate the success or failure of the project by January 15, 1973, and the same group that screened the applications would form the nucleus of the evaluation committee. Fifth, an affirmative opinion from legal counsel on any legal questions would be needed.[27]

Vice Provost Russell insisted that the residence was not a move toward separating the black and white segments of the student body and that three-fourths of the black students would still be interspersed in other residences. Alan Kors "asked whether acceptance of the proposals would be a major policy change in the University and questioned what criteria would be used to determine 'blackness' and whether non-blacks would be systematically excluded from the black residence." Provost Reitz replied that "it was not the intent of the proposals to develop a separatist motion within the University. Rather, they reflect the fact that a certain segment of the University community has difficulties in getting through the transitional period [of the freshman year]."[28] Provost Curtis Reitz also termed the residence idea "a modest proposal" and emphasized that it would "not entail the development of any kind of separatist pattern in the University." The University Council discussed the issue for half an hour but was not asked to take any action on it. The administration, however, had signaled conditional approval of the proposal, subject to certain provisions, on a one-year experimental basis.[29]

Local media quickly disseminated news of this decision. On March 11, 1972, the *Philadelphia Inquirer* ran a banner story on its Metropolitan Page, more than seven columns in width, emblazoned with the headline "Penn to Build Black Dorm as Orientation Center." The article was generally positive and devoted a good deal of attention to Associate Dean of Students Conrad Jones. He emphasized the difficulties faced by students from high schools and neighborhoods that were totally black, who were suddenly thrown into an environment that was 90 percent white. He also said the residence "could not be called segregation in reverse, because segregation is involuntary and forced. This is separation by choice."[30]

An editorial in the *Philadelphia Daily News* attempted to show "both sides" of the issue, saying that the black students' proposal for an all-black dormitory and studies center "has certain merits and a certain danger." The editorial quoted Conrad Jones as saying, "Our first large class of black freshmen in 1969 went through hell. . . . Students from black homes and high schools often have difficulty adjusting to the whites they find all around them and you cannot integrate unequals." Jones, like Provost Reitz, emphasized that the program would be limited to 90 freshmen and sophomores. He indicated that there were 335 black freshmen and sophomores, out of a total black undergraduate population of 550. Furthermore, "All of the activities in the black center will be open to the entire Penn community."[31] The *Daily News,* however, also noted the danger when a group "retires into its own special enclave." It warned that

Though the blacks may have to get to know themselves and to understand their black identities, they also have to get to know and understand their white classmates. Equally important, the white students must get to know and understand the blacks. An all-black situation may tempt both races to the luxury of not facing up to the fact that all of us must, sooner or later, learn to live in an integrated world. A lesson that's been postponed by too many of us for too long.[32]

The *Philadelphia Tribune,* which proclaims itself the oldest surviving African American newspaper in continuous circulation, ran a story on March 14 characterizing the proposal as "controversial." It did recognize, however, that only 90 of the approximately 550 African-American undergraduates at Penn would live at Low Rise North, and quoted Vice Provost Russell as saying "three-fourths of the Black students would still be interspersed into other residences."[33] Nevertheless, the *Tribune* also ran an editorial, which sought to remind African American students that, only a decade earlier, "The breaking down of exclusion of Blacks from dormitories in predominantly white universities and colleges was a national issue. . . . Now that the discriminatory bars against Black students are down and all facilities are open to them, Blacks, obsessed with the militancy of Black Awareness, are demanding that they be placed on reservations in college freedomland. They are turning the clock backward in their militant thrust."[34]

A Chorus of Opposition

During March 1972 the proposal for a black residence and cultural center encountered numerous obstacles and roadblocks. First, on March 20, it was revealed that Faculty Senate Chairman Henry Abraham had called for a special meeting of the Faculty Senate for April 5 to discuss the proposed residence.[35] Also, amid considerable media attention, on March 26 the local North-Central Philadelphia branch of the National Association for the Advancement of Colored People (NAACP) criticized the plan. President Juanita Green, of the North-Central Chapter, criticized the advocates of separate black residences on college campuses as "misguided, misinvolved and misinformed in their quest to turn back the clock 100 years." President Green claimed to represent "those in the community who have suffered miseries untold to bring about integration" and accused the students proposing separate facilities of being segregationists. She lamented: "These students are the cream of our crop. And the administrators are the cream of our educational crop. They should be pioneering in ways to work together, not in ways to make the races separate." Furthermore, she said, "Segregation enforced by blacks against whites is as legally and morally wrong as segregation enforced by whites against blacks."[36]

On March 28 the organization of Black Faculty and Administrators (BFA) issued a statement criticizing delay by the administration, and John Wideman declared, "By hesitating, the administration intends to build failure into the plan." Furthermore, the Black Faculty and Administrators stated, "We realize the administration's concern for the expression of sentiment by the Faculty Senate, . . . but we were not led to believe the proposal would be conditional upon the Faculty Senate's approval." The BFA insisted that action was needed immediately to ensure the proposal's success, to complete the selection of students, and to distribute leases and select residential advisers for the upcoming year. The BFA called upon the administration to "keep faith with its intention announced at the University Council meeting, Wednesday, March 8."[37]

This was followed by an equivocal advisory opinion from the university's legal counsel, the firm of Drinker, Biddle and Reath. The firm advised, "The proposal may be subject to attack under a large number of constitutional and statutory provisions." Yet it also indicated that "the adoption of the proposal on a trial basis" would probably not involve the university "in any substantial immediate risk of criminal penalties, financial damage or forfeiture." It warned, however, that "persistence by the University in such a course following warnings or preliminary findings of illegality may, under some circumstances, involve risks you would find unacceptable."[38] To make matters worse for the advocates of the black residence proposal, it was reported that the Pennsylvania Human Relations Commission had informed the law firm that it would test the proposal in court if it were implemented.[39]

At the same time, one can easily imagine that the central administration now found itself besieged on all sides and caught in a cross fire from the campus black community, adverse media attention in the city of Philadelphia, the external rumblings of the local NAACP and the Pennsylvania Human Relations Commission, and the internal grumbling of the Faculty Senate. Indeed, some members of the Faculty Senate had prepared a resolution that ran: "Resolved that the Faculty Senate is opposed to the establishment of any racial or religious criteria for residence in any University operated housing unit or subdivision thereof."[40]

On April 3, two days before the scheduled Faculty Senate meeting, about fifty black students staged a demonstration on College Green. They criticized delay by the provost, and expressed the view that they had been "lied to" and were being used as a "political football." They denounced the forthcoming special meeting of the Faculty Senate as "an unprecedented act," demanded that leases be sent to students who wished to live in the program immediately, and insisted that President Martin Meyerson or Provost Reitz "certify publicly in writing that the Faculty Senate vote will have no bearing on the project."[41]

The same day the Black Faculty and Administrators held a press conference and also issued a statement that defended the black residence proposal and denounced the leadership of the Faculty Senate. The BFA statement acknowledged the alienation felt by many black students in a predominantly white environment. It claimed: "Segregation is forced separation which dehumanizes and degrades the spirit; it is immoral, unlawful, and unjust. On the other hand, a voluntary plan for Blacks to come together for academic and cultural enrichment is in the highest tradition of morality, and will strengthen rather than weaken the human spirit." It also noted, "Because all cultural and academic affairs offered by the Center will be open to all members of the University community, both Black and White, the Center will contribute to the enrichment of the academic and cultural experience for a wide spectrum of the University family." Among the speakers at the BFA press conference were Bernard Anderson, William Meek, John Edgar Wideman, William Adams, Conrad Jones, Thomasina Reed, and James Robinson.[42] Here, again, concerted pressure by the African American faculty and administrators in support of the students played a crucial role in holding the proverbial feet of the administration to the fire. Although this study emphasizes student activism, there *was* an African American community at Penn, which included faculty, administrators, support staff, and employees. This segmented community was, in turn, linked to the wider black Philadelphia community off campus.

The following day, April 4, 1972, Provost Reitz met with a group of African American students, most of whom were applicants for the proposed black residential center. Reitz promised a final decision by Thursday, April 6, but also said the failure to get a black faculty member to live in the residence was an obstacle to the approval of the plan. He also indicated that the proposal would have to be modified to comply with city and state ordinances that prohibited residential activities that are exclusive to any one race. Some of the students objected, however, that there were fraternities on campus that did not accept blacks, yet no one had charged them with violating the said ordinances. In addition, they criticized the Faculty Senate as a "lily-white organization" and questioned its role in the matter.[43]

Tensions on campus mounted, and the frustrations of black students found expression in some unorthodox ways. Some black students were unhappy with the way the *Daily Pennsylvanian* had been covering the debate about the proposal to establish a residence for African American students. On Tuesday, April 4, 1972, following the meeting with Provost Reitz, a few black students allegedly demanded to check the notes of the reporter who covered the meeting for accuracy, and at that time they threatened to destroy copies of the newspaper. Later they expressed a wish to check the final draft of the story. On Wednesday, April 5, an unknown number of black students allegedly carried out the earlier threats and confiscated and destroyed several thousand copies of the paper.[44] Those familiar with a similar act of confiscation in 1993 will appreciate that history sometimes appears to repeat itself. Subsequently, on April 13, a statement from the Committee on Open Expression condemned the theft.[45]

As April 4 drew to a close, the prospects for President Meyerson's and Provost Reitz's approval of the proposal for a dormitory for black students looked rather bleak. There was intense and vocal opposition among many members of the faculty, and the campus was deeply divided. In this climate of acrimony, as is evident from the confiscation episode, relations between more militant black students and the *Daily Pennsylvanian* were badly strained. Would the administration proceed with such a controversial step if the Faculty Senate strenuously objected? Would black students tamely and peacefully submit to being denied something that many of them said they desperately wanted and needed? A fateful decision had to be made, and the campus held its collective breath.

A special meeting of the Faculty Senate had been scheduled for April 5, to discuss the question and offer the advice of the faculty to the administration.

That morning, the *Daily Pennsylvanian* printed an editorial ironically entitled "Deliberate Speed." It criticized the failure of liberal faculty members to participate in the Senate and said that "too many liberal faculty members have long stayed away from Senate meetings, convinced the body is dominated by a small group of their conservative colleagues. If there were ever a meeting that liberal faculty members should attend, this is it and we suggest they turn out in full." Moreover, echoing the sentiments of black students, the editorial continued:

University officials are apparently ready to let threats of legal action block the program without ever testing the matter in court, a position that suggests a rather weak commitment. If officials here believe in the merits of the program, as they profess to, then they should be willing to defend them in court. Should the Human Relations Commission or any other agency threaten legal action, the matter should be settled in a court of law; the University's decision should not be based upon a legal opinion that is in no way conclusive.[46]

The Faculty Senate Has Its "Say"

The criticisms by black students and the *Daily Pennsylvanian* seem to have hit their mark. Liberal faculty members did indeed attend the Faculty Senate meeting, and by all accounts it was a heated affair. Dr. Michael Cohen, reputed author of the original resolution, asserted the residence plan would violate principles of integration. He suggested that hiring only black resource personnel in the program would lead to discrimination. Dr. Benjamin Hammond, an African American faculty member in the Dental School, said, "It is utterly unrealistic to think that any of us can live in an all-black world or that black people in America can continue to live in isolation." Dr. Martin Seligman said the project involved "a systematic exclusion of whites" and the "hostility and suspicion" present in black–white relations at the university "is not alleviated by walling blacks and whites off from each other."[47]

In defense of the proposed residential program, Vice Provost Humphrey Tonkin emphasized the need for the project to assist in the "cultural transition" between life in a black community and life at the predominantly white university. He observed that the Cohen resolution "shows no particular awareness that there is such a problem at all." John Edgar Wideman spoke on behalf of the plan, as did Cathy Barlow.[48] Pressed by Dr. Jean Crockett as to whether white students would be allowed to participate in the program, Barlow is reported to have said, "Theoretically, if a white student is truly committed to learning about black culture and truly has the same need to have a black resident advisor, to live with black faculty and to have a black freshman advisor to advise him he is welcome to participate in the program, but I doubt that one would."[49]

Liberal Law Professor Howard Lesnick offered a substitute resolution that commended the administration for "committing serious efforts to maximizing the educational opportunities of black students." The Lesnick resolution also called for the creation of a Senate committee to study the project once it was in operation. The Senate voted on the Lesnick alternative—and if it failed, it could then turn to the original resolution opposing "the establishment of any racial or religious criteria for residence."[50] Rather to the surprise of many, the Senate voted 82 to 71 in favor of the Lesnick substitute. In voting for the Lesnick alternative, the Faculty Senate effectively rejected the original resolution. It also rejected a resolution that would have declared it "in favor of the establishment on an experimental basis of a black residence program basically in line with the program approved by the University administration, provided however that participation both residential and non-residential in this program be open to all students of the University regardless of race." The Lesnick alternative created the study committee for the project. It also asked the provost to appoint a member of this committee to the review committee, which would evaluate the success of the program and advise as to whether it should be continued after the one-year trial period.[51]

The following day, Thursday, April 6, 1972, Vice Provosts the Reverend Jack Russell and Humphrey Tonkin announced that the university definitely would proceed to operate a residential center in fall 1972, open to *all* freshmen and sophomores "who have a particular interest in and commitment to black culture, and a particular need for the educational opportunities and services which the Center and its environment will provide." It was pointed out that the residential program would include a speakers series and a library (subsequently named in honor of Paul Robeson). Furthermore, this wording of the purpose and rationale for the program was selected to indicate the possibility that white students with an interest in learning about black (African American) culture might also reside in the dormitory. This wording was also intended to soften the "exclusionary" nature of the original proposal. Forty-three black students had applied to live in the residential center.[52]

A six-member interracial committee of faculty and administrators, plus one student, was appointed to review applications.[53] African American students had articulated their desire and "felt need" for autonomy and a cultural space of their own. On this occasion, perhaps surprisingly, they got most of what they wanted.

CHAPTER NINE

"A PROGRAM FOR ANY UNDERGRADUATE OF ANY RACE"

Black people must redefine themselves, and only *they* can do that. Throughout this country, vast segments of the black communities are beginning to recognize the need to assert their own definitions, to reclaim their history, their culture; to create their own sense of community and togetherness.

—Kwame Ture and Charles V. Hamilton, *Black Power,* 1967

During the winter and early spring of 1972 the university community had debated a proposal from black students that a residence be established for African American students. What the Faculty Senate and administration approved was a residential program for *any* undergraduate student of *any* race or ethnicity who was interested in learning more about Afro-American culture. Initially it was called the W. E. B. Du Bois Program, and the residence opened in August 1972. Later it was made a "college house." Here we can compare the formation of Du Bois House with a similar program at Cornell, called *Ujamaa* and describe the subsequent development of Du Bois College House in its struggle both to survive and to justify its existence. Du Bois House has persisted into the new century, and stands as testimony to the enduring desire of African American students at Penn to preserve their own culture and autonomy.

The Example of Cornell

Penn's decision to proceed with the formation of Du Bois College House, on an experimental basis, was not without precedent, for, in fact, the experiences of Penn and Cornell University were very similar. In 1963 Cornell had twenty-five African-American undergraduates. In 1965, with a grant of $250,000 from the Rockefeller Foundation, Cornell began to bring in black students whose Scholastic Aptitude Test scores ranged from 900 to 1100. Cornell Trustees established an intensive recruiting, guidance, and counseling program called the Committee on Special Educational Projects (COSEP). With the increase in the number of black students, the Afro-American Society was formed in 1966. In 1968 black students asked for a separate residence for black students, and Cornell established a cooperative house for women of any racial background who were in COSEP. There were some whites, Puerto Ricans, and Native Americans in COSEP, but in 1969 all thirteen of the women at Wari House happened to be African Americans. Most of the one hundred black female undergraduates at Cornell lived in dormitories or apartments, however. In 1969 fifteen African American men lived in a residence called Elmwood House.[1]

Although Penn was in a major metropolitan area, Cornell was located in quiet, racially homogeneous Ithaca, New York, with a population of 29,750 in 1969. Therefore, the size of the population of the university's site would not seem to be the determining factor at work in these two institutions. At Penn, as at Cornell, campus social and residential life had traditionally been dominated by the fraternities, some of which had once chosen to admit members on the basis of religion or race. Hence, there were "white" Jewish, Protestant, and Catholic fraternities. The number of black students may have been so small in the years immediately following 1965 that it was hardly possible to form black fraternity and sorority houses.

Furthermore, without a strong alumni network and funds, it would have been impossible to obtain a house—even with an adequate number of members. Consequently, one tentative interpretation of this development might be that African American students found it necessary to turn to the universities to achieve through public or institutional means what may otherwise be described as private or communal purposes. If black students had possessed the private resources from wealthy alumni or foundations to purchase or lease fraternity houses and fund social and cultural centers, there might have been an alternative to asking the institutions to provide these resources. After all, the Newman Center provides for the social needs of its Catholic constituency, and the Hillel Foundation funds the Hillel centers for Jewish students. Wealthy fraternity and sorority alumni support fraternities and sororities, but African American students, so recently arrived at Penn and Cornell in large numbers, had no such private resources to call upon.

By 1968 the African American students at Cornell demanded an Afro-American Studies program with a black director, and in September 1968 Cornell formed a committee to outline such a program. The black students at Cornell also demanded a black social center.[2] The trajectory at Penn is very similar to that at Cornell. In creating Du Bois College House, the authorities at Penn were certainly aware of events at Cornell and other universities. Indeed, articles and materials on similar activities at Cornell and elsewhere can be found in Penn's archives. Penn was not acting in isolation or in a vacuum.

The Inception of Du Bois College House

Following the decision by Penn to establish the Du Bois residential program, criticism continued on campus. Off-campus difficulties with the NAACP and the Pennsylvania Human Relations Commission also persisted. On April 5, John Wideman, Conrad Jones, and Cathy Barlow met with members of the Pennsylvania Human Relations Commission, but apparently no minds were changed. Meanwhile the Reverend Wycliffe Jangdharrie, of the Metropolitan Council of the NAACP, insisted that, "regardless of how you word it, it's reserved for black students only and as far as I'm concerned it's segregation in violation of Title VI." He asked, "Who's interested in a black dorm but blacks?"[3]

Meanwhile, on April 12, Provost Reitz publicly reaffirmed to the University Council that "an administrative decision has been made to proceed with plans for a black residence center; it is noted that a resolution adopted by the Faculty Senate was generally supportive of this proposal."[4] On April 21, 1972, the campus learned from the *DP* that the forthcoming "black residential program" would be called the W. E. B. Du Bois Residential Program,[5] and that Dr. Patrick Cole would be returning to Penn, to the History Department, in the fall and would serve as a faculty fellow in residence at the Du Bois Residential Program. Previously, in 1970 and 1971, Cole had taught West African history, and had received a Ph.D. from King's College, Cambridge.[6]

Media coverage attempted to strike a balance between deploring a demand for a "segregated, black-only" center and emphasizing that the dormitory would be "open to all." The *Philadelphia Daily News* was the most positive, with a story under the headline, "Penn to Open Black Center with Integrated Dorm Unit." The story emphasized that Penn had "ruled out black student demands that the center be restricted to blacks," and the "library, lectures and seminars would be open to all members of the university regardless of race." The article also specifically mentioned that Patrick Cole, an assistant professor of history, and Burney Hollis, a visiting lecturer in English, would be resident faculty persons.[7]

The *Evening Bulletin* was much more critical. The statement that "students of any race could apply for spots in the dorm" was immediately undercut by quoting Cathy Barlow as saying that she "doubted there will be any whites in the dorm when it opens." The headline read, "Penn Dorm for Blacks Reflects Steady Rise in Separatist Sentiment," and it was followed by the recollection that, in 1968, members of the Society of African and Afro-American Students (SAAS) "held a blacks-only meeting at the university's Christian Association to hear prize fighter and Black Muslim minister Muhammad Ali."[8]

A *Bulletin* editorial the previous day had declared:

There is enough mutual hostility between blacks and whites already at integrated campuses without having to institutionalize it in the form of black-only facilities and academic courses. . . . Instead of aiding their adjustment, however, the sanction of separate dorms, clubs and academic programs often works against assimilation. . . . This is not to deny a place to black studies and activities. But such programs must remain open to all students if they are not to become enclaves of black separatism. The University of Pennsylvania reached a compromise when it recently authorized establishment of a residential center which will have as its focus black culture but which will be open to all students. Even here there is a danger in unwittingly fostering a center, which may by its very nature and emphasis, end up catering to blacks only. But at least it avoids the formal establishment of a racially separate facility.[9]

The *New York Times* noted that whites were not formally excluded, but that, "because the concept of the program and the content of its remedial counseling and teaching will be directed exclusively to black identities, campus observers believe there is little chance that a white student would apply for admission." The article also quoted an unidentified official at the Department of Health, Education and Welfare as saying: "On the basis of two previous attempts to establish all-black living quarters at Antioch College and Cornell University, the department would find any racial exclusionary language in the program's official description would violate Title 6 of the Civil Rights Act of 1964."[10]

Despite the controversy, Du Bois College House opened at the end of August 1972. A plaque installed there later reads, in part, "On this site, the W. E. B. Du Bois College House was established on the 31st day of August, 1972, for students wishing to study and foster Afro-American culture within a residential environment at the University of Pennsylvania."[11] At the formal dedication ceremony, which occurred belatedly in 1981, President Sheldon

Hackney read the inscription on the dedicatory plaque. The keynote speaker was Ozell Sutton, president of Alpha Phi Alpha (the nation's first black fraternity). Penn alumnus and former trustee, Philadelphia Deputy Mayor George Burrell was among the more than two hundred people who attended the ceremony. The gala evening also included a performance by the Fisk Jubilee Singers at the Zellerbach Theatre and dramatic readings by Cicely Tyson.[12]

Cathy Barlow, who had been the moving force behind the original proposal for a black student residence, served as the administrative director of the program during 1972–73, and Dr. Burney Hollis, a visiting lecturer from Morgan State College, served as a faculty fellow (living-in-residence) along with Patrick Cole. There were also five graduate fellows.[13] Typically one or two faculty fellows lived at the House, along with several graduate fellows who served as counselors. Usually about ninety students lived in the House and they comprised about one-fifth of the black undergraduate student population. Most African-American undergraduates at Du Bois House lived there for a year or two, and then either moved elsewhere in the residence system or off campus. Rarely did a student remain there all four undergraduate years. Thus, Du Bois House was one experience among many.

In 1972–73 Burney Hollis inaugurated a literary magazine, called *Ulozi,* at the Du Bois House, and taught a seminar in Afro-American Literature there. There were twenty-four students in the seminar, all African American, of whom one-third were residents of the program, and some were from Morgan State University. During that year, Du Bois House also provided a meeting place for a gospel choir and black drama group, both of which included many students who did not live at the House.[14] Beginning in September 1974, Dr. Howard Arnold (Social Work) served as the first housemaster of Du Bois College House.[15] During 1974–75 Du Bois House inaugurated its *Uchoraji* Art Gallery, with monthly exhibitions.[16]

A Renewed Chorus of Criticism

Following approval of Du Bois College House by the administration on April 6, 1972, many voices continued to be raised against the residential program. A sampling of them follows. In a bitter critique, Steven Fadem wrote that it was

tragic that less than a decade after Schwerner, Goodman and Chaney died, those who opposed segregation were called bigots. . . . It makes one wonder whether years of civil rights activism to gain equal freedoms for an "oppressed" minority haven't been cruelly twisted around in our faces. Admissions standards are lowered and concessions continually granted, through capitulation, to make amends for centuries of inequality, and now the very moral, legal, Constitutional principles under which we acted are reversed, perverted, and prostituted in the name of equality.[17]

A letter from Michael Meyers, then a senior at Antioch College (which had also established a black-only residence), appeared in the *Daily Pennsylvanian* on April 27. Meyers, who is black, wrote:

The frustrations that black students feel when they come up against the cruel prejudices of the white majority are understandable, but black students, because they are black, must prepare themselves and be prepared for continued struggle. One cannot obtain self-confidence, dignity or a positive self-identity in a house segregated from the real world, in a living facility where there is an insidious, tacit requirement for avoiding the real. . . . In the real world black students will not be given the chance to retreat into a disneyland of racial breast-beating. Like it or not, the real world is white, and it is racist.[18]

In a similar vein, Larry Fine complained:

What on the part of whites would justly be termed segregation and racist, the University has chosen to view euphemistically as "nation-building" and "search for identity". . . Rather than attempting to integrate a student into a "university experience" (not a white experience or a black experience) the existence of a black dorm will serve only to further polarize the campus and inhibit anything beyond superficial interaction.[19]

The impression that Penn had approved a "black-only" facility proved exceedingly difficult to rectify. On April 20, 1972, the *Chicago Daily Defender,* a venerable African American newspaper, observed that the University of Pennsylvania had rejected a proposal for a black-only living and counseling center and that the provost had ruled that all students must be admitted to the project. But, the *Daily Defender* continued, "In so ruling, the institution skirted possible legal objections from state and federal civil rights officials. For the residence and study project would have carried with it terms that could result in its being all black in fact." The editorial noted the bitter irony in that "the attempt at residential exclusion and separate academic projects reached its height just at the time when matured blacks everywhere were fighting for open housing as the surest way of bringing down the black ghetto walls that keep black folk out of the main stream of American society."[20]

African American Penn student Wilson Jones noted that critics of Du Bois College House said it would *cause* polarization. But, he contended, "Realists know that whites and blacks (barring a few) don't come from well integrated neighborhoods. They also know the immoral, low, and wrong things some white folks do to keep their living environments segregated. . . . If whites and blacks live in geographically distinct areas, why play 'integration' for four years under the pretense of education?"[21] Jones seemed to be suggesting that, in the "real world," homogeneous neighborhoods and residential patterns already existed, and more often than not it was residential integration that was a fantasyland. Du Bois College House did not create polarization. Perhaps it merely mirrored the separation that already existed.

The External Investigations

During its first few years of operation the Du Bois Residential House remained the object of criticism and hostile scrutiny. The Reverend Wycliffe Jangdharrie of the NAACP inquired whether the NAACP could sue the "black dorm," and a white graduate student lodged a complaint, but the American Civil Liberties Union indicated that a proper complaint would have to come from an undergraduate at Penn, because Du Bois was an undergraduate residence.[22] The Pennsylvania Human Relations Commission and the Higher Education branch of the Civil Rights Office of the Department of Health, Education and Welfare (HEW) investigated Du Bois House.

Although black residences at Vassar and on the Livingstone campus of Rutgers University closed in 1975, the HEW investigation of Du Bois continued without consequence.[23] In the end nothing came of the investigations. If there had been a white undergraduate who wanted to live at Du Bois, and this individual had been denied admission to the House, solely on the basis of race, there might have been grounds for a complaint of racial discrimination. But the House had not denied admission to any white student who wished to live there. There had been no discrimination. What continued to make some people unhappy however was the perception of "separatism." This was really the clash in ideological perspective between the desire of assimilationists to be color-blind (to erase consciousness of race and color in a nonracial society) and the desire of pluralists and nationalists to be race conscious and to value highly their racial and ethnic identity in a multiracial, multiethnic, multicultural society. What black students were really guilty of was a "failure of assimilation."

White Students at Du Bois College House

By 1976 there were white students living at Du Bois, which established that anyone of any race who wished to live in the College House could do so. As one example, in 1976–77 a white student, Marian Dorn, lived at Du Bois, as one of the very first to do so.[24] Indeed, in March 1977, while the *Bakke* case was being considered by the Supreme Court and the campus debated the issue of Affirmative Action, Marian Dorn and her African American roommate Kimberly Edmunds wrote a letter to the *Daily Pennsylvanian* defending the need for it. Among other things, the authors took issue with those who advocated a race-neutral standard based solely on "merit."[25]

Likewise, in the spring of 1981 a white student named Robert Zagerman applied to live in Du Bois College House for the following academic year (1981–82). In a *DP* article in April 1981, Zagerman explained that he had lived in the Quadrangle as a freshman, but said he "felt out of place" there. He said he had grown up in Willingboro, New Jersey, in a racially integrated neighborhood and school system. He listened to WDAS radio station, a black station in Philadelphia.[26]

Zagerman described the atmosphere in the Quad as very homogeneous. And the university seemed very isolated from the surrounding black community. In his sophomore year he moved to Low Rise North, and lived on the third floor, above Du Bois House. Low Rise North is the name of the four-story building that contains Du Bois House (on its first and second floors). Residing at Low Rise North in his sophomore year enabled him to live in an environment that he found more diverse and familiar, in proximity to people of different backgrounds, and where he felt "more comfortable." He had friends who were black and lived at Du Bois. One of them, Philip Cuffey, said "You can't stereotype people. A few white guys lived here two years ago, and everything was cool. Bob is a real positive brother." Black student and Du Bois House resident Robin Renee Johnson said, "I no longer look at Bob as being white. I look at him as being Bob." Zagerman said that only one black person told him she did not want white people to live at Du Bois. He added, "She's a racist—against whites. I'm a bigger person than she is. She's as bad as the person who writes 'nigger' in a high rise elevator."[27] Zagerman also expressed sympathy for the condition of being in the minority, saying, "How would someone [white] feel if the school was 95 percent black? If the people in that vast majority don't seem to care about you it can make you hard. I think the general attitude towards blacks around here is negative or indifferent. A lot of people probably would prefer not to see blacks on this campus."[28]

Robert Zagerman said that when he chose to live at Du Bois House he was not looking for publicity or attention, nor was he trying to "prove a point." He simply wanted an atmosphere that reflected the diversity he had been accustomed to in his hometown of Willingboro, New Jersey. He said that when he was a sophomore he had friends who lived at Du Bois, and they and House Master Denis Cochran Fikes encouraged him to apply to live there. He lived at Du Bois House for one year, on the second floor, while a junior, and in his senior year returned to an upper floor of Low Rise North. When asked about his experience at Du Bois House, he said he had "loved living there." A small handful of blacks seemed as if they would have preferred that he not be there, but he felt that the overwhelming majority accepted him. He said if he were to be an undergraduate again, he would make the same choice and he had no regrets about living there.[29]

In time it became apparent that those who criticized the House on the grounds of "racial exclusion" against whites had a very weak case. As the experiences of Marian Dorn and Robert Zagerman prove, there was no one who wished to be included or who wished to reside at and participate in Du Bois House who was being excluded or denied the opportunity to do so.

Surviving in the Midst of Adversity

Despite its critics, Du Bois College House continued to grow. In 1973–74, the new administrative director was William Harvey, a Ph.D. candidate in English. He remained until academic year 1975–76. During 1973–74 a course in college reading and study skills was taught at Du Bois, and its library began to expand. Soon there were a gospel choir, a literary magazine, and an art gallery.[30] Over time, a greater emphasis was placed on African American culture and less on the special "counseling needs" of African American students. The "downside" of an emphasis on counseling needs had been that it inadvertently reinforced the image of all black students as being academically "at risk," remedial, and deficient. This negative labeling stigmatized black students and fed into perceptions that

African American students were not really qualified for admission but had been accepted only to meet affirmative action targets and quotas.

Unfortunately, the never-ending criticism sometimes caused African American students to feel besieged—as if they were living on a hostile campus. The House is located adjacent to a high-rise dormitory of more than twenty floors. On occasion racial epithets have been yelled from the taller building, and eggs, water balloons, and other objects thrown at persons walking by Du Bois College House. In fall 1981, there were bomb threats.[31] But Du Bois College House has survived despite all of this.

Through all the turmoil, controversy, and uncertainty of the first few years, Faculty Master Professor Howard Arnold was a guiding and stabilizing influence. Although he did not live in the House, he was a voice of calm and a pillar of strength. He and other members of the black faculty resolutely defended the House from criticism when many others sought to undermine and destroy it. Professor Arnold's commitment and devotion to the College House endeared him to its residents.

During 1973–74, Irving McPhail (Education) served as a faculty fellow at Du Bois College House and as an adviser in the College. Leslie Carter served as assistant director during 1974–75, and the graduate fellows included Don Maynard (Engineering) and Rita Smith (a Ph.D. candidate in Psychology). In 1975–76 doctoral candidate Lorraine Howard and Professor Gerald Jaynes (Economics) served as faculty fellows. Law student William Sims III succeeded William Harvey as administrative director in the summer of 1976. In 1977 Professor Mary Rhodes Hoover (Education) succeeded Howard Arnold as house master. Doctoral candidates Lorraine Howard and Jacqueline Wade served as faculty fellows at that time, and Professor Ernest Wilson III (Political Science) served as a faculty fellow during 1978–79. House Master Hoover was followed in 1978 by Faculty Master Valarie Swain-Cade, and in 1980 by Denis Cochran-Fikes. In the mid- and late 1980s house masters included Dr. John Roberts (Folklore), Dr. Allen Green (History), and Dr. Risa Lavizzo-Mourey (Medicine). All these faculty members and graduate fellows serving at Du Bois were African American despite the paucity of black faculty in these years.

Over the years Du Bois College House has maintained a very active schedule of guest speakers and social and cultural activities, and these have been and are open to the entire university community. In February 1974 the noted African American historian Benjamin Quarles, of Morgan State College, gave a lecture (in Stiteler Hall), which was cosponsored by the Morgan–Penn Cooperative Project, the Afro-American Studies Program, and Du Bois House. The lecture commemorated the birth of W. E. B. Du Bois.[32] Other speakers at Du Bois House itself have included Kwame Ture, Vincent Harding, Rosa Parks, Ali Mazrui, Bishop Desmond Tutu, Harold Cruse, C. Eric Lincoln, David Bradley, Sonia Sanchez, Harriette McAdoo, Gloria Naylor, and Toni Cade Bambara, among many others.

Despite controversy and misunderstanding, Du Bois College House continues and has become a permanent part of the University of Pennsylvania. Yet, if one were to pick up the *Daily Pennsylvanian* for any year between 1972 and 1999, one would find letters similar to those described above, alleging separatism, voluntary segregation, and reverse discrimination against whites. A perfect example of this genre would be a column in which Albert Gorden wrote, "The conclusion is that Du Bois House is a revolting example of de facto segregation, it probably is illegal and *if it isn't it should be* [emphasis added]. Du Bois House tacitly fosters, abets and provokes racial polarity at Penn."[33] One is reminded that in the nineteenth century Protestant Americans were profoundly agitated by the "inexplicable" attachment of the Irish Catholics to their priests and their Catholicism. The pronounced tendency of the Irish to "cling" to their religion affronted wasps who expected immigrants not only to acculturate, but also to convert. The attachment of African Americans to their ethnic identity and their efforts to preserve their culture seem to excite similar consternation today.

Other Thematic Houses

Du Bois College House was not the only thematic residence. In fact, in the 1970s Penn established a variety of them. In 1972 the university established the International Program, consisting of two floors of High Rise East, where foreign students and American students lived together in an environment devoted to cross-cultural exchange. This included exposure to music, art, film, language, and cuisine. Ambrose Davis served as program director and was also the director of the Office of International Programs. Penn established the Romance Languages College House, in 1973, with a floor for students who wished to learn Spanish and a floor for those wishing to learn French. Subsequently this was expanded to provided floors or wings for those wishing to learn German and Italian, and the name changed to Modern Languages College House. This setting would provide an immersion experience, with the language of study spoken almost exclusively on the respective floors and with activities designed to teach students about the cultures of Spain, France, Germany, and Italy. So these students not only learned a language but learned about the art, music, literature, film, history, and cuisine of the people who spoke the language as well.[34]

In 1973 the university established the Arts House, for students with a special interest in the visual arts (painting, sculpture, graphics, and photography). It even had its own darkroom. In 1974 Penn inaugurated the Japan Program, a residential program on a floor in Harrison House. Brent and Hiroko Evans served as the resident graduate fellows. The program featured exposure to Japanese art, film, and cuisine, and lectures on other Japanese topics. Subsequently, the program was expanded to include Chinese and other Asian cultures and became the East Asia Program.

In 1976 the university sponsored the Health and Society College House (later called Ware College House, after its benefactor). This was a residential program for students with a special interest in issues of health, science, and society. Premed students and majors in the biological basis of behavior flocked to it, and Dr. Samuel Martin was named its first master. Previously he had been a resident scholar at Dunster House at Harvard.[35] All these "thematic" residential programs brought together students who shared a common interest. Yet, somehow, when students who shared an interest in African American culture came together in a residential setting, they were doing something "separatist" and "exclusionary." Somehow their actions were deviant and constituted "voluntary segregation."

Some Euro-American students have lived at Du Bois, as we have seen, yet far too few have availed themselves of the opportunity for what could also be described as an "immersion experience" in African American culture. One cannot avoid asking "why?" Perhaps it reflects a view that there is no African American culture to learn about, or a view that there is nothing of worth in African American culture. Perhaps white students imagine that they already know all there is to know about African Americans and their culture. Or perhaps it simply reflects indifference, and the fact that many white students aren't terribly interested in the African American culture or experience. Or could it be that learning about a people's history and culture in a classroom is such a different matter from living with the people? It might also reflect a healthy willingness to leave African American students alone when they request it. Yet, more than twenty-five years later, one is haunted by a paraphrase of the Reverend Janghdarrie's question: "Who is interested in black culture except black people?" Perhaps therein lies the crux of the problem.

Du Bois College House has survived investigation, criticism, and misunderstanding. Though still much maligned in some circles, it has proven itself tenacious and resilient. Moreover it has flourished—in large part, because black students, faculty, and the campus community insist that it should be available as an option for those who desire it. And it is testimony to the rejection of rapid assimilation and to the persistence of a distinctive sense of African American peoplehood, identity, and affinity.

Although Du Bois House endured, the House of the Family went into eclipse. In July 1974 the House of the Family building (3914 Locust Walk) was vacated, as the university contended repairs were needed to bring the structure into conformity with fire regulations. Soon thereafter, the Provost's Office decided to locate the Department of Public Safety (now the Penn Police Department) in the building.[36] Although the House of the Family disappeared after 1974, Du Bois College House became its heir and successor. In Du Bois College House, the House of the Family lives on.

A Delicate Matter: Differences in Cultural Styles

Du Bois College House grew out of the desire of some black students for an all-black residence hall. The university could not and did not meet this demand in such a bald form. Instead, it provided a program for any undergraduate student of any race who wished to study and foster African American culture in a residential setting. To critics, this was merely a subterfuge, a clever evasion, via a de facto black residence by another name. Opponents deemed it a shrewd way to allow a black residence on campus without actually admitting that it was one.

Cathy Barlow was the moving force behind the drive by African American students to establish Du Bois College House. Therefore, it is fitting to return to her earlier words. She had written, "Rather than developing a sense of belonging, a sense of community with the University, the incoming Black freshmen experience a deep sense of alienation because the University is a white-oriented institution."[37] She and her fellow authors said it was vital "that Black students, especially in their freshman year, have the alternative of discussing problems and ideas with Black residence counselors and academic advisors." The authors also lamented that "Black students were expected to adjust themselves in whatever manner necessary to function in the white environment into which they had been thrust. They were expected to adapt their thinking, their aspirations, their life style to conform with white middle class values."

Moreover, they charged, "The Black student is dispersed throughout the University residences and is therefore denied the comfort and understanding of his peers."[38] Black students also rejected the contention that Du Bois House caused polarization. Racially homogeneous neighborhoods and residential patterns already existed in society. Du Bois College House merely reflected that reality.

These statements by black students speak to the evident sense of isolation that some of them felt as they were immersed for the first time in a predominantly white social environment on a residential basis. For them, this immersion produced "culture shock" and a startling awareness of differences in cultural styles. One mundane example of this is as simple as preferences in music. White students at Penn in the late 1960s and early 1970s generally listened to "rock" music and local radio stations such as WMMR and Penn's own WXPN. Black students generally listened to rhythm and blues or the "Motown" sound and local station WDAS. At parties sponsored by white fraternities or by dormitories, the music generally was "white" rock music or heavy metal. African American students missed "their" own music and were turned off by these parties. A second mundane example could be cuisine. White social gatherings were famous for wine and cheese. At the risk of stereotyping African American students, many of them would have preferred "soul food"—or just some fried chicken and potato salad.

On the first warm day of spring, white students flocked onto the lawns to sun bathe. Rarely did one see African Americans sunning themselves. Blacks and whites even differed in which barber shop or hair parlor they went to. Some white students seemed to think it was a prank to spray shaving cream on one another. When white students, who thought that they were just playing around, sprayed shaving cream on some black students, the latter sometimes retaliated. In one such episode, the black student involved, enraged over the shaving cream squirted on his expensive leather coat, "beat up" the white student—and was charged with assault. The incident was eventually mediated.[39]

Although this statement may seem to invoke another stereotype, some of the African American students arriving at Penn in the late 1960s and early 1970s, from inner-city public school backgrounds, were described by contemporaries as "rough" and "confrontational." In contrast, African Americans who attend private, predominantly white preparatory schools are often socialized differently and carry themselves in a "preppy" manner that more closely approximates the "cultural style" of white middle-class Americans.[40] By white upper- and middle-class standards, this style is considered more polite, refined, or genteel. Conversely, in other circles, it may be viewed as "WASPification," "Anglo-Saxonization" or "middle-classification."[41]

The statements of students such as Cathy Barlow reflected a profound sense of alienation and estrangement. They themselves said that they did not feel a sense of belonging or community. They said that they perceived the campus environment as hostile and unwelcoming, and felt as if they were unwanted intruders. They said that, at best, white students and faculty seemed indifferent to them. The black students perceived that somehow there was an unwritten and unspoken expectation that *they* were supposed to assume the burden of adapting to the white Anglo-Saxon culture and assimilating into it. European immigrants might have chosen to come to America, and assimilation into the dominant British American culture might have been part of their price for immigrating. But enslaved Africans and their African American descendants had never asked to be brought to America. They had made no implicit bargain to assimilate into the dominant culture. Furthermore, the British American culture portrayed itself as superior and universal, while black culture was "narrow, parochial and particular." Interaction was not a two-way street. The two cultures, black and white, did not meet one another halfway, as equals, with mutual respect, but instead, blacks encountered a one-way street. *They* were expected to assimilate into the dominant (superior) white culture. It absorbed *them.* The process was neither mutual nor reciprocal.

Yet the expectation of assimilation is precisely what black students recoiled against. They wanted a first-rate education at a world-class institution of higher learning and they wanted to acquire the technical and professional expertise Penn had to offer. But some of them did not want to have to assimilate into the dominant white (Anglo-Saxon) culture. Apparently, some students were not willing to pay this price. The demand for Du Bois College House reflected both a negative reaction against the pressure to assimilate into what students found to be an alien culture and a positive attraction toward group affinity. It was also a negative reaction against the perception that the white environment was hostile to them and stigmatized them as intellectually, academically, and culturally inferior, and hence as "undeserving" of admission.

For black students, this was just the same old white racism with a different rationale: not the naked assertions of biological inferiority of the Jim Crow era but pseudoscientific allegations of intellectual and cultural inferiority. African Americans suspected that, if a black student had a 4.0 G.P.A. and an SAT score of 1600, some whites would still dislike that person and feel superior to him or her. Blacks students felt that (many) whites from affluent backgrounds simply resented that blacks had intruded into what had once been their exclusive Ivy League preserve, broken up their monopoly, and forced them to "share" the University with "others." For black students, the hand-wringing over declining standards was simply a rationalization and a convenient excuse for racial antipathy and class prejudice.

At Du Bois College House black students found relief from the burden and pressure of constantly trying to fit into someone else's culture, especially when that "someone" was perceived as condescending or afflicted with a superiority complex. Du Bois House was a source of solace and nurturance for some African American students in a way that the rest of the campus was not. Some black students felt that there was something that they were being denied and deprived of, something they needed—and could get at Du Bois House— which would enhance their academic performance and their sense of well-being. Whatever this need for a sense of community and belonging was, progressive whites seem to have understood that it was something that some black students wanted and needed, and they could assent to it.

African American students also had to learn the social skills of interacting and coping with members of a different race—on a full-time basis—where, suddenly, they were in the minority and felt unwelcome in a hostile environment. This emotional and psychological challenge was new to many of them. And it is a challenge that Euro-American students, who usually are not in the minority, do not face. Even Catholics and Jews, who find themselves in the minority in settings that are predominantly Protestant or Gentile, still share a dual layer of commonality with WASPs as whites and as people of European ancestry. It is also worth noting that Afro-American students, even into the twenty-first century, can go through four years of college without even once having a class with a black professor. Euro-American students do not usually go through four years of college without ever having a class with a white professor. Afro-American students at predominantly white colleges frequently experience being the only black person in a classroom. White students rarely have the experience of being the only person of their "race" in a class full of black students.

Part of what had to be learned by African Americans were the differences in "cultural style" not only between the so-called races but also among socioeconomic classes. African American students, especially those who were in the first generation in their families to attend college and who were from working-class, inner-city backgrounds, had to learn the cultural style of Euro-American students who often were from wealthy, affluent, upper- and middle-class suburban backgrounds. The interaction involved not only the visible dimension of race and ethnicity, but also the sometimes invisible and intangible dimension of socioeconomic class. This required them, in some sense, to become bicultural. They had to know both "codes." (Furthermore, it was not as if there were only two codes: They might need to become proficient with several.)

Many white students were coming to Penn from privileged suburban backgrounds where they knew few if any black students—and the few black people they did know were their maids, gardeners, janitors, or other subordinates. I would suggest that the "racial tension" that sometimes manifested itself between black and white students at Penn was, in part, the result of friction between white students from privileged, racially homogeneous, middle-class and upper-class backgrounds rubbing elbows with black students for the first time—with some of the latter from inner-city, public school, working-class backgrounds. A class dynamic was conflated with a racial one. This was exacerbated by the tendency of some white students to regard themselves as qualified and deserving, based on "superior" academic merit or achievement, while stigmatizing all or most blacks as remedial, undeserving, and unqualified. Of course, while preferences based on race were patently "unfair," these students felt no qualms about preferences based on unearned privilege as the children of alumni or faculty members.[42] The resentment by white students (and some faculty) was tinged with condescension and contempt, Little wonder, then, that apart from rudimentary civility in the classroom, library, and dining hall, some black students wanted as little to do with those white snobs and bigots as possible. In the eyes of (some) black students, the friendliness of well-meaning whites could easily be outweighed by the contemptuous attitude of other whites. The "superiority complex" of (some) whites fueled an equal and opposite reaction on the part of blacks. Nevertheless, against this background, the majority of black students did not live at Du Bois House and many had white roommates. The benefits to be derived from a Penn education were worth the "hassles," and black students certainly realized that they would have to "contend" for an education and an opportunity for upward mobility. For most of them, their overall experience was positive.

It also bears repeating that over time Penn became more adept at identifying good "feeder schools" and recruited a greater proportion of its African American students from such sources. Thus, more of them are already "socialized" to the white middle- and upper-class cultural style. Furthermore, at any given moment, only one-fifth of the black undergrads at Penn live at Du Bois House.

At some level, by 1972 the Meyerson administration had realized the difficulty that some African American students experienced, and agreed to establish Du Bois College House as a temporary coping mechanism. President Meyerson said, in an interview with a campus newspaper, that "many black students feel neglected. . . . If so many of our fellow black students feel that they are not being given the educational sustenance they need, and this is a claim of white students as well, then there should be some set of alternatives for them: the black center is one of these alternatives."[43] Liberal and progressive whites were responsive to the crisis of adjustment that some blacks faced. Undoubtedly the Penn administration looked forward to the day when no African American student would feel the need for such a residence any longer. Yet that day has not quite dawned. In the meantime, Du Bois College House stands as a monument to double-consciousness. Many African Americans seek to be bicultural, to preserve their own ethnic culture and to be Americans at the same time. Many do not want assimilation. They are cultural pluralists. The House could not have been given a better namesake than the complex and enigmatic prophet, W. E. B. Du Bois.

CHAPTER TEN

THE SIT-IN OF 1978 AND
THE UNITED MINORITIES COUNCIL

At the present time, integration as a solution to the race problem demands that the Negro foreswear his identity as a Negro. But for a lasting solution, the meaning of "American" must lose its implicit racial modifier, "white." Even without biological amalgamation, integration requires a sincere acceptance by all Americans that it is just as good to be a black American as it is to be a white American.

Here is the crux of the problem of race relations—the redefinition of the sense of group position so that the status advantage of the white man is no longer an advantage, so that an American may acknowledge "Negro ancestry" without apologizing for it. . . . [African Americans] live in a society in which to be unconditionally "American" is to be white, and to be black is a misfortune.

—Lewis Killian and Charles Grigg, *Racial Crisis in America*, 1964

Between 1972 and 1978, the black student movement at Penn was preoccupied with questions of maintaining the number of black students admitted to the university and increasing the number of African American faculty members. A detailed examination of these issues is beyond the scope of the present study. However, student dissatisfaction with the glacial pace of change mounted. In March 1978 a massive student sit-in rocked the apparent calm and tranquility of the University of Pennsylvania. This came at a time of budget cuts and unpopular, controversial decisions. Penn was phasing out the popular School of Allied Medical Professions. The Annenberg Center for the Performing Arts was in danger of being closed, over the vehement objection of students involved with the performing arts. Sports clubs were slated to be eliminated. In this climate, disaffected elements of the student body revolted. The full story of the sit-in of 1978 could well be a book unto itself, and thus it is also beyond the scope of this chapter. During the course of the 1978 sit-in, however, which was for the most part triggered by white students, the Black Student League (BSL) occupied an administration building, the Franklin Building, and essentially held its own sit-in within-a-sit-in. It used the occupation as its own bargaining chip and advanced its own agenda—separately from the white-led undergraduate student government.

The BSL demanded implementation of the recommendations of the Report on the Task Force on Black Presence. And it took the lead in creating the United Minorities Council (UMC) as an umbrella group of undergraduate racial-minority student organizations. The BSL closed ranks with the Puerto Rican, Mexican American, other Latino, Japanese American, Chinese American, and Korean American student organizations to create a united front. This chapter focuses on the sit-in of 1978, as the process by which the "racial" minority groups drew together to form the United Minorities Council in March 1978, and the implications of these events. The formation of the UMC may be seen as an unmistakable sign that the black nationalism and Black Power movement of the 1960s, which had strongly influenced the black student movement at Penn between 1967 and 1972, was evolving into a conception of cultural pluralism and African American ethnicity. With this conception of identity, African Americans would come to view themselves as an ethnic group, with a distinctive culture of their own, along with other ethnic groups in a pluralistic and multicultural society. The UMC stands as powerful testimony to the embrace of a vision of ethnic diversity and cultural pluralism on the part of African American students at Penn by 1978.

The Larger Context: Severe Budget Problems and Unpopular Cuts

Perhaps the single greatest contributing factor in the uprising of 1978 was that Penn was experiencing financial difficulties and running a deficit. Simply put, the accumulated deficit by 1978 was approximately $12–13 million.[1] Against this background of financial stringency, the Meyerson administration felt compelled to make harsh choices and reduce expenditures. These cuts, however, generated such a backlash of resentment that the positions of the provost and the president eventually became untenable.

Instead of across-the-board cuts, President Meyerson saw the need for "selective excellence." Of course, if decisions were to be made on the basis of selective excellence, it would be necessary to determine excellence through some process of evaluation, rating, and ranking. An Academic Planning Committee would do this work of "evaluation."[2] Not surprisingly, given the financial condition of the university, Penn had raised tuition for 1975–76.[3] Still, the financial situation continued to deteriorate, and the trustees insisted upon a balanced budget.[4] With these mounting deficits, there was intense pressure to balance the budget.[5] The administration in response sought to hold down costs, limit the size of increases in the faculty, and cut programs. In this fiscal context, it stumbled into conflict with the leadership of the faculty on several fronts.

A second critical factor that brought the faculty and the Meyerson administration into intense conflict was a decision to phase out the School of Allied Medical Professions (SAMP). It taught occupational therapy, physical therapy, and medical technology, and was widely regarded as one of the best such schools in the country. Without relating the details of the termination of SAMP, however, the decision to close the school proved be an immensely unpopular one that embittered some of the faculty. The administration also stumbled into a terrible fight with the unions when it sought to fire its 343 housekeepers (many of whom were African Americans). The unions flexed their political muscle, and Penn's appropriation from the Commonwealth came under attack in the State Assembly at Harrisburg. To save its appropriation, Penn was forced to settle with the union.

In his report to the trustees on the state of the university on January 13, 1978, President Meyerson attempted to emphasize the themes of achievement and adversity, but he also underscored the fact that Penn had the smallest endowment of all the Ivy League schools. Budget projections predicted a "shortfall" of $5 million for 1978–79.[6] The pressures on the administration to balance the budget were relentless.

In this climate, on February 23, 1978, Provost Stellar announced that the professional theatre programs of the Annenberg Center would be slashed as of the following academic year (fall 1978). Efforts to raise funds for the center had proved less than successful. Following the announcement of the theatre program curtailment, Steve Roth, vice chair of the Undergraduate Assembly (the undergraduate student government) protested, "This step may help balance our budget but it moves us one step closer to mediocrity."[7] Annenberg School Dean George Gerbner, Professor of Communications Amos Vogel, and Undergraduate Assembly Chair Trish Brown all condemned the Annenberg cutbacks.[8]

The impending downsizing of the Annenberg Center enraged the performing arts community, but for many other students the proverbial red flag was the cut in athletics. On February 23rd, the same day that Stellar announced that the Annenberg Center was likely to close, Athletic Director Andy Geiger announced that, because the Department of Intercollegiate Athletics had run a deficit of $500,000 the previous year, it would be necessary to eliminate the women's hockey club, men's and women's gymnastics, women's badminton, and men's ice hockey. The cuts would affect ninety athletes and at least one full-time coach.[9] For students, the projected cuts in the Annenberg Center and athletic programs were the triggers that precipitated the sit-in of 1978.

The College Hall Sit-in of 1978

At the turbulent Undergraduate Assembly (UA) meeting of March 1, Vice Chair Steve Roth offered a resolution calling for the resignation of President Martin Meyerson. However the UA defeated the motion. Kenneth "Teek" McNeil, BSL officer and UA member, denounced the UA for ineffectiveness and offered a motion that the student government disband. This, too, was defeated. McNeil asserted, "We're supposed to have input and we don't and if we don't there's no reason for us to be here." He condemned the UA as a "farce" and resigned in protest.[10] A rally to protest the budget cuts was scheduled for Thursday, March 2, at 11 A.M. It had been organized by the UA, under the leadership of Vice Chair Steve Roth. Roth, Annenberg Center Director Stephen Goff, and others addressed the crowd, but when Provost Eliot Stellar spoke, he was booed, and some students threw snowballs and eggs. Others chanted "Marty must go."[11]

At noon, at the conclusion of the rally, and apparently to the surprise of the Undergraduate Assembly, a group of students rushed up the stairs of College Hall and into the building. They were followed by the mass of students attending the rally, who soon were inside the offices of Faculty Arts and Sciences Dean Vartan Gregorian. It was widely believed that the students who initiated the rush into College Hall were disaffected members of the ice hockey and other sports teams. The UA followed in their footsteps, lest it be left behind and deemed to be irrelevant. Thus began a sit-in that swelled to eight hundred students and would last four days, until the early morning of Monday, March 6.[12]

Once inside, the students formed a Student Committee on University Priorities (SCOUP) and formulated several demands. These included reinstatement of the gymnastic and badminton teams, reinstatement of professional theatre at Annenberg, the implementation of nonvoting representation of students on the Board of Trustees, the demand that all trustee meetings be held while classes were in session, and the right of upcoming graduates to have sole say over the choice of their commencement speaker.[13] On Saturday some progress was reported when President Meyerson and Trustee John Eckman promised to raise the additional $125,000 needed to enable the Annenberg Center to continue for another year.[14]

The BSL Occupies the Franklin Building

Amid the chaos and confusion BSL President Sheryl George sought a seat on the Negotiating Committee of SCOUP and sought to have the concerns of minority students added to the six original demands. George did win election to the committee on Thursday night, but evidently she felt the concerns of minority students were being overlooked. Accordingly, at 5 A.M. on Friday morning, March 3, the BSL decided to pursue its own policy.[15] The BSL, as the self-proclaimed organization for African American students, conceived of itself as independent, and as such, it dared to act on its own.

The BSL decided that, while the Undergraduate Assembly managed the sit-in at College Hall, the BSL and minority students would occupy a building of their own (the Franklin Building) and negotiate from a position of strength with both SCOUP and the administration. Whereas College Hall housed the offices of the president, provost, and dean of arts and sciences, the Franklin Building was the financial hub of the university. It housed the Bursar's Office, the comptroller, the Cashier's Office, the Payroll Office, accounting, the Registrar's Office, and computer processing. If College Hall symbolized the university as an academic institution, the Franklin Building symbolized the university as a corporation and the largest private employer in the City of Philadelphia. Just after 9 A.M. on Friday, March 3, officers of the BSL roused students at Du Bois College House from their beds. At 10 A.M. black students occupied the first two floors of the building and remained there for the duration of the College Hall sit-in, which lasted until past 3 A.M. on Monday morning, March 6.[16]

Sheryl George stressed that this action was in solidarity with and in support of the action at College Hall. In fact, it was also designed to give the minority students leverage. If they were not satisfied with the demands drawn up by

SCOUP, the minority students would have the option of maintaining a separate sit-in at the Franklin Building even after the College Hall sit-in had concluded. Sheryl George was insisting that the minority community could act and speak for itself, and if it had to go its own way, then it could and would.[17]

On Saturday, March 4, 1978, the "racial" minority student organizations formed an umbrella organization, the United Minority Council (UMC). This was one of the most significant and tangible achievements of the sit-in. At the time the "minority" student organizations were the BSL, the Mexican American or Chicano student organization (MEChA), the Caribbean American Intercultural Association, the Chinese Students Association, Korean Cultural Society and Japanese American Student League. Sheryl George previously had maintained that she represented the "minority students" on campus. President Meyerson challenged this assertion, suggesting that she spoke for (some) black students only and not for Mexican American or Asian American students as well. By formalizing a relationship with the MEChA and the Asian American undergraduate student organizations, the BSL helped to create an entity that could legitimately and credibly claim to speak on behalf of minority students collectively—or at least their organizational memberships. The UMC further enhanced the legitimacy of the BSL. This coalition strengthened the bargaining power of the BSL and each of the racial "minority" student organizations.

During the sit-in the UMC formulated the following demands: that an Ad Hoc Committee on Financial Aid and Admissions be made a standing committee; an official commitment be made to the presence of Chicano, Latino, and Asian minorities; a Third World Center be established; and that the recommendations of the Black Presence Task Force be issued and implemented in total. The Black Presence Task Force had recommended the hiring of more black faculty members and the funding necessary to implement this. These and other demands were presented to SCOUP (the Negotiating Committee at College Hall) on Sunday morning, and as a result, the original list of six demands formulated at College Hall grew to thirty-one.[18]

Settlement of the Sit-in

At College Hall, negotiators agreed to reinstate the gymnastics, badminton, and golf teams, though not hockey. This would be matched by $50,000 in cuts elsewhere. It had been agreed on Saturday that "the highest priority effort" would be made to raise $125,000 for the Annenberg Center. The administration also agreed that at least students should have the "major say" in selecting their commencement speaker. The trustees then agreed to one student and one faculty voting member for one year, on an experimental basis (ultimately made nonvoting). It was also agreed that two of the three full trustee meetings would be held while classes were in session (September to May). The president and provost also agreed to assist members of the ice hockey team in transferring to other schools.[19]

On Monday, March 6, 1978, a committee of members of the United Minority Council met with Provost Stellar to discuss implementation of the ten minority student demands agreed to by the president and provost the previous day. One of the ten minority demands had been that this meeting take place. The BSL demanded that a report called the Black Presence Task Force Report (of June 1977) be published in the university's official record, the *Almanac*. This was done on March 21, 1978. The UMC demanded that it be recognized by the university. It also demanded that the provost and vice provost commit themselves officially to guaranteeing the presence of Chicano, Latino, and Asian students at the university, in a manner similar to the recognition of the presence of blacks as stated in the McGill Report. Provost Stellar affirmed this commitment. The UMC expressed concern about the future and budgeting of the Office of Supportive Services, and demanded that its budget and those of other minority-oriented programs be reexamined. The UMC also demanded a Third World Center, a demand that eventually was met. It also stipulated that money for minority-oriented programs be included in the forthcoming Campaign for the Eighties, the fundraising drive, a recommitment to minority faculty, administration, and student recruitment, and the implementation "in total" of the recommendations of the Task Force on Black Presence.[20]

In March 1978 the BSL and the UMC met with a modest degree of success and certainly breathed a bit of life into the implementation of the recommendations of the Task Force on Black Presence. Eventually, the Campaign for the Eighties did raise funds for minority presence, and a committee of faculty members was established to oversee how the money was used. The occupation of the Franklin Building by the BSL was a brilliant and successful strategy. The actions of March 1978 marked a resurgence of the kind of activism black students had exhibited in 1969 and 1970.

After some years, the university did fulfill its promise, in a modified form, to create a Third World Center. In November 1982 Penn purchased a building at 3708 Chestnut Street, which became the Albert Greenfield Intercultural Center and the home of the United Minorities Council (the original "minority" by then had been pluralized) with the blessing of the trustees.[21] Rene

Abelardo Gonzalez became the first director of the center in 1983 and retained that position until 1993. The center provided offices for the student member organizations and facilities for guest speakers, films, and social activities. As its name implied, the Intercultural Center became a place where exchange among students of different cultural backgrounds could take place in an organized way.

In many ways, however, the student "victory" was illusory and even Pyrrhic. The students had not sought to destroy the Meyerson administration or drive it from office. They merely desired to extract some concessions from it. Instead, the student sit-in wounded the administration so severely that it paved the way for a faculty revolt that *did* topple the president and the provost. The faculty criticized the administration for caving in to the demands of the students. In response, on April 20, 1978, Provost Eliot Stellar announced his intention to resign by the end of the calendar year. On April 28 the Faculty Senate met "to assess the performance of the central administration," and it became apparent that even the sacrifice of Eliot Stellar was not enough to appease the faculty. Usually, about one hundred twenty-five faculty members attended meetings of the Senate. At this meeting, however, the turnout was huge, with over seven hundred in attendance. The Senate Advisory Committee recommended to the Senate its (earlier) resolution of April 25. It stated, in part, "The Senate instructs the Senate Advisory Committee to establish a faculty panel to review faculty concerns about the administration and to pursue with the administration measures to *reestablish an atmosphere of confidence . . .* and to report back to the Senate no later than the fall meeting" (emphasis added).[22] A motion of "no confidence" was defeated, but the damage was done. One by one, members of the administration began making their exit. On September 6, 1978, President Meyerson publicly announced he would resign as president by June 1981.[23]

The ouster of Eliot Stellar claimed another casualty as well, as he had been an advocate for minority admissions and in the past had personally intervened to induce reluctant deans of admissions to admit black students. Indeed, this may have been one of the "sins" that conservative members of the faculty held against him. Hence, it is possible that, in spring 1978, the "lameduck" provost was in no position to pressure the undergraduate admissions system to admit more than a minimal number of black students. The incontrovertible fact is that, in September 1978, only 104 black students matriculated at Penn, the smallest number since 1969. The BSL regarded this as a disaster. Black admissions had become a casualty of the fall of Eliot Stellar.

End Gains

The occupation of the Franklin Building by the Black Student League and the other racial minority student organizations during the sit-in of March 1978 marked a crucial assertion of political autonomy and self-determination. The BSL had stepped out on its own and charted its own course, rather than subordinating itself to the Undergraduate Assembly. The formation of the United Minorities Council (UMC) may be interpreted as an expression of solidarity with other people of color. In this aspect, the actions of the BSL resembled the efforts of the Black Panthers, or the students in the San Francisco State College strike of 1968, to build coalitions with other Third World peoples and organizations.

An important factor in the creation of the UMC at Penn was the emergence and cultivation of a mutually cooperative relationship between the BSL and the Mexican American student organization (Movimiento Estudiantil de Chicanos de Aztlan, or MEChA) in the early 1970s. In April 1974 Louis Escareno, a Mexican American student and chairman of MEChA, filed a complaint with the Department of Health, Education and Welfare (HEW), charging the university with violating its affirmative action plan and failing to admit enough Mexican American students. In late September, Escareno also met with Bolivar Rivera, chairman of the Committee on Spanish-Speaking Peoples, which advised Pennsylvania Governor Milton Shapp. According to the Admissions Office, at the time, the entering class of 1974 had included sixteen Mexican Americans and two mainland Puerto Ricans (as distinct from those from the island).[24] In October 1974 Louis Escareno and former BSL chairman Craig Inge joined forces to condemn the university for what they perceived as efforts to cut minority admissions.[25] Thus, the roots of the coalition between African American and Mexican American students at Penn, or at least of their respective organizations, can be documented as far back as 1974. It is noteworthy that the issue that gave urgency to the perception of a mutually shared and advantageous need for cooperation was the maintenance of and increase in the number of African American and Mexican American students matriculating at Penn. The BSL and MEChA were also allies in 1974 in demanding restoration of the prefreshman summer program.

To be sure, all was not blissful harmony between the BSL and the other non-European groups. Many black students still regarded the historic black-white polarity as primary, and subjectively they still felt that blacks had been oppressed "more" than anyone else in the United States because of the extent, severity, and duration of chattel slavery. Nevertheless, the Black Panthers had spoken of the need for solidarity among people of color. The Panthers had also cooperated with radical, progressive white groups such as Students for a Democratic Society (SDS). Black students and Mexican American students had joined together in support of the student strike at San Francisco State College in 1968. The BSL now followed these examples.

African American students at Penn were being pressed—directly and personally—by their Latino and Asian American peers to expand the conception of domination and subordination to include *all people of color,* not only people of African extraction. For some African American students, their undergraduate experience at Penn was not only the first time that they had spent a significant amount of time with white students, but it was also the first time they had met and interacted with Latino and Asian American students and peers. In this sense, exposure to the Latino and Asian Pacific students expanded the horizon of understanding of African-descended students and broadened their awareness of the shared commonalities of subordination. The creation of the UMC suggests that the leadership of the BSL was moving beyond an awareness of "black" interests only and toward a coalition with other groups of color.

The UMC is testimony to an effort to build solidarity and a united front with other nonwhite, nondominant, historically subordinated groups. Evidently, by 1978 the BSL at Penn had embraced the discourse of cultural pluralism. African American students met and interacted with Mexican Americans, Puerto Ricans, Latin Americans, and Asian Pacific students, and this began to broaden their understanding beyond a binary preoccupation with white versus black.

The Emergence of African American Ethnicity

By the late 1970s, at Penn, black students began to see themselves not simply as members of a black "race" but also as one "group" among many in a pluralistic American society. They began to perceive that *everyone* in American society has a culture and is a member of some group into which they were born, as a matter of lineage, ancestry, and background. *Everyone,* therefore, has a culture and an ethnicity (or combinations thereof) as one of their layers or aspects of identity. These groups into which people are born are, in fact, ethnic groups, and ethnic groups can be aggregated together into "races." Indeed, ethnic groups are constitutive of "races" and are one of the raw materials or ingredients from which the idea of race is socially constructed. From the discovery of cultural pluralism and multiple ethnic groups (in addition to "races"), it took only a small additional step to perceive people of African extraction in the United states as not only a racial group but as a *cultural* group, and an *ethnic* group, as well. The recognition and consciousness of African American ethnicity became a new layer of identity along with or in addition to consciousness of color and "race."[26]

I suggest that lurking beneath the surface of what black students at Penn were saying and doing in the 1970s was a recognition of cultural pluralism and an *implicit,* emergent conception of Americans-of-African-extraction as an *ethnic* group. By 1978 the black student movement at Penn was certainly evolving in this direction. By 1978 one was able to see that the avowed black nationalism of the 1960s was merging with and evolving into the avowed cultural pluralism of the 1970s and 1980s.

The pluralist view can countenance the idea that Americans-of-African-extraction in the United States, with a distinct sense of peoplehood, might be or are an ethnic group in American society, with a unique culture of their own. It can also perceive that African-descended people throughout the New World (and Europe and elsewhere) were part of an African diaspora. This synthesis is called *African American ethnicity.* Furthermore, some proponents of African American ethnicity combine that belief with the conviction that the members of this ethnic group should not assimilate, but should struggle instead to preserve their distinctive group culture. Then, one may further perceive Americans-of-African-extraction as a segment of a transoceanic and diasporic "black" racial group and as an interest group among other ethnic groups and interest groups in American society.

African American ethnicity as an ideological stance and orientation rests on the premise that the original ancestral ethnic or "tribal" identity of African people brought to the New World in the transatlantic slave trade was lost here. Under the regime of slavery members of specific African ethnic groups, such as the Ibo, Yoruba, Mende, Ashanti, Bini, and Bakongo, underwent a process of deculturation in which successive generations lost their ancestral languages. They acquired a new identity as black Americans (or Americans of African extraction). They were treated alike at the hands of Europeans and Euro-American people in the New World. Out of this emerged a syncretized, *conglomerate or composite* identity, which in the United States is referred to as African American. This new identity is not a duplicate of the specific original African ancestral ethnicities (Yoruba, Ibo, or Ashanti), but is derived from them and combined with creative elements of innovation. After all, culture is not merely a static received tradition but a living (sometimes intermittent and discontinuous) process of invention and reinvention. In the 1960s and 1970s, black Americans were constructing (or reconfiguring) a new identity.[27]

The concept of African American ethnicity envisions "the people" as an extended family, implicitly sharing a common ancestry in Africa. Thus all black or African-descended people are bound by (real or imagined) ties of blood kinship.[28] One may recall that the Greek word *ethnos,* in its pristine sense, referred to a group characterized by common descent.[29]

If one conceives of the members of the African-descended group in the United States as an ethnic group, then the sense of peoplehood becomes black or African American *ethnicity.* If one believes that the black people constitute a *nation,* or national minority, then the sense of peoplehood becomes black *nationalism.* Furthermore, Walker Connor has argued—and I concur—that the congruence of ethnicity and nationalism produces *ethnonationalism.*[30] The supposed "separatism" of the BSL may reflect this ethnonationalism, though not a full-blown desire to partition the United States into a white country and a black country. Regardless of which concept (ethnicity or nationalism) one employs, however, there should be no doubt that this sense of groupness resembles the type of sentiment that Edward Shils (1957) and Clifford Geertz (1963) had described as "primordial" (as distinct from civic).[31]

The formation of the UMC at Penn in 1978 suggests that some African American students were embracing the vision of America as a multiracial, multiethnic, multicultural, pluralistic society. It also strongly attests to a conception of *group pluralism.*[32] This conception might not have been fully articulated or developed in 1978, but it is reasonable to infer that the African American student movement was evolving in that direction.

For these reasons, with respect to the African American student movement at Penn, I suggest that between 1967 and 1978 the paradigm of assimilation was challenged by the ideologies of Black Power, black nationalism, and pluralism, and over time the perspective of cultural pluralism and African American ethnicity became more pronounced. The UMC is a critical piece of evidence, and an important, tangible expression of a pluralist conception. The awakening of cultural pluralism would, in time, have profound consequences for the project of assimilation into a color-blind society. At Penn, at least, the birth of the UMC was a declaration that some Americans of color had rejected the goal of rapid assimilation and repudiated an earlier vision of the integration of detached, atomistic individuals into a society that sought to eradicate consciousness of difference.

CHAPTER ELEVEN

ASSIMILATION, PLURALISM, AND
NATIONALISM–SEPARATISM

No other group would submit to being led by others. Italians do not run the Anti-Defamation League of B'nai B'rith. Irish do not chair Christopher Columbus Societies. Yet when black people call for black-run and all-black organizations, they are immediately classed in a category with the Ku Klux Klan.

—Kwame Ture and Charles V. Hamilton, *Black Power,* 1967

Throughout this book I have traced the continuing impact of black nationalism and the ideology of Black Power on African American students at Penn into the 1980s, especially the influence of Kwame Ture and the black "cultural revolution" of the 1960s. Yet it is fair to ask just how widespread nationalist and separatist sentiments are among African American students. Are these sentiments "representative" of black students or held only by a vocal minority?

In the absence of a survey or some type of statistical analysis, it is impossible to answer this question in a quantitative way (and that is not the method of this book). Nevertheless, the activities of African American students offer some insight into answers to this question in reflecting a range of responses through the 1980s and into the present. After surveying three orientations among black students in a predominantly white university and society— assimilation, pluralism, and "separatism"—I find that many if not most African American students at Penn (and probably elsewhere) are cultural pluralists and are bicultural. Most African American students do not seek to separate and withdraw from the campus (or society), but wish to participate in *both* their own ethnically homogeneous institutions and the larger society as well, while pursuing upward mobility without assimilation.

Two Tripartite Models

In 1983 Dr. Jacqueline Wade completed a dissertation entitled "Black College Students' Adaptive Modes: Making It at Penn."[1] She began with a model of institutional racism that included the stigmatization of African Americans as inferior (of course, the model of stigma is derived from Erving Goffman). Wade asked how African American students adapt and respond to institutional racism, and in her case study of Penn delineated three types of response. The first adaptive mode, which she described as characteristic of "Black students," was separatist. These students sometimes retreat into a parallel world of their own, preferring to live in all-black settings and to associate almost exclusively with other blacks. Their attitude toward whites is rejectionist.

The second pattern of response is that of students who are "Black Americans." To some degree these students identify with the middle-class values of individualism, competition, and achievement and aspire to a professional, white-collar lifestyle. At the same time, however, they have a positive sense of black identity. They associate with both blacks and whites. The third pattern identified by Jacqueline Wade was students "who happen to be black." These students tend to de-emphasize their blackness. They do not wish to accentuate it and distance themselves from anything explicitly "black." They wish to be perceived simply as a "person" or as an "individual" and eschew group labels. They identify closely with white, middle-class values, and could be described as highly assimilationist and Eurocentric. Wade's study is indispensable for any investigation of the African American student experience specifically at Penn. William Van Deburg, in *New Day in Babylon* of 1992,[2] also presents a similar tripartite model that suggests that African Americans tend to cover an ideological spectrum that ranges from assimilationism to pluralism to nationalism.

My study confirms what Wade and Van Deburg suggested earlier. Among African American students one can find a range of perspectives. There are some who are rejectionist in their views, are highly alienated from the white dominant culture, and openly display their anger and contempt. This seems to be closely correlated with a more nationalist or "separatist" orientation emphasizing in-group solidarity, organizational homogeneity, and empowerment. These students identify very strongly with Malcolm X, Minister Farrakhan, Kwame Ture, and black economic and cultural nationalism. There are some students who are assimilationists (per Wade, those blacks who just happen to be black). For the most part these students are invisible. They are trying to "blend in" and hence are rarely heard from and are the least noticed. Furthermore, that would seem to be the way they want it. Such students would be exceedingly unlikely to join or actively participate in the BSL, live at W. E. B. Du Bois College House, attend black social events, join a black fraternity or sorority, or attend a speech by Minister Farrakhan, the Reverend Jesse Jackson, or even a "moderate" black spokesperson from the NAACP. This is their choice, and they have every right to that choice.

Observation suggests, however, that at Penn the great majority of African American students resemble Wade's category of "Black Americans" or Van Deburg's category of pluralists. In a word, they are bicultural. They embrace their African American identity with a sense of pride and wish to preserve their own culture and learn more about their history and heritage. They may embrace black or African American ethnicity. They sympathize with the search for empowerment and appreciate the need for in-group solidarity and organizational self-determination. They, however, also identify with the middle-class aspirations of white-collar professionalism and upward mobility. They may hope to go on to law, medical, or business school. And they participate in *both* ethnically homogeneous black organizations (the Black Wharton Undergraduate Association, Black Pre-Law Society, Black Pre-Health Society, the BSL, a black fraternity or sorority, the Gospel Choir), and majority organizations (the Undergraduate Assembly, Houston Hall Board, Performing Arts Council). A few examples will illustrate these different orientations.

The Black Student League at Penn has always been conscious of itself as an advocacy organization exerting pressure on the institution in order to advance the interests of African American students and improve the quality of campus life for them. Furthermore, since the late 1960s, the BSL had *in practice* reserved full membership for persons of African descent only. Even in the 1980s this ideological orientation persisted and, in some respects, became even more pronounced and noticeable. This was dramatically reasserted in 1986 when the BSL denied full membership to a white student. This episode raised new questions about the assumptions of integration and also revealed the persistence of the issue of "separatism."

In order to follow this "thread" of inquiry, however, it will be necessary to leap forward in the historical narrative and omit full discussion of a number of intervening events. In 1979 African American students reacted forcefully against an incident in which guests at a white fraternity party thought it would be amusing to dress up in Ku Klux Klan robes. In the winter and spring of 1985 students held massive protests against a lecturer who referred to the black students in his legal studies class as "ex-slaves." There were instances of urine being thrown on blacks at the Quadrangle dormitories. In January 1986 the Penn trustees refused to divest immediately some $93 million worth of stocks and securities in companies doing business in South Africa. Instead, they opted for what appeared to be—at best—a five-year plan for gradual divestiture. These incidents deeply alienated black students and polarized the campus. They also contributed to a hardening of attitudes on the part of black students at Penn and an openness to the Nation of Islam. In this climate, a student who was a member of the Nation of Islam was elected as chairman of the BSL.

Conrad Muhammad and the Nationalist Pattern

The disputed BSL elections of March 1986 were the best attended in years. The four candidates included Glenda Grace, Chris Salley, and incumbent BSL Vice Chairman Erik Williams. The fourth candidate was Conrad Tillard (now Muhammad),[3] a transfer student from Middlebury College and a member of the Nation of Islam. None of the four received a majority of the vote and therefore, under the provisions of the BSL constitution, there was a run-off election between the two candidates who had received the most votes. They were Glenda Grace and Conrad Muhammad. Although the vote count was not publicly revealed, the outgoing officers who presided over the election declared Muhammad to be the winner.[4]

In an interview after the election, Muhammad said, "Essentially, the thrust of my campaign was that I could provide the kind of leadership which would unify all segments of the black student population at Penn based on similarities instead of differences." Asked about his affiliation with the Nation of Islam, Muhammad responded, "Islam is my religion, [but] I feel that my religion will not affect my ability to govern the BSL, any more than Kennedy's Catholicism affected his ability to govern the U.S., any more than the Rev. Jesse Jackson's Christianity would have affected his ability to govern the U.S." Other members of the newly elected Executive Committee were Vice Chair Kimberly Jones, Corresponding Secretary Howard Sanders, Recording Secretary Musau Dubinga, and Treasurer Rhonda Fredericks.[5]

Conrad Muhammad was entirely open and candid about his membership in the Nation Of Islam. At no time, nor in any way, did he make any effort to hide it or to deceive anyone about it. In voting for him, therefore, one may surmise that the members of the BSL were making a conscious choice. One might infer that the members of the BSL were choosing the candidate who they thought would be the most forceful and effective advocate and would confront and engage the university and struggle against racism. This sentiment was especially strong in view of the 1985 demonstrations against a lecturer who referred to black students as "ex-slaves" and the foot-dragging of the trustees on the university's South Africa–related securities. The members of the BSL probably were voting for the candidate they felt was most likely to be a strong leader, but this does not mean they were necessarily endorsing Muhammad's personal views or those of the Nation of Islam.

The Exclusion of Thornbury from Full BSL Membership

Muhammad's term got off to a controversial start in September 1986, when freshman Sydney Thornbury asked if she could join the BSL. She was a white student, whose father had been involved in the 1963 March on Washington. Muhammad opposed her joining: "Any white person that plans to join is either part of a plan to disrupt the BSL, or they are being selfish. . . . The purpose of the Black Student League is as a support mechanism to facilitate the needs of black undergraduates at the University of Pennsylvania. . . . She does not need the BSL in the sense that other [black] students need it."[6]

Thornbury, however, insisted she was "sincerely" interested in black concerns. She said, "I think Conrad's hurting the BSL. . . . I think the BSL's hurting the blacks more than it's helping them." Furthermore, she said, "There's got to be more people on campus that feel this way—and not just whites. . . . There are a lot of people on the campus who are afraid to say that black people are wrong—and God forbid the administration should stand up to the BSL." She added, "Maybe the blacks on campus don't feel like they have any other forum [than the BSL]." In addition, she stated, "You cannot allow a segregationist sect to exist on campus." She insisted she wanted to help the black community. Muhammad, however, responded: "Many whites want to help blacks, on their terms. . . . Why doesn't she help us on our terms?"[7]

This issue provoked a debate within the BSL and the African American community itself and precipitated a furor on the campus. It also struck directly at the heart of the issue of black "separatism." Kwame Ture (Stokely Carmichael) could not have fictionalized a better drama. The Thornbury controversy and Muhammad's initially adamant insistence on racial homogeneity within the BSL illustrated the continuing influence of the ideas of Malcolm X and Kwame Ture.

Thornbury attempted to meet with Vice Provost Jim Bishop, but at the time he was "not available." He did state, however, that he could not comment other than to say that the information available to him was insufficient to determine if there was a matter for the university to act on.[8]

On September 16, *Daily Pennsylvanian* Managing Editor and columnist Felipe Albuquerque entered the fray with a lengthy attack on the Nation of Islam and Minister Farrakhan.[9] On September 19, the *Daily Pennsylvanian* printed a response by Muhammad, in which he essentially defended the Nation of Islam, claiming that an element of the university community was trying to undercut the unity of the black community and that the Albuquerque column was but one in a series of events designed to attack the leadership and members of the BSL. He also expressed the view that "we are different people, our concerns are different and clearly our interests are different." There could be peaceful coexistence between blacks and whites on a college campus, but only on the principle of mutual respect.[10]

Some black students, such as Jill Robinson, defended the right of whites to join the BSL. She wrote that she did not see how one white student, or even one hundred, would disrupt the BSL. She believed every one must be judged as an individual.[11] Philip Remaker condemned Muhammad for separatism and isolationism.[12] April Claytor, however, compared Thornbury to a male friend of her's who wanted to serve as a counselor for Women Organized against Rape. He felt he could offer an additional attribute to the counseling experience and aid women victims of rape in understanding that all men are not to blame. Nevertheless, the man's offer of "help" was denied because, as Claytor put it, "Regardless of his sincerity, the effect could be detrimental to the victim." Claytor concluded, "Support is welcome if it is sincere, but allow us to be our own counselors and address our concerns. We are not looking for a patron."[13] Still others were incensed that Thornbury should presume to know what was best for blacks, rather than respecting their right to self-determination and their right to decide for themselves what was best for black people. It seemed too much like paternalism.

On September 24, President Hackney, Provost Ehrlich, and Vice Provost Bishop issued a carefully worded statement. It condemned both "overt separatism" and "attempts to exacerbate existing suspicions among groups." It also urged constructive discussion that aims toward the amicable and positive resolution of conflicts. Apparently the administration felt the students should work out their problems among themselves through continued dialogue.[14]

Part of the debate centered on the BSL constitution of 1972, under which it was recognized by the Student Activities Council,[15] which provided for a category of associate (nonvoting) membership. Accordingly, on September 25, the BSL offered Thornbury associate membership, and Muhammad emphasized that the exclusion of Thornbury from full membership had not been his personal capriciousness, but rather had been the policy and practice of the organization for decades.[16]

Yet, ultimately, Sydney Thornbury decided not to accept the offer of associate membership, in part because she did not want to be a "token" member.[17] She also issued a statement explaining the evolution of her views. She condemned right-wing conservatives for martyring her and charged that they were manipulating her. She expressed regret that the Nation of Islam was taking over the BSL and wondered if the separatism of the BSL really reflected the views of most black students and fairly represented them, or if they were being manipulated by a few "angry young men." She also indicated she had come to realize that, if the Black Student League were forced to admit whites, then the campus gay student organization would have to admit heterosexuals, and the women's groups would have to admit men. She worried that, under these circumstances, the Non-Discrimination Code, which was originally intended to protect the rights of minorities, would be twisted around to deny them rights. In a particularly soul-searching passage, she wrote: "And yes, I have come to the conclusion that there is a certain right to be had in a group of people of the same origin standing up for what they believe in solely with other people of that origin. That is a very hard statement for me to make because it is the very opposite of what I previously believed."[18]

She felt, however, that minorities working alone in their own groups can only achieve so much. She felt there was a genuine need for a group on campus "to provide a forum for where all interested people can voice their concerns, raise concerns, and hopefully find a solution to the racism problems" of Penn.[19] What she had in mind, though she did not specify it in her letter, was perhaps something like the Congress of Racial Equality (CORE) before 1966, or the NAACP, or the Urban League. And, indeed, there was no reason why truly sincere whites who were opposed to racism could not form an organization whose membership would include blacks who chose to participate in an integrated organization. But this was different from trying to force the BSL to become that organization.

To her credit, Sydney Thornbury did go on to participate in such a group, the Progressive Student Alliance (PSA), which was a vocal interracial group that opposed racism, sexism, homophobia, anti-Semitism, and all the "ism's." It consistently supported efforts at divestiture, and (later on) adoption of the racial and sexual harassment policies. It particularly provided a "home" for progressive whites who wished to be involved in the campus effort against racism, but were not welcome or accepted in the BSL.

In-Group Self-Determination as a Norm

Absent a statistical survey, it is impossible to say to what degree Conrad Muhammad was "representative" of black students. It would seem, however, that many if not most African American students felt the BSL should be for African Americans exclusively. These same students would have said it was also perfectly okay for a campus chapter of the Sons of St. Patrick to admit only Irish and Irish American students, or for the Knights of Columbus to admit only Italian Americans. Increasingly, African American students saw the BSL as parallel to ethnic associations, or even to private religious organizations such as the Hillel Foundation (a Jewish organization) or the Newman Centers (Catholic student centers). The similarity to ethnic associations is that their memberships are based on an aspect of identity; the issue is complicated by the fact that both Hillel and the Newman Centers are private foundations.

Sociologists Ralph H. Turner and Lewis Killian have suggested that social movements involve a process which they call "normative transformation."[20] Often social movements challenge traditional patterns and norms and seek to establish a new norm—the *emergent norm*—in place of older established ones. The emergent norm may involve a rejection or revision of previous notions of justice. In the contest between the established social order and the oppositional movement, "The ultimate and most enduring product of a movement is either the repudiation of the revised conception of justice or the establishment in the society of the revised conception."[21]

The belief that black racially and ethnically homogeneous organizations are necessary, appropriate, and desirable has been reasserted as a fundamental premise and axiom of much of black nationalism and self-determination over the last thirty-five years. This belief is actually centuries-old (at least as old as the black church in Philadelphia and the "Negro conventions" of the 1840s and other "complexional" institutions). It has also influenced conceptions of cultural pluralism as a form of ethnic self-determination. Remembering Andrew Bryan, Richard Allen, and Prince Hall, we can see this actually represents the *reassertion* of an old norm, challenging the "universalist" ethic of the "color-blind" civil rights movement.

As noted, however, many in the larger society see this as "voluntary segregation" and "reverse discrimination." Furthermore, segments of the dominant culture have sought to ignore, dismiss, and devalue the tradition of ethnic-group self-determination because it runs at cross-purposes to the project of assimilation and erasure of difference and because it contradicts the narrative of a triumphalist, positivist civil rights movement. Nevertheless, despite the controversy, the ideological perspective of in-group (or ethnic- or ethnonational) self-determination remains strong among the generation of African Americans who have "come of age" since 1960. It is part of an enduring legacy of black nationalism, pluralism, and autonomy. The denial of full membership to Sydney Thornbury by the BSL is dramatic evidence of the persistence of the nationalist, separatist, self-determinationist orientation among black students at Penn as late as the fall of 1986.

Bicultural Patterns among Black Students

In contrast, there are many other examples of black students who participated in both black activities and the mainstream life of the campus. In 1973, Ruth Ann Price, an African American student and upper-class adviser in the Black Advising Program, was elected to the Undergraduate Assembly and to the University Council. She also was elected to the Steering Committee of the University Council (an advisory body to the president).[22] In 1974–75, two African American students, Robert Wilson and Gary Greene, became members of Penn's literary society, the Philomathean Society. Kenneth McNeil, president of the BSL (1978–79), and BSL chairman Russell Brooks (1979–80), both of whom lived at W. E. B. Du Bois College House in 1978–79, were also members of the predominantly white Undergraduate Assembly (the undergraduate student government). Although they were advocates on behalf of the black student body, they did not retreat into separatism and withdraw from participation in the larger university. Indeed, in 1980–81, Russell Brooks served as treasurer of the UA. He went on to become a member of the Board of Trustees as a recent alumnus.

In 1985–86 Glenda Grace served on the Houston Hall Board (an advisory board that oversaw the Student Union building). In 1987–88 Quintus Jett, an African American student, was elected to the Undergraduate Assembly and served on the University Council. He did not, however, eschew identification with the black community, as an assimilationist might have done. That same year, Lolita Jackson was a columnist for the *Daily Pennsylvanian*.[23] In April 1988 Miriam "Duchess" Harris, an African American, was elected vice chairperson of the Undergraduate Assembly, where she served with UA Chairman Keith Wasserstrom. She was also an advocate on behalf of black students. In April 1990 Duchess Harris was elected chairperson of the UA, becoming the first African American to lead the predominantly white undergraduate student government. Thus, she could only have been elected with support from white students, which suggests that some white students were able and willing to look past race and color to accept African American participation and even leadership. Harris said, "We need a UA chair who can break down the barriers of this campus and unify its students."[24]

One could give many other examples of African American students at Penn who participate in both their own "closed" intraethnic or endoethnic organizations and in majority organizations whose membership is "open" as well. Membership in the first organizations does not preclude participation in the others, and the two are not mutually exclusive. In much the same way, within society at large, an individual may belong to an exclusively ethnic voluntary association, and yet this does not preclude membership in a religious body, union, neighborhood association, fraternal association, political party ad infinitum.

Separatism Not Pluralism and Vice Versa

As remarked on previously, there is also a pattern of "dual organization" at Penn. Thus, there are preprofessional organizations such as the Black Wharton Undergraduate Association, Black Pre-Law Society, Black Pre-Health Society, and the Society of Black Engineers. These organizations date from the early 1970s and typically sponsor guest speakers who describe how to get into law or medical school. They also assist students in preparing résumés, finding summer internships, and securing jobs. In the mid-1970s African American students at Penn formed their own honor society, called Onyx. Barry Jordan and Edward James were early presidents of the organization. In April 1989 Jillian Johnson took the lead in organizing the Black College Association. It became an academic support group for African American students in the School of Arts and Sciences (SAS), intended to assist with peer advising, selection of majors, and career choices.[25]

Just as many fraternities and sororities, historically, have been all white, and some have been identified as Catholic or Jewish fraternities, so, too, there are historically black fraternities and sororities. At Penn one finds chapters of fraternities such as Alpha Phi Alpha and Kappa Alpha Psi, and Groove Phi

Groove Social Fellowship. In the 1970s there had been a chapter of Omega Psi Phi Fraternity as well. There are also chapters of Alpha Kappa Alpha, Delta Sigma Theta, and Zeta Phi Beta sororities. In 1982 black students established their own newspaper, *The Voice*. In 1989, through the efforts of Altoine Scarborough, it was succeeded by *The Vision*. At times there were also the Black Drama Ensemble and the Black Arts League.

Although some might decry African American fraternities and sororities and "dual organizations" as "separatist" (or ethnically homogeneous), in fact African American students tend to be bicultural. The use of the term "separatist" to describe this behavior is misleading and constitutes an ideological attempt by the dominant culture to discredit something it does not like or understand. As Malcolm X pointed out, separatism is *withdrawing* from society, rather like the Mennonites and Schwenkfelders. True black separatism is territorial nationalism, wherein groups such as the Republic of New Africa seek to partition the United States to make five states in the South a separate, independent, African American nation–state. Black students at Penn had no such aspirations. Similarly, white "separatists" want a "white homeland" in Idaho, Montana, and other western states.

Most African American students are not "segregating" themselves into ethnically separate organizations only and withdrawing from participation in the larger campus or society. Rather, they are participating in their own in-group voluntary associations and also participating in and interacting with the larger society. This behavior reflects pluralism and biculturalism, not separatism. If it is separatism, it is a separatism that implicitly presupposes that Americans-of-African-extraction are an ethnic group (and a national minority) within American society. Per Kwame Ture, the purpose of (ethnically) homogeneous organizations is not to withdraw from society into some permanent isolationist enclave, but rather to organize a power base from which to prepare *to enter the mainstream* and successfully *compete within it.*

Nor is this so remarkably different from the plethora of ethnic and identity associations one finds at Penn or other universities. In 1990, for example, the Student Activities Council at Penn also listed the Armenian Club, Canadian Club, German Club, Greek Club, International Students Association, Irish Club, *Jewish Quarterly,* Jewish Social Action Committee, Lesbian, Gay and Bisexual Alliance, Lubavitch House Students Association, Muslim Students Association, Pakistan Society, Penn Christian Fellowship, Penn Women's Alliance, Scottish Society, Society of Women Engineers, Turkish Students Association, Ukrainian Students Association, Wharton Asian Association, and

Wharton Women, among many others, as "recognized" organizations at the university.[26] "Recognition" meant that these groups had members who were Penn students and were entitled to use university facilities, but it did not necessarily mean the university funded the organizations. Although some of the organizations listed above are composed of international students, African American students also wished to preserve their distinctive cultural identity. After four hundred years of white supremacy, African American culture sometimes stands as a national minority culture in relation to the dominant Anglo-Saxon culture.

In this rich mosaic of pluralism and voluntary associations, it can be seen that the activities of African American students are not somehow deviant and aberrant. It is perfectly natural for people who share something in common to come together in a voluntary association based upon some aspect of their identity (whether race, ethnicity, religion, gender, or sexual orientation). It is also natural for people who share a common interest, whether politics, art, music, theatre, sports, an academic discipline, or a profession, to come together in voluntary associations.

To assimilationists, however, group pluralism looks like separatism. They seem unable to distinguish between the two. Of course, what both pluralism and genuine separatism have in common is what they are *not:* And what they are not is Anglo-conformity. And here the logic and the ulterior motive behind the tactic of equating pluralism with separatism is revealed (or betrayed). This "confusion," whether calculated or otherwise, obfuscates the real issues. It also exacerbates the mutual misunderstanding that continues to divide black and white. The real conflict is a tug-of-war between the vision of a *raceless,* nonracial society of assimilated, Anglo-conforming individuals sharing a common culture that seeks to obliterate consciousness of difference, and a *multiracial,* multicultural, race- and color-conscious, pluralistic society that seeks to value and cherish difference.

Black Students Nonrevolutionary

The bicultural pattern described here also demonstrates the obvious: African American students at Penn were *not* revolutionaries, and few of them ever pretended or claimed to be. Rather, they are individuals seeking to achieve economic upward mobility. Many hope to utilize their skills and knowledge for the benefit of the black community. Their purpose, however, is not to overthrow capitalism in a revolutionary upheaval or to seize state power, but to expand the ranks of the black middle class and open the doors of opportunity so that everyone can be "middle class." For if white-supremacist racism is a great enemy of black people, the other great enemies are superexploitation, poverty, deprivation, and joblessness.

The vision of many students (however utopian or reformist) would be a society in which racialist doctrines of the superiority of one group and the inferiority of another, stigmatizing stereotypes, and demeaning and violent treatment of others based on race, color, or ethnicity have all been abandoned. In this ideal society, all black people would have a "good education" and a "good job" and be prosperous and middle class; all black people could enjoy the "good life" in America. This would be a society where every black person who wished to do so could live in a spacious home with a nice car, a yard, and a pool in the suburbs (it could be an affluent black suburb such as Prince George's County, Maryland). And in this vision, no black person would be consigned to live in a congested neighborhood in a rowhouse in a drug- and crime-infested, inner-city slum. This would not dissolve the black community or even the black neighborhood. It would merely dissolve the slum. In this vision, no black person is involuntarily unemployed, or homeless, or without a prescription plan and health insurance and childcare. (Naturally, one would wish the same for non–African Americans as well.) This vision is not separatism. Instead, it is the dream of economic opportunity, material abundance, and upward mobility, without Anglo-conformity or forced assimilation, for all Americans. In a phrase, it is a vision of humanist cultural pluralism.

But there is, within this vision of a middle-class utopia, no guarantee of a critique of the excesses of capitalist exploitation and the tendency to place the pursuit of private and corporate profit over the welfare of people. Thus, to extrapolate from Robert Allen's critique of cultural nationalism,[27] although the vision of cultural pluralism is in opposition to assimilation and white cultural imperialism, it may not go far enough in critiquing the roots of exploitation, poverty, and oppression in the system of global capitalism. Cultural pluralism, then, by itself, may not be sufficient. It may be merely a stepping stone or a building block that can open the way for other more oppositional and liberating possibilities.

The danger is that cultural pluralism could become simply "ornamental,"[28] and that a black bourgeoisie tied to the fruits of capitalism could become content and complacent, and then begin to blame the condition of the black underclass and the poor on the poor themselves. So long as nearly one-third of African Americans, however, continue to live at or below the poverty level, it is likely that most African Americans will find it impossible *not* to be conscious of the oppressive aspects of capitalist inequality. The average African American knows that it is a sin for anyone to be hungry, homeless, or involuntarily unemployed in the midst of plenty in the richest nation on earth. The black working class and underclass are the sources from which nationalism and pluralism and socialism in the black community, in the twentieth century (since Garvey), have flowed and been replenished and renewed. Since the 1960s the black intelligentsia and literati have aligned themselves with these classes. A black middle class connected to its ethnic group roots culturally could also serve as an advocate in the struggle to obtain economic justice and to ameliorate excessive inequalities of wealth by expanding and extending the "safety net" of the social welfare state. Thus, the black middle class (reminiscent of Du Bois's "talented tenth") should be neither idolized nor demonized. It may choose the path of assimilation and serve as a neocolonial buffer group for corporate America, or it may become the ally of the black working- and underclass in the struggle to further humanize and democratize the distribution of wealth. Much will depend upon which class alliances the middle class may choose.

CONCLUSION

THE REVOLT AGAINST ASSIMILATION

The history of the American Negro is the history of . . . strife—this longing to attain self-conscious manhood, to merge his double self into a better and truer self. In this merging he wishes neither of the older selves to be lost. He would not Africanize America, for America has too much to teach the world and Africa. He would not bleach his Negro soul in a flood of white Americanism, for he knows that Negro blood has a message for the world. He simply wishes to make it possible for a man to be both a Negro and an American, without being cursed and spit upon by his fellows, without having the doors of opportunity closed roughly in his face.

—W. E. B. Du Bois, *The Souls of Black Folk,* 1903

Most of this book has been structured as a narrative description and chronological account of the impact of the Black Power ideology, the Black Arts movement, and black pride on the African American student movement at Penn, in the period from 1967 to 1990. This narrative has been based on archival, documentary research. I have attempted to show that Black Power and black pride inspired a "cultural revolution" nationwide, which was reflected locally in the activities of black students at Penn. Thus, I have sought to link the "macro" and the "micro." The Black Power ideological revolt of the 1960s helped to give rise to a revolution in black identity and a cultural revolution that continues on the cusp of the twenty-first century, in the form of multiculturalism and Afrocentrism. But this revolution has vastly complicated the vision of an "integrated" society as a "color-blind" society. Today many Americans are still trying to come to terms with this "failure," as it appears that the dream of an integrated society somehow got sidetracked and became a casualty of ethnic squabbling. In anguish, many people wonder, "Where did the 'movement' go wrong?" In particular, the ethnic revival reflects strong resistance to assimilation not only by African Americans but by Spanish-speaking Mexican Americans, Puerto Ricans, and other

Latinos, and by Asian and Pacific Americans as well. This revolt against assimilation challenges fundamental assumptions about American life and society, and it is based in part on a critique of assimilation as cultural imperialism. After the narrative of events in the previous chapters, this final chapter is largely interpretive and structured as an extended commentary.

Counterassimilation at Penn

The ideological perspective of the Black Power, Black Consciousness, black pride, and Black Arts movements—and black nationalism more generally—in the period 1967 to 1990 emphasized in-group solidarity, self-determination, autonomy, and independent institutions. It emphasized pride in culture and the rejection of assimilation. It advocated a positive race-conscious and ethnically conscious approach to identity, as opposed to a nonracial, "raceless," color-blind approach that augured the erasure of difference or consciousness of difference. Imbued by this ideology, a significant portion of the African American students at Penn were members of the Society of African and Afro-American Students (SAAS), a racially (ethnically) exclusive student organization, which changed its name to the Black Student League in 1971. African American students agitated for the formation of an African American Studies Program and, less successfully, a dormitory for black students.

They also developed a pervasive pattern of "dual organization." These dual organizations included the black preprofessional organizations, the Black College Association, and their own publications, *The Voice* and a minority student newspaper called *The Vision*. Local chapters of national, historically black Greek-letter fraternities and sororities were established. At the graduate level there were parallel black organizations in the Medical School, Law School, Wharton M.B.A. Program, School of Social Work, Engineering School, and a campuswide umbrella group. A Black Alumni Society was also formed. This pattern of creating independent dual organizations is a reflection of the imperative toward in-group self-organization and autonomy.

Of course, I cannot claim here that the pattern of dual organization and biculturalism described in this book was "representative" of *all* students of African extraction at Penn in the period. There are assimilationists as well as pluralists and nationalists in the African American community. There may have been some assimilationist Afro-American students at Penn, but they were students who happened to be black, and certainly would not have joined the BSL or lived at Du Bois College House or participated in a black preprofessional association. By choice, they would have been invisible—and they had every right to that choice. Pluralists *choose* to be pluralists. They choose to embrace their communal origins, but they do not seek to impose compulsory identification with communal origins on anyone.

Nevertheless, while creating their own autonomous culture-within-a-culture, African American students and other students of color also participated in the life of the wider campus, including student government, the Philomathean Society, and the major campus newspaper, *The Daily Pennsylvanian*. In this respect they were not really separatists—rather, they were bicultural.

A similar pattern exists in American society at large, with the various associations of black lawyers, M.B.A.s, journalists, psychologists, law enforcement officers, firefighters, fraternities, sororities, Masonic lodges, black state legislative caucuses, the Congressional Black Caucus, ad infinitum. The members of these associations participate in both their private, African American organizations and in the desegregated public domain as well. Many African Americans, however, aspire to function as a *group-for-itself*, with a tradition or organized self-interest, not merely a *group-in-itself*. In this self-help endeavor, they seek to emulate what other ethnic groups have done. Furthermore, they are merely continuing an old tradition of group self-determination through independent institutions that can be traced back at least as far as Richard Allen, Prince Hall, and Andrew Bryan—as old as the United States Constitution. Thus, to elaborate upon a thesis introduced by Harold Cruse in 1967, there has also been a tradition of independent in-group (ethnic) institutions—which could be characterized as pluralist—running parallel to the traditions of integration–assimilation and nationalism–separatism.[1]

African American undergraduates at Penn went on to graduate schools or pursued careers as doctors, lawyers, engineers, broadcast journalists, psychologists, actuaries, business people, and educators. Among those who had not come from the black middle class to begin with, many rose into its ranks after graduating or going on to professional schools. Most would describe their experiences at Penn as rewarding, challenging, and worthwhile. Most coexisted peacefully with white students, many of whom were probably well-meaning. Penn was, for most African American students, an escalator toward upward mobility and life as white-collar, college-educated professionals. But upward mobility and cultural assimilation are not the same thing. If the purpose of a Penn education was to facilitate upward mobility, Penn succeeded. If the purpose of a Penn education was to produce assimilation and the obliteration of consciousness of difference, for a substantial number of students, the effort failed. Most African Americans probably do not wish to assimilate culturally into the dominant Anglo-Saxon culture (undergo Anglo-conformity)[2] any more than Catholics wish to convert to Protestantism. Yet, like Catholics, African Americans certainly desire upward mobility.

Revolt against Assimilation in Society at Large

With the narrative of events at Penn in the foreground, it is possible to see these events as a reflection of wider social forces—at work in the country at large—in the background. Fundamentally, what has been taking place is a process of cultural contest(ation) between the ideals of race-consciousness and the eradication of consciousness of race (and group identity). It is the struggle between two competing versions of integration. One version of integration believes that equality requires the obliteration of attention to difference, and the reduction of persons to individuals—pure and simple. The other version seeks recognition and consciousness of difference, with respect for those differences, and consideration of group characteristics (such as historic disadvantage and discrimination).

On one side stand the advocates of assimilation. As Maria Lugones and Joshua Price argue, assimilation, at its greatest extent, seeks to erase the culture of other groups.[3] It aims at the creation of monoculturalism, which is the belief that the United States is—or should be—a nation with one culture.[4] That "select" culture is the English-speaking Anglo-Saxon culture, which often sees itself *not* as one particular culture among many but rather as "beyond culture" because it embodies the "universal." In a sense, then, it becomes normative, taken for granted, and invisible to the Anglo-Saxons (and the Anglo-conformed) themselves.[5]

Assimilationists seek to erase difference or the consciousness of difference—especially in matters of public policy—and desire a nonracial, race-neutral, raceless society. This society would be "color-blind," and distinctions on the basis of race, ethnicity, religion, gender, sexual orientation, or other aspects of identity would be minimized. In their view, "equality" means the erasure of consciousness of difference.[6] The assimilationists want a monocultural and preferably monolingual society, with one universal, cosmopolitan, "common" culture. Everyone will be homogenized to become only an American, only an individual. These individuals would be purged of their "particularistic" ties to communal origin and identity, such as race, ethnicity, religion, and class.

President Woodrow Wilson expresses this view forcibly and simply in 1915: "America does not consist of groups. A man who thinks of himself as belonging to a particular national group in America has not yet become an American."[7] Particularism, which Arthur Schlesinger Jr. analyzes, is bad for America because it promotes "fragmentation," the "disuniting of America," and "tribalization."[8] This ignores the question of people holding on to their communal origins *voluntarily*, by choice, because they like them and want to do so, as opposed to being "chained" to an identity or assigned to one by the state in some compulsory fashion.

In an assimilated society, individuals would be raceless ("de-raced"), de-ethnicized, nonsectarian (presumably secularized), classless people. Detached from "constricting" communal ties, these atomized individuals could be judged and rewarded solely on the basis of merit, qualification, and "universalistic, objective criteria." Conveniently, this would obviate demands for compensatory treatment from women and minorities, as members of historically disadvantaged *groups*. In a society of atomized individuals, identity groups and claims based on membership in such groups would have no proper place.

Opposing the project of the erasure and obliteration of consciousness of difference are the cultural pluralists and multiculturalists. Their vision of "integration" is different. For pluralists and (many) black nationalists, race consciousness is paramount. They reject the vision of a homogenized, color-blind society in which people are asked to renounce or subordinate their communal ties with respect to race, ethnicity, religion, and other dimensions of identity. Instead, pluralists celebrate and cherish diversity and multilingualism. They demand respect for difference.

The contest between the project of monocultural, Eurocentric erasure and assimilation (on the one hand) and cultural pluralism (on the other hand) is what has fueled the "culture wars" of the last thirty-five years. This "culture war" represents a cultural *revolt* by (many) African Americans, Spanish-speaking Latinos, and Asian Americans, who simply refuse to comply with the demand for monoculturalism and rapid assimilation. These latter, historically subordinated groups, do not seek to be culturally incorporated or assimilated into a white Anglo-conformed society. They are struggling to transform America into a multiracial, multicultural society—a syncretized society—in which a new social contract can be written. In this society, a new "common," shared culture can be created through a multilateral process of negotiation rather than being unilaterally imposed by white, Anglo-conformed elites.

The "universalists" who trumpet a "common culture" rarely specify the content of this purported "shared" culture. They also cannot specify the commonly shared "values" to which they allude (hence the rejoinder, *"Whose values?"*). They presuppose the existence of the very thing that still remains to be created! Furthermore, the demand that nonwhites "assimilate" is really a demand that African Americans and other historically subordinated groups (including women of all races) accept the "rules of the game" that elite white men have already established and that people of color had no part in creating. In effect, they are being asked to accept blindly the rules of the game that someone else has established—after the game has already started.[9] As Michael Parenti observes:

Loyalty to Americanism became loyalty *to the system as it was* [is], an acceptance of the dominant credo of a capitalist culture . . . that ours was the "most perfect system. . . ." While strenuously propagating an ideological acculturation, dominant white Protestant America discouraged any tampering with *the ongoing arrangements of class privilege and power* [emphasis added] which was the material base of structural non-assimilation."[10]

The revolt against assimilation and a restrictive view of individualism, merit, and qualification represent a refusal to "accept the system *as it is*" and blindly conform to it. Instead, the insurgents are questioning the existing social contract and demanding that it and the "ongoing arrangements of class privilege and power" be reviewed and changed. The advocates of the color-blind society reject consciousness of race, color, historic group disadvantage, and claims to compensatory treatment or consideration as a threat to universalism and individual meritocracy. This is, however, more than a debate about abstractions. Perhaps so many African Americans persist in embracing the discourse of cognizance of group identity and claims to compensatory treatment because they believe that the material advantages potentially to be gained from a race- and ethnically conscious public policy far outweigh what little a policy of raceless, color-blind, "individual meritocracy" seems to offer. It would be quite naive to imagine that questions of discourse and ideology bear no relationship to the material and economic interests that may be served or are at stake or risk. As yet, for many African Americans, the ideology of color-blind meritocracy seems to have too little of a material nature (an economic payoff) to offer.

Furthermore, the advocates of race consciousness argue that white supremacy is not simply slavery, Jim Crow segregation, disenfranchisement, ghettoization, or even the superexploitation of the labor of people of color and their disproportionate proletarianization.[11] It is more than being "marginalized" and relegated to the economic underclass.[12] White supremacy, carried to its logical conclusion in the cultural sphere, would produce cultural genocide and the complete erasure or annihilation of a people's culture.[13] The revolt against white supremacy (in its guise of cultural imperialism) is taking place in the realm of culture and language.[14] (For examples, there are the Spanish-speaking and Chinese-speaking immigrants who refuse to renounce bilingualism in favor of monolingualism.) In the past, as Anglo-America sought to assimilate the immigrants from southern and eastern Europe, "whiteness" and Anglo-conformity were the traits that bound together an "American" identity. The immigrant Irish, Germans, Scandinavians, Italians, Poles, and other Europeans could subordinate their ethnic identities, which were then subsumed beneath the umbrella of European origin and "whiteness." But such a bond cannot win the allegiance of people of color. A new, broader inclusion is needed, with which to base a multiracial (as opposed to only white) "American" identity. One suspects that—subconsciously—all too many Americans still think of America as a "white" country that has some Native American, black (of African extraction), brown (Latino), and yellow (East Asian) people living in it (rather as guests, with the Anglo-Saxons as the "original" [usurping] owners and hosts). One fears that too many white Americans subconsciously assume, because they have been the "majority" in the past and remain the majority at present, that, therefore, America "belongs" to them "more" than to people of color. Perhaps not enough Americans perceive of the United States as a multiracial country and shared property, in which people of color are the joint *owners*.

The great irony of the last fifty years is that, as desegregation proceeded, many African Americans were forced to rethink exactly what it was they wanted from "integration." By the time that some whites began to dismantle the system of legalized segregation in 1964, African Americans discovered that many whites expected them to give up their distinctive identity and to assimilate. It is, as if for centuries, while black people were trying to assimilate, white Americans "would not have them." Blacks were not permitted to assimilate (either by acculturating or amalgamating) no matter how hard they tried to do so. By the time that the liberals and moderates of white America were prepared to tolerate assimilation by blacks, most African Americans were no longer interested in it. Indeed, what African Americans wanted was power-sharing and socioeconomic upward mobility—without cultural assimilation. Under these circumstances, the belated gift of an opportunity to "assimilate" came to be perceived as a Trojan horse.

Many African Americans have refused to play the upward mobility game by the previously established rules. This defiance on the part of African Americans may seem to express the height of audacity. But African Americans, who first arrived in the United States in 1619, do not perceive themselves as immigrant *newcomers* who must adopt the ways of their "host." After nearly four hundred years of residence, African Americans feel coeval with the Anglo-Saxons, who arrived permanently in 1607, and do not feel the need to accept blindly their "established" rules.

Today, the balance of social forces in this country is slowly changing, as millions of Mexican Americans, diverse Latin Americans, Haitians, Dominican Republicans, Filipinos, Chinese, and other East Asians stream into America year after year. Many of the immigrants from the Western Hemisphere and the Philippine Islands are "mixed race" people who reject the simplistic binary categories of "black" and "white." They are blurring the distinction and challenge the past orthodoxy that a person must be either one "race" or another. Increasingly, they assert a biracial or even multiracial identity. The best-known example of this today is the golf champion "Tiger" Woods, whose ancestry is a mixture of African American, Caucasian, Native American, Filipino, and Thai (he refers to himself as "Cablinasian"). According to the U.S. Bureau of the Census, between 1970 and 1995, the number of interracial couples increased from 310,000 to 1,392,000. In that time span, the number of marriages between blacks and whites, specifically, more than quintupled, from 65,000 to 328,000.[15] As the Latino, Filipino, and mixed-race groups increase in size, they will become a force to be reckoned with, and the balance of social forces may change.

The 1996 census revealed that African Americans comprised 13 percent of the U.S. population, Latinos constituted about 10 percent, Asians represented 4 percent, and 1 percent was made up of Indians, Eskimos, and Aleuts. In 1995, 74 percent of Americans classified themselves an "non-Hispanic whites."[16] Perhaps a majority of three-fourths feels that it can safely disregard the feelings of the minority. But it is one thing to reject cultural pluralism and multilingualism when only one-fourth of the American people are African American, Latino, Asian American, and Native American. It may be quite a "different ballgame" when the so-called racial minorities make up fully half the population (as may happen in the next fifty years). Then, the United States may look more like Cuba or Brazil or the countries of Latin America than like an extension of Europe. Indeed, it is possible that what we are witnessing, in our time, is the beginning of the Latin Americanization of the United States.

The trajectory of black student activism at Penn is merely a reflection of the wider social process of the "culture wars," and it represents a cultural revolt against rapid assimilation. It reflects opposition to the project of incorporating people of African extraction and other people of color into a monocultural, Anglo-conformed, dominant culture that still worships at the altar of Europe and still pretends to be superior, universal, and to have the "best values."[17] Thus far, the post–World War II "liberal" vision of a homogenized, nonracial, raceless, color-blind society of detached individuals, to be judged solely by "universalistic" and "objective" standards of merit, has been confounded. The opposition consists of social forces that seek to pluralize America to create a race-conscious, multiracial, multiethnic, multicultural, multilingual society that will countenance compensatory measures as redress for historic discrimination and disadvantage.

At issue is a matter as simple as respect. Imagine the person who says, "In order for me to respect you and treat you decently as a fellow human being, I must obliterate consciousness of your difference as a person of color (or as a woman or as a homosexual)." This implies that, if the first person were conscious of the second person's race, ethnicity, gender, or sexual orientation as different from his own, then he could not respect that person or treat that person equally or decently. But if my respect for you depends upon pretending to ignore your difference, and I would denigrate you or treat you adversely if I heeded your difference, then there is no basis for mutual respect, cooperation, or allegiance. Pretending to ignore one another, in the name of phony "toleration," is no basis for constructing a common culture. Pluralists want to be respected *with* their racial, ethnic, and other differences, not because they camouflage them. To say that we can only respect others if they are like us, or are the same as us, is narrow and childish. Such a shallow policy will engender little sense of loyalty or allegiance among people of color. Nor would it *deserve* their loyalty and allegiance.

Perhaps we cannot move in one smooth step to the nonracial, postracial, purely individualistic society without going through the intermediate phase of the multiethnic, multilingual, multiracial, race-conscious society. When we learn to respect people even as we are fully conscious of their difference, then we can cast difference aside as insignificant.

Many people of color, and progressive whites, resist the project of the homogenized, Anglo-conformed, raceless, denatured society of abstract, universalist individuals. But the creative task of constructing and negotiating—multilaterally—a more democratic, humane, and pluralistic alternative has barely begun. At the beginning of a new millennium, we are reminded that "demography is destiny." It is possible that the multicultural, multiracial rainbow is the "manifest destiny" of America. But only time can tell whether we have the courage to embrace that destiny. If and when we do, perhaps then America really will become the "melting pot" that it has so often claimed to be.

ACKNOWLEDGMENTS

We all stand upon the shoulders of those who came before us and lent us a helping hand when we needed it. In that spirit, I wish to acknowledge my indebtedness to those who have helped and encouraged me in completing this book.

I wish to express my gratitude to my colleagues Rodney Carlisle and Janet Golden, of the Rutgers History Department, who provided invaluable advice in the preparation of this manuscript and generously shared their time and offered support. I am also thankful to Robert Engs, who first encouraged me to pursue a doctoral degree and later directed my dissertation with both patience and constructive criticism. I also thank Phil Scranton, who read an earlier draft of the manuscript, and my other colleagues in the History Department at Rutgers–Camden. I thank an anonymous reader, known to me only as "Reader A," for cogent criticism and advice. I am especially grateful to John Bracey, who read the manuscript and offered valuable suggestions. I thank Rutgers University for a Faculty Academic Study Program leave in autumn 1997, which allowed me to devote myself to research at the University of Pennsylvania Archives. Grateful acknowledgment is also given to the Rutgers Research Council for a subvention grant. I also wish to thank Drew Faust, Murray Murphey, Elijah Anderson, Janice Radway, Larry Gross, Mel Hammarberg, Mary Rhodes Hoover, Sybil Lipschultz-Lichtenstein, and Julie Aparin for their support.

Over the years a number of individuals have encouraged me to persevere through the endurance test called the academic profession. I thank Lamont Lee, Melvin Wilbourn, Joyce Pressley, Valarie Swain Cade McCoullum, Jacqui Wade, Dan Scott

Butler, Houston Baker, Ralph Smith, Ernie Wilson, Francille Wilson, Rose Smith, Rita Smith, Terri White, Howard Arnold, Peter Vaughan, Orneice Dorsey-Leslie, John Roberts, Donald Cunnigen, Barbara Cassel, Jim Gray, Ruth Wells, Rene Gonzalez, Cora Ingrum, Amelia T. Smith, Karen Byrd, Will Edwards, Jonathan Muse, Leland Butler, Cynthia Riggs, Allison Emery, Tom DiValerio, Joe Watkins, Elena (Ellie) DiLapi, Gloria Gay, and Tom Henry for their words and deeds of support. Likewise, I thank Helen Davies, Bob Davies, Kim Morrisson, Robert Rutman, Sohrab Rabii, Jacob Abel, Noam Lior, Barbara Stevens, Steve Steinberg, Fran Walker, Nick Constan, and Bill Epstein for their counsel.

I thank Loretta Carlisle of the History Department at Rutgers University for her superb secretarial support, and Mark Lloyd, Gail Pietrzyk, James Curtiss Ayers, and Jim Duffin for their invaluable assistance at the University of Pennsylvania Archives. I also thank Bruce Wilcox, Carol Betsch, and Mary Capouya of the University of Massachusetts Press for their endless patience with my "million questions."

A word of thanks is also in order for my comrades and fellow activists in the "movement(s)," including Bill Westerman, Eli Pringle, David Kenosian, John Nevius, Lissa Hunt, Michael Polgar, Ellen Somekawa, Eric Joslyn, Vincent Phaahla, Barth (Kwaku) Yeboah, Priyethan Seebadri, Mickal Kamuvaka, George Spencer, Pedro Ramos, Deirdre White, Susan Fisher, and Patrick Hagopian. I also thank William "Skip" Knight, Sheryl George, Kenneth McNeil, Russell Brooks, Ralph Murray, Alma Bone, Eric Elie, Charles Henderson, Traci Miller, Melissa Moody, Travis Richardson, William Molette, Conrad Muhammad, and Reuben Brown. In their courageous actions, I came to know that the black student movement lives on.

I am indebted to my partner, David B. Rose, who has been a devoted friend and companion. I also thank my family, which has tolerated my "egghead" eccentricity with charity and indulgence for so many years. My debt to them is so great that I must thank Justine, Valerie (and Steve), David, Michael (and Sherri), Kenneth, and Timothy individually. I also thank the members of my "adoptive" family, Denise Holland, Sylvia Ferreabough Brooks, Eleanor Matthews, Marilyn and Garrett Allen, Norma and George Hayes, and Sylvester and Elaine Rose.

I wish to acknowledge the *Almanac,* at the University of Pennsylvania, for permission to reprint material from the Report of the Task Force on Black Presence, Section II.C., presented to the Trustees of the University of Pennsylvania, June 9, 1977. Published in *Almanac* 24, no. 24 of March 21, 1978.

I also gratefully acknowledge the *Daily Pennsylvanian* for permission to quote from its editorials of 3 November 1967, 25 February 1972, and 5 April 1972, and to utilize the following letters to the editor: Billy Riley, "Exclusive Freedom," 7 November 1967, 4; Drake Turrentine, "Immoderate Tone," 9 November 1967, 4; Mary Lovett, "Some SAAS," 10 November 1967, 6; Joel Aber, "Sick Society," 13 November 1967, 4; George Royal, "An open letter, updated," 31 October 1968, 2; Steven Fadem, "Letter to the Editor," 6 April 1972, 2; Wilson Jones, "Defending the Black Dorm," 19 April 1972, 2;

Michael Meyers, "Black Residence: Where It's Been . . . ," 27 April 1972, 2; Larry Fine, ". . . And Where It May Go," 27 April 1972, 2; April Claytor, "Student Defends BSL's Black Only Admissions Policy," 24 September 1986, 4; and Sydney Thornbury, "Questioning," 26 September 1986, 4.

Grateful acknowledgement is also due to the *Daily Pennsylvanian* for permission to quote liberally from the following articles: "Black Residence Demands," 18 February 1972, 4; Michael Silver, "Faculty Senate Accepts Black Residence Proposal," 6 April 1972, 1, 8; Margot Cohen, "Du Bois House Living: Student Bridges Racial Barrier," 2 April 1981, 1, 3; Jeffrey Goldberg, "Procedural Problems Mark BSL's Election," 28 March 1986, 7; Robert Pasnau, "White Student Not Allowed in BSL," 19 September 1986, 1, 10; and Jeffrey Goldberg, "Student Turns Down BSL Offer," 16 October 1986, 1.

I also thank the *Daily Pennsylvanian* for permission to use the photograph of April 5, 1968, which appears on the jacket of this book.

NOTES

Introduction: Dual Organization on the Predominantly White Campus

1. The term "movement–organization" is derived from Mayer Zald and Roberta Ash, "Social Movement Organizations: Growth, Decay and Change," *Social Forces* 44 (1966): 327. Simply put, this is the idea that movements can become institutionalized in the form of a movement–organization that acts as a watchdog, lobby, or advocacy group on behalf of the issues of concern to the movement in question. Examples of movement-organizations might include unions, welfare rights organizations, ethnically based organizations, political action committees, women's groups, gay rights organizations, and the like.

2. A plaque at the site indicates that the residence was dedicated on February 21, 1981. It had been referred to as a "college house" and not merely a living–learning program or "project" since the late 1970s.

3. It should be noted that technically Penn was not segregated. Four African Americans were enrolled at Penn in 1879, and of these the first to graduate was James Brister, from the Dental School, in 1881. Until the mid-sixties, however, there were relatively few African American students at Penn. In September 1968, for example, sixty-two African American undergraduates matriculated at Penn (James Cass, "Can the University Survive the Black Challenge?" *Saturday Review* 52, no. 25 [21 June 1969]: 68).

4. William Van Deburg, New Day in Babylon. Manning Marable makes a similar

point about the impact of black nationalism in *Race, Reform, and Rebellion,* while Harold Cruse contrasts black nationalism and pluralism with the "noneconomic liberalism" of the Civil Rights Movement in *Plural but Equal.*

5. Malcolm X was one of the very first African Americans to speak and write of a black "cultural revolution," in the "Statement of Basic Aims and Objectives of the Organization of Afro-American Unity" in June 1964; see George Breitman, *The Last Year of Malcolm X,* 111. Harold Cruse also analyzed, developments in the 1960s as a cultural revolution. See his "Behind the Black Power Slogan," in *Rebellion or Revolution?* 247; and idem, "The Fire This Time," in Edward Greer, *Black Liberation Politics,* 396–97. Kwame Ture and Maulana Karenga employed the term "cultural revolution" as well.

6. The term "cultural revolution" stands in contrast to political revolutions that involve the seizure of state power (such as the French Revolution) or national revolutions (such as the American) wherein an "indigenous" group overthrows a foreign or colonial elite. Social revolutions involve changes in the relationships of power among social classes (such as the Bolshevik and Chinese Revolutions).

7. The concept of "Anglo-conformity," as used here, is borrowed from Milton Gordon, *Assimilation in American Life.* Technically, the process referred to as assimilation is "acculturation." It is a process of culturally absorbing or incorporating people by having them internalize and adopt a culture. Biological assimilation or absorption is "amalgamation," in the sense of intermarriage.

8. See Clayborne Carson, *In Struggle;* Manning Marable, *Race, Reform, and Rebellion;* Robert L. Allen, *Black Awakening in Capitalist America;* Raymond Hall, *Black Separatism in the United States;* and William Van Deburg, *New Day in Babylon.*

9. For useful definitions of black nationalism, see E. U. Essien-Udom, *Black Nationalism,* 20; John Bracey Jr., August Meier, and Elliott Rudwick, *Black Nationalism in America,* lvi–lx; John Bracey Jr., "Black Nationalism since Garvey," in Nathan Huggins, Martin Kilson, and Daniel Fox, *Key Issues in the Afro-American Experience,* vol. 2, 261; Rodney Carlisle, *The Roots of Black Nationalism,* 1–6; and Wilson Jeremiah Moses, ed., *Classical Black Nationalism,* 1–42, especially 1–8.

10. Essien-Udom, *Black Nationalism,* 20. John Bracey Jr. explicitly invokes this definition in "Black Nationalism since Garvey," in *Key Issues in the Afro-American Experience, vol. 2,* 260.

11. See Elijah Muhammad, "What the Muslims Believe" and "What Do the Muslims Want?" Quoted in Bracey, Meier, and Rudwick, *Black Nationalism in America,* 404. The authors reprinted this from *Muhammad Speaks* (the weekly newspaper of the Nation of Islam), July 31, 1962. See also Van Deburg, *New Day in Babylon,* 140–44.

12. For an excellent discussion of the Republic of New Africa, see Van Deburg, *New Day in Babylon,* 144–49.

13. See Huey Newton, *Revolutionary Suicide,* and George Jackson, *Blood in My Eye.*

14. Quoted in Hall, *Black Separatism,* 34.

15. See, for examples, Albert Cleage Jr., *The Black Messiah* (1968) and *Black Chris-*

tian Nationalism (1972); and James Cone, *A Black Theology of Liberation* (1970) and *God of the Oppressed* (1975).

16. Elijah Muhammad, "What the Muslims Believe." Quoted in Elijah Muhammad, "What Do the Muslims Want?" Quoted in Bracey, Meier, and Rudwick, *Black Nationalism*, 406. The authors of *Black Nationalism in America* reprinted this from *Muhammad Speaks,* July 31, 1962.

17. Maulana Karenga, *The Quotable Karenga,* quoted in James Barbour, ed., *The Black Power Revolt,* 165; and Karenga, *Introduction to Black Studies,* 133.

18. Karenga, *Introduction to Black Studies,* 133.

19. Kwame Ture and Charles V. Hamilton, *Black Power: The Politics of Liberation in America,* 46.

20. Ibid., 47.

21. Ibid., 44.

22. Ibid., 45.

23. For further discussion of the themes of internal colonialism, see Michael Hechter and Margaret Levi, "Ethno-Regional Movements in the West," in *Nationalism: An Oxford Reader,* ed. John Hutchinson and Anthony D. Smith, 184–95. For a discussion of the role of uneven economic development, and the resentment that it may generate, see Tom Nairn, "The Maladies of Development," ibid., 70–76.

24. See Walker Connor, Introduction to *Ethnonationalism: The Quest for Understanding,* xi; and his essays therein: "American Scholarship in the Post–World War II Era," ibid. 49; "A Nation Is a Nation, Is a State, Is an Ethnic Group, Is a . . ." 94; "Ahistoricalness: The Case of Western Europe," 165–91; "Man is a N(r)ational Animal," 195–209; and "When is a Nation?" 210–26.

25. Malcolm X was a pioneer among African Americans in his use of the term "cultural revolution." Harold Cruse also analyzed the trajectory of events in the 1960s this way. See his "Behind the Black Power Slogan," in *Rebellion or Revolution?* 247; and idem, "The Fire This Time," in Edward Greer, *Black Liberation Politics,* 396–97; Van Deburg, *New Day in Babylon,* 10.

26. Van Deburg, *New Day in Babylon,* passim.

27. Hall, *Black Separatism,* 1.

28. The major proponent of the "melanin hypothesis" is Frances Cress Welsing. See her *The Isis (Yssis) Papers: The Keys to the Colors,* 1–16; and see Michael Bradley, *The Iceman Inheritance.*

29. For a cogent, detailed discussion of black culture, the Black Aesthetic, the Black Arts movement and the critique of white culture, see Van Deburg, *New Day in Babylon,* especially chaps. 4–6.

30. The concept of "Anglo-conformity," as used here, is borrowed from Milton Gordon, *Assimilation in American Life: The Role of Race, Religion, and National Origins,* 85, 88–114. Technically the process referred to as "assimilation" is "acculturation." It is a process of culturally absorbing or incorporating people by having them internalize

and adopt a culture. Biological assimilation or absorption is "amalgamation," in the sense of intermarriage.

31. Michael Parenti, "Assimilation and Counter-Assimilation: From Civil Rights to Black Radicalism," in *Power and Community: Dissenting Essays in Political Science,* ed. Philip Green and Sanford Levinson, 173–94.

32. Ture and Hamilton, in *Black Power.* This was consistent with the view of Harold Cruse that African Americans previously had "lacked a history of the *politics of organized self-determination*" (author's emphasis). See his *Plural but Equal,* 252. The phrase "group-for-itself" parallels Karl Marx's description of the transformation from being a *class-in-itself* to becoming a conscious *class-for-itself.*

33. See Gordon, *Assimilation in American Life,* 85, 88–114.

34. Here I borrow the term of Vincent P. Franklin, as expressed in *Black Self-Determination: A Cultural History of African American Resistance.*

35. The Wharton School of Finance and Commerce is the business school at Pennsylvania.

36. Over time some of these organizations have adopted the use of the term "African American" in place of black. As of 1987, "black" was still being used by student organizations at Penn; however, since that time a shift from black to African American has begun. Thus, some of the organizations referred to here as "black" might today be called African American. As an example, the Organization of Black Faculty, Administrators, and Staff changed its name in 1989 to the African American Association.

37. Here I have borrowed the term "autonomy" from Peter Eisinger, as discussed in "Ethnic Conflict, Community-Building, and the Emergence of Ethnic Political Traditions in the United States," in *Urban Ethnic Conflict,* ed. Susan E. Clarke and Jeffrey L. Obler, 1–34.

38. Van Deburg, *New Day in Babylon,* 25.

39. For a discussion of the persistence of ethnic feeling and rejection of rapid assimilation among European immigrant groups and their American-born progeny, see Michael Novak, *The Rise of the Unmeltable Ethnics.*

40. For a fuller discussion of the roots of the black nationalist tradition, see Essien-Udom, *Black Nationalism;* Rodney Carlisle, *The Roots Of Black Nationalism;* Bracey Jr., Meier, and Rudwick, *Black Nationalism;* Theodore Draper, *The Rediscovery Of Black Nationalism;* Wilson Jeremiah Moses, *Classical Black Nationalism.*

41. Charles M. Christian, *Black Saga: The African American Experience,* 45.

42. Martin Delany was the author of *The Condition, Elevation, Emigration and Destiny of the Colored People of the United States Politically Considered* (1852). He popularized the doctrine that black people in America were a "nation within a nation," comparable to the Irish under British rule, the Poles under Russian rule, and the Hungarians under Austrian (Hapsburg) rule.

43. For a discussion of separate black enclaves and towns after the Civil War, see Carlisle, *Roots of Black Nationalism,* 90–101, 114.

44. Consider his 1897 essay "The Conservation of the Races," in *W. E. B. Du Bois, Writings,* ed. Nathan Huggins, 813–26. Consider also chap. 1 of Du Bois's 1903 *The Souls of Black Folk,* and also his "Does the Negro Need Separate Schools?" *Journal of Negro Education,* 4, no 1 (July 1935): 328–35.

45. Here I utilize the concept of "group affinity" as employed by Iris Marion Young, in "Five Faces Of Oppression," in *Multiculturalism from the Margins: Non-Dominant Voices on Difference and Diversity,* ed. Dean A. Harris, 70–71.

46. Robert L. Allen, *Black Awakening in Capitalist America.*

47. Ibid., 119.

48. Jacqueline E. Wade, "Black College Students' Adaptive Modes: Making It at Penn," Ph.D. dissertation, University of Pennsylvania, 1983. Wade uses a tripartite model consisting of students who happen to be black, black Americans, and black students. Equivalent categories might be assimilationists, bicultural pluralists, and nationalists. Van Deburg discusses assimilationism, pluralism, and nationalism in *New Day in Babylon,* 25. Harold Cruse argued in 1967 that African American history has oscillated between two poles, integration or inclusion and nationalism–separatism. See his *Crisis of the Negro Intellectual,* 5–6, 264, 291, 333–34, 563–64.

Chapter 1. To Open the Doors of Opportunity

1. Marvin Lyon Jr., "Blacks at Penn, Then and Now," in *A Pennsylvania Album,* ed. Richard S. Dunn and Mark F. Lloyd, 43.

2. Ibid.

3. Sadie T. M. Alexander, "A Clean Sweep," *Pennsylvania Gazette,* March 1972, 30–32.

4. Marvin Lyon Jr., "Blacks at Penn," 45.

5. Ibid.

6. Kendall Wilson, "Ivy League's First Black Captain Honored by Univ. of Penn's Dental School," *Philadelphia Tribune,* 4 March 1980, 11.

7. John Edgar Wideman, *Brothers and Keepers,* 28–33.

8. In 1996 the University of Pennsylvania Press reissued *The Philadelphia Negro,* with an introduction by Dr. Elijah Anderson. This commemorated the 1999 centenary of the original publication.

9. "The Morgan State College–University of Pennsylvania Cooperative Project," brochure, 1973, in Records of the Office of the Vice Provost, 1967–1975, UPA 6.7, box 23, "Morgan State Project" file, University of Pennsylvania Archives (hereafter UPA). Researchers are forewarned that box and folder numbers or names of all Penn administrative records may change as the collection grows or is reorganized.

10. "Morgan State to Start Student Exchange Plan," *Daily Pennsylvanian* (hereafter *DP*), 16 November 1966, 1.

11. "Admissions Policy for the Undergraduate Schools of the University of Pennsyl-

vania," Dan McGill, Chairman of the Committee on Undergraduate Admissions, August 1, 1967, p. 2, in Office of the Provost Papers, UPA 6.4, box 72, folder 9, UPA.

12. *Regents of the University of California v. Bakke,* 1978.

13. "University Acceptance of Black Students up 44% over Last Year," *DP,* 16 April 1968, 1.

14. "Report Explains University's Structure, Admissions Process," excerpts from "An Organizational Sketch," a report released by the Vice Provost's Office as part of the university's accreditation review by the Middle States Association, published in *DP,* 15 November 1974, 4. See Middle States Evaluation document, Koons draft, 1974, in Records of the Office of the Vice Provost, 1967–1975, UPA 6.7, box 23, "Middle States Evaluation folder," UPA.

Chapter 2. Years of Discord, 1967 and 1968

1. "Dick Gregory Speaks Here," *DP,* 29 March 1967, 1.

2. "Ain't Gonna Shuffle No More," Episode 5 of PBS's *Eyes on The Prize II* (Blackside Productions, Boston, 1990).

3. Eric Turkington, "Campus Black Power Triumphs," *DP,* 6 November 1967, 3.

4. William Thompson, "Negroes Must Unite to Survive in White World, Clay Tells Penn Students," *Philadelphia Inquirer,* 1 November 1967, 7. As Thompson was admitted to the meeting, it seems likely that he was an African American.

5. Ibid.

6. "Not Here," editorial, *DP,* 3 November 1967, 4.

7. Ibid.

8. Ibid.

9. Billy Riley, "Exclusive Freedom," *DP,* 7 November 1967, 4.

10. Ibid.

11. Drake Turrentine, "Immoderate Tone," *DP,* 9 November 1967, 4.

12. Ibid.

13. Mary Lovett, "Some SAAS," *DP,* 10 November 1967, 6.

14. Ibid.

15. Joel Aber, "Sick Society," *DP,* 13 November 1967, 4.

16. Ibid.

17. Mark Lieberman, "Ali Urges Separation of Races," *DP,* 7 March 1968, 1.

18. Mike Treat, "Militant F. McKissick to Predict Black Future," *DP,* 16 November 1967, 5.

19. Dennis Wilen, "'Whitey Needs Shock,' McKissick Declares," *DP,* 17 November 1967, 1.

20. Cecil J. Burnett, "A Truce to Nonsense about That Liberal Myth: Painless Progress," *DP,* 18 January 1968, 2, 3, 6.

21. Robert Savett, "Condition of Blacks 'Steadily Worsening,' Declares Bond," *DP,* 13 November 1968, 1.

22. Incidentally, George McGovern and Andy Warhol also spoke at Penn in the spring semester of 1969. Advertisement, *DP,* 30 January 1969.

23. J. L. Teller, "Poet Calls for Black Autonomy," *DP,* 18 February 1969, 1.

24. Ibid.

25. Ibid.

26. See George Breitman, *The Last Year of Malcolm X: The Evolution of a Revolutionary,* 45.

27. Ture Kwame, and Charles V. Hamilton, *Black Power,* 44.

28. Ibid., 43.

29. Ibid., 46.

30. Ibid., chap. 3, passim.

31. Malcolm X, *The Autobiography of Malcolm X,* 246.

32. Ibid., 344.

33. Ture and Hamilton, *Black Power,* 47.

34. Ibid., 49.

35. Ibid., 51.

36. Quoted in Clayborne Carson, *In Struggle,* 205.

37. Quoted in Breitman, *Last Year of Malcolm X,* 44.

38. Quoted in ibid., 49.

39. Quoted in ibid., 48.

40. Ture and Hamilton, *Black Power,* 80.

41. Kwame Ture (Stokely Carmichael), interview by William A. Price, *National Guardian,* 4 June 1966, 1, 8, 9.

42. In the final chapters, I revisit this issue and relate it to the enduring African American impulse toward self-organization and self-determination. This tradition did not begin with the black nationalism of the 1960s, but may date back at least as far as such figures as Richard Allen, Absalom Jones, and Prince Hall in 1787.

43. "King Killed in Memphis; Cities in Fear of Rioting," *DP,* 5 April 1968, 1.

44. Berl Schwartz, "Campus Mourns King; 60 Negroes Lead Vigil," *DP,* 8 April 1968, 1.

45. David Kaye, "Students Defy Mayor's Orders; 56 Seized by Police at Rally," *DP,* 9 April 1968, 1.

46. Ibid; Robert Savett, "Arrested 55 Demand Hartwell 'Disassociate' the University from 'Racist City Government,'" *DP,* 17 April 1968, 1.

47. Judy Teller, "'Guilt' and 'White Racism' Are Stressed at Town Meeting," *DP,* 10 April 1968, 1.

48. "Civil Rights Bill Passes House; Ivy Papers, SAAS Support It," *DP,* 11 April 1968, 1.

49. "SAAS Black Week to Open with Rally." *DP,* 11 April 1968, 1, 3.

50. Stephen Marmon, "SAAS Denounces University for Handling of Discrimination Case," *DP,* 30 April 1968, 1, 2.

51. Ibid.

52. Ibid.

53. Ibid.

54. Ibid.

55. This story was shared with me by Rasool Berry, who was preparing an oral history of the black student movement at Penn, in August 1997.

Chapter 3. The Sit-in of 1969

1. "University Acceptance of Black Students up 44% over Last Year," *DP,* 16 April 1968, 1.

2. "Report Explains University's Structure, Admissions Process," excerpts from "An Organizational Sketch," a report released by the Vice Provost's Office as part of the university's accreditation review by the Middle States Association, published in the *DP,* 15 November 1974, 4. See Middle States Evaluation document, Koons draft, 1974 in Records of the Office of the Vice Provost, 1967–1975, UPA 6.7, box 23, "Middle States Evaluation" folder, UPA.

3. James Cass, "Can the University Survive the Black Challenge?" *Saturday Review* 52, no. 25 (21 June 1969): 68.

4. Barbara Slopak, "Dean to Boost Black Admissions," *DP,* 29 January 1969, 1.

5. Report to the Plenary Session of the Trustees of the University of Pennsylvania, 4 May 1967, in the Office of the Provost Papers, UPA 6.4, box 72, folder 37, UPA. See also "The History of Spice Rack," *DP,* 31 March 1967, 5.

6. For more information on the University City Science Center, see "A Summary Report regarding the Formation of the University City Science Center," in ibid.

7. "STOP Leaders Reject Harnwell Plan for Referendum," *DP,* 27 April 1967, 1; "Sit-in Perspective," *DP,* 28 April 1967, 4; "Air Force, Penn end Spice Rack," *DP,* 13 September 1967, 1.

8. Berl Schwartz, "Protesters Sit in Recruitment Centers," *DP,* 2 November 1967, 1; and "Chaplain Johnson Gets Names of anti-Dow Chemical Protesters," *DP,* 9 November 1967, 1.

9. Lawrence Beck and Stephen Kerstetter, "Redevelopment Uproots People as It Eliminates Blight," *DP,* 23 January 1967, 1; and David Kaye, "UCSC Site Still Holds 14 Unwelcome Tenants," *DP,* 20 February 1969, 5.

10. Sue Lin Chong, "University City Home Owners Fight Planners to Save Homes," *DP,* 6 December 1966, 5.

11. Stephen Marmon, "Gov. Shafer Signs Bill Creating Authority," *DP,* 7 December 1967, 1.

12. "Harnwell to Retire in 1970," *DP,* 20 January 1969, 1.

13. Stephen Marmon, "SDS Pickets Greet Trustees," *DP,* 20 January 1969, 1.

14. Berl N. Schwartz, "Residents To Fight Center Demolition," *DP,* 27 January 1969, 1.

15. "Sunday, Jan. 26," editorial, *DP,* 27 January 1969, 2; and "Looking Back," *DP,* 29 January 1969, 2.

16. "400 Sleep in College Hall to Protest USCS Policies," *DP,* 19 February 1969, 1, 5, 3.

17. Ibid.

18. Renewal Housing was the name of a local community group, and it was regarded as an outgrowth of the Reverend Edward Sims's Volunteer Community Resource Council. See "Demonstrators Will Respond to Trustee Proposal," *DP,* 20 February 1969, 1, 2.

19. "400 Sleep in College Hall to Protest," 1.

20. Ibid., 2.

21. "Demonstrators Will Respond to Trustee Proposal," 1, 2.

22. "Black Leaders Join Students; List Demands," *DP,* 21 February 1969, 1.

23. "Final University Agreement with the Community," *DP,* 25 February 1969, 2; "Demonstration Agreement," *Almanac* 15, no. 7 (March 1969): 3; "Development Commission Set Up; Six-Day Demonstration Ends," ibid., 1, 3, 4, 6.

24. "College Hall Sit-in Ends; Community Committee Forms," *DP,* 24 February 1969, 1.

25. The story of the Science Center–Mantua sit-in of 1969 warrants an entire book itself. Here, I have given only a cursory description. Additional detailed information about the Quadripartite Committee is to be found in Records of the Office of the Secretary, UPA 8, University Council, Committees, box 178, 1969–70, Quadripartite Committee on University–Community Development folder, UPA.

26. See Minutes of the Trustees' Urban Affairs Committee, 8 October 1970, in Records of the Office of the Secretary, UPA 8, Committees, box 178, "Urban Affairs Committee, 1970–1971" folder, UPA.

27. The housing was built on Market Street between 39th and 40th Streets in the 1980s.

28. Critics of Frank Rizzo, who was then Chief of Police, regarded him as an amalgam of "Bull" Connor, of Birmingham infamy, and the fascist dictator Benito Mussolini.

29. One may ask why SAAS "waited for SDS," and black students did not initiate the sit-in themselves. Perhaps, in 1969, SDS at Penn was better organized or more militant or focused than SAAS. Some members of SDS "had something to prove" and wanted to "expose the hypocrisy of the system." They were looking for an issue as a means to that end. My impression is that SAAS became directly involved in the College Hall demonstration only after it became clear that black community activists from Mantua would

support the sit-in. Thus, SAAS may have perceived itself as acting in support of the black community rather than merely as an ally of the mostly white SDS.

30. Some observers would point out that it has only been since World War II that the Ivy League schools have placed their focus on "merit." Traditionally, these schools had cared more about wealth and family background.

31. The benefits and advantages that may flow from the accident of birth to affluent parents can hardly be described as "earned." None of us can claim to have earned, by our own individual effort, what our parents or grandparents achieved. *They* earned and achieved it: *We* did not. As offspring, usually, we merely inherit.

32. Robert T. Blackburn, Zelda F. Gamson, and Marvin W. Peterson, "The Meaning of Response: Current and Future Questions," in *Black Students on White Campuses,* ed. Marvin W. Peterson et al., 310.

33. Marvin W. Peterson and Roselle W. Davenport, "Student Organizations and Student Life," in ibid., 199.

34. Blackburn, Gamson, and Peterson, "The Meaning of Response," in ibid., 319.

35. Patricia Gurin and Edgar Epps, *Black Consciousness, Identity, and Achievement,* 224.

36. Ibid., 279.

37. See Gurin and Epps, "Collective and Individual Achievement Polarized, Independent, or Integrated?" 339–54, and "Collective and Individual Achievement—Putting It All Together," 355–406, in ibid.

38. Ibid., 260.

39. George Royal, "An Open Letter, Updated," *DP,* 31 October 1968, 2.

40. Ibid.

41. Ibid.

Chapter 4. Reflections in the Mirror, Reflections in the Curriculum

1. E. Franklin Frazier, *The Negro in the United States,* rev. ed., 680–81.

2. Nathan Glazer and Daniel P. Moynihan, *Beyond the Melting Pot,* 2nd ed., 53.

3. Ibid.

4. Norman Podhoretz, "My Negro Problem—And Ours," *Commentary* (February 1963): 101.

5. See Robert Blauner, *Racial Oppression in America,* especially chap. 4, "Black Culture." My analysis in this chapter borrows from Blauner and is heavily indebted to him.

6. Bennett Berger, "Soul Searching," review of *Urban Blues* by Charles Keil, in *Trans-Action* (June 1967): 57.

7. Ibid., 57.

8. See Blauner, *Racial Oppression,* 117.

9. See Carolyn B. Murray and J. Owens Smith, "White Privilege: The Rhetoric and

the Facts," in *Multiculturalism from the Margins: Non-Dominant Voices on Difference and Diversity*, ed. Dean A. Harris, 139–53.

10. For a discussion of the "invisibility" of the dominant Anglo-Saxon culture, see Maria Lugones and Joshua Price, "Dominant Culture: *El deseo por un alma pobre* (The desire for an impoverished soul)," in ibid., 103–27.

11. The resemblance of the black pride–black consciousness movement to Marcus Garvey's theme of black pride is very striking and significant. The black pride movement of the 1960s recapitulates the black pride theme of Garveyism, as well as the "race-love" of Alexander Crummell and Henry McNeal Turner. Garvey can be thought of as the father of black pride and black cultural nationalism in the twentieth century. In content, the black pride of the 1960s was Crummell's, Turner's, and Garvey's minus the emigrationism. This illustrates the rediscovery and the resurfacing, in the 1960s, of aspects of the subterranean black nationalist legacy of the past.

12. For the anthropological concept of a revitalization movement, see Anthony Wallace, "Revitalization Movements," *American Anthropologist* 58, no. 2 (April 1958): 265–81.

13. "The Morgan State College–University of Pennsylvania Cooperative Project," brochure, 1973, in Records of the Office of the Vice Provost, 1967–1975, UPA 6.7, box 23, "Morgan State Project" file, UPA. Researchers are forewarned that box numbers and folder names may change as the collection grows or is reorganized.

14. "Morgan State to Start Student Exchange Plan," *DP*, 16 November 1966, 1.

15. "Morgan State Receives Grant to Continue Joint Efforts with University," *DP*, 17 September 1968.

16. Justine Rector to Lawrence Klein, "Quantitative Report of Faculty–Student Exchange . . . , 30 April 1973, p. 7, in Records of the Office of the Vice Provost, 1967–1975, UPA 6.7, box 23, "Morgan State Project" folder, UPA.

17. Ibid., 9.

18. "Annual Report of the Morgan State College–University of Pennsylvania Cooperative Project, 1972–1973," in ibid.

19. "Appointments: Morgan–Penn Project," *Almanac* 19, no. 3 (12 September 1972): 5.

20. "Annual Report of the Morgan State College–University of Pennsylvania Cooperative Project, 1972–1973."

21. "Morgan State Project: Helen Davies," *Almanac* 19, no. 16 (19 December 1972): 5.

22. "Morgan–Penn: Five More Years," *Almanac* 20, no. 33 (7 May 1974): 3.

23. "Annual Report of the Morgan State College–University of Pennsylvania Cooperative Project, 1973–1974," p. 2. See also "Report on Students' Evaluation of the Morgan State College–University of Pennsylvania Cooperative Project, 1972–1973," p. 4.

24. "Black Past Is Topic of New Course," *DP*, 8 February 1968, 1.

25. Rona Zevin, "Professor to Teach Negro History," *DP,* 19 March 1968, 1, 2.

26. Stephen Rutter, "Black Students Ask for New Instructor of Class," *DP,* 15 November 1968, 1.

Chapter 5. The Sojourn of the Afro-American Studies Program

1. Letter of charge to members of the Rieber Committee, dated 10 March 1969, in Records of the Office of the Secretary, UPA 8, Committee Files, box 145, "Afro-American Studies Committee, 1967–1972" folder, UPA. See also University of Pennsylvania News Bureau Release, 24 March 1969, in UPF 8.5, News Bureau–Subject Files, box 7, "Afro-American Studies" folder 11, UPA; and "Goddard Announces Formation of Black Studies Committee," *DP,* 24 March 1969, 1.

2. Phyllis Kaniss, "Committee to Establish Black Studies Program Sets Goals," *DP,* 25 March 1969, 1, 3; "Afro-American Studies Committee Appointed," *Almanac* 15, no. 8 (April 1969): 1, 6.

3. "Report of the Rieber Committee," 28 April 1968, Records of the Office of the Secretary, UPA 8, Committee Files, box 145, "Afro-American Studies Committee, 1968–1969" folder, UPA.

4. Kaniss, "Committee to Establish Black Studies Program," 3; and Andrew Wallace, "Penn Group Named to Plan Black Studies," *Philadelphia Inquirer,* 24 March 1969, 1, 14.

5. Phyllis Kaniss, "Black Students Express Mixed Reactions to Plans for Program," *DP,* 26 March 1969, 1.

6. "Report of the Committee on Afro-American Studies" [Rieber Committee Report], 28 April 1969.

7. Igor Kopytoff, "Statement of Dissent," 28 April 1969, ibid.

8. Herbert Wilf, "Statement of Dissent," 28 April 1969, ibid. See also Bob Hoffman, "Black Studies: A Question of Form," *DP,* 10 November 1969, 3.

9. Samuel Klausner, "Statement of Dissent," 28 April 1969, Records of the Office of the Secretary. See also John Riley, "Group Is Named on Black Studies," *DP,* 30 September 1969, 1; Joseph R. Daughen, "Separate School of Black Studies Urged at Penn by Special Committee," *Sunday Bulletin,* 8 June 1969, 1, 7.

10. David Goddard, "Letter to Members of the University Council," 30 April 1969, Records of the Office of the Secretary, UPA 8, Committee Files.

11. "Minutes of the Special Meeting of the University Council," 8 May 1969, ibid.

12. "Phillips Group Dissolves; Establishes Research Group," *DP,* Special Summer Edition, 1 July 1969, 8.

13. Ibid.

14. "Minutes of the Meeting of the Steering Committee of the University Council," 3 July 1969, and Memorandum from Almarin Phillips to Bernard Wolfman, "Report of the Chairman of the *Ad Hoc* Council Committee on Black Studies," 16 Sep-

tember 1969, Records of the Office of the Secretary, UPA 8, Committee Files, box 145, "Afro-American Studies Committee, 1968–1969" folder, UPA.

15. Ibid., 3 July 1969, in Records of the Office of the Secretary, UPA 8, Committee Files, UPA 8, box 145, "Afro-American Studies Committee, 1968–69" folder, UPA, 1.

16. Ibid., 2.

17. Claudia Cohen, "Barlow Proposes Black School," *DP,* 11 September 1969, 3.

18. Bernard Wolfman, "Minutes of the Steering Committee of the University Council," 7 July 1969, Records of the Office of the Secretary, UPA 8, Committee Files, box 145, "Afro-American Studies Committee, 1968–1969" folder, UPA.

19. "Memorandum of Meetings of the Steering Committee of the University Council, September 10, 23, and 29, 1969," and "Minutes of the University Council," 15 October 1969, pp. 2–3, Records of the Office of the Secretary, UPA 8, University Council, Papers and Minutes for Meetings, 1967–1978, box 283, file folder 5 ("24 September 1969–11 February 1970"), UPA; also Bernard Wolfman, "Re: Black Studies," *DP,* 1 October 1969, 4; "Black Center Organized; Council Weighs Black Studies," *Almanac* 16, no. 1 (September 1969): 1, 5.

20. Hoffman, "Black Studies: A Question of Form," 1.

21. Judy Teller, "An Analysis of Selected Areas in Black Studies at the University," 4 September 1969, p. 34, Records of the Office of the Secretary, UPA 8, box 156, "Afro-American Studies Committee, 1969–1970" folder, UPA.

22. Ibid., 39.

23. Joan Rieder, "Cathy Barlow Resigns Black Studies Position; Committee Halts Work," *DP,* 21 January 1970, 1; Phyllis Kaniss, "SAAS Plans to Establish Its Own Black Studies Program," *DP,* 23 February 1970, 2.

24. Kaniss, "SAAS Plans Its own Black Studies Program," 1.

25. Ibid.

26. Ibid., 2.

27. Claudia Cohen, "Black Studies Group Will Continue Activity," *DP,* 24 February 1970, 1.

28. "Final Report of the University Council *Ad Hoc* Committee on Black Studies," April 1970, pp. 4–5, Records of the Office of the Secretary, UPA 8, Committee Files, box 156, "Afro-American Studies Committee, 1969–1970" folder, UPA.

29. Ibid., 8.

30. Ibid., 7, 8. See also "Black Studies Report," *DP,* 27 April 1970, 4.

31. "Separate Statement of Robert Mundheim and Robert Schrieffer," Addendum to the Final Report of the University Council *Ad Hoc* Committee on Black Studies, April 1970, p. 15.

32. Murray Gerstenhaber, "Statement on the Rieber Committee's Report Recommending the Establishment of a School of Black Studies," 18 May 1969, Records of the Office of the Secretary, UPA 8, Committee Files, box 145, "Afro-American Studies Committee, 1968–1969" folder, UPA.

33. See letter to Werner Gundersheimer, 17 May 1970, and Gundersheimer reply, 20 May 1970, in ibid., box 156, "Afro-American Studies Committee, 1969–1970" folder, UPA.

34. "Final Report of the University Council *Ad Hoc* Committee on Black Studies," April 1970, 3–4.

35. "Statement of the Committee of Undergraduate Deans," R. Jean Brownlee, Chairperson, 19 October 1970, in Records of the Office of the Secretary, UPA 8, University Council Materials, 1963–1989, Papers and Minutes for Meetings, box 283, folder 7 ("9 September 1970–10 February 1971"), UPA.

36. "Recommendation of the Steering Committee on the Report on Black Studies," in agenda and materials for the University Council meeting of November 11, 1970; and Minutes of the University Council meeting of November 11, 1970, in ibid.

37. Anita Sama, "U. Council Approves Black Studies Dept.," *DP,* 10 December 1970, 1.

38. Minutes of the Meeting of the University Council, 9 December 1970, pp. 3–6, in Records of the Office of the Secretary.

39. Jonathan B. Talmadge and Mark McIntyre, "Black Studies Move Criticized," *DP,* 11 December 1970, 1, 7.

40. Maurice Obstfeld, "Wideman Replaces Walmsley as Black Studies Comm. Chairman," *DP,* 6 December 1971, 1.

41. "News in Brief: Black History: Robert Engs," *Almanac* 18, no. 27 (14 March 1972): 1, 8.

42. News release from University of Pennsylvania News Bureau, dated 2 December 1971, UPF 8.5, News and Public Affairs, Subject Files, box 7, folder 12 ("Afro-American Studies II"), UPA.

43. Obstfeld, "Wideman Replaces Walmsley," *DP,* 6 December 1971, 1; and "Editorial Perspective: Nov. 21–Dec. 4: Black Studies: Genesis of a Program," ibid., 4.

44. In 1997 the Afro-American Studies Program celebrated its twenty-fifth-anniversary year. Engs celebrated his twenty-fifth year at the university. See Robert Engs, "Twenty-Five Years of Afro-American Studies," *Almanac* 29, no. 32 (29 April 1997): 24.

45. Kathe Archdeacon, "Univ. Names New Black History Prof.," *DP,* 2 March 1972, 1; "News in Brief: Black History: Robert Engs," 1, 8.

46. Peter Conn to Dean William Stephens, "Report on Black Studies," 7 August 1970, in Records of the Office of the Vice Provost, 1967–1975, UPA 6.7, box 20, folder 7 ("Afro-American Studies, 1967–1972"), UPA.

47. John Murphy, "Black Studies Committee Formed to Convince U. of 'Legitimacy,'" *DP,* 18 September 1973, 1.

48. After 1993, Provost Stanley Chodorow transferred responsibility for the Afro-American Studies Program from his office to the School of Arts and Sciences.

49. Engs, "Twenty-Five Years of Afro-American Studies."

50. Lee Levine, "Engs Selected to Coordinate Plan to Recruit Notable Black Faculty," *DP,* 19 October 1973, 1, 7; "Minority Faculty Recruiting: Robert Engs," *Almanac* 20, no. 7 (9 October 1973): 1; Eliot Stellar, Provost, Memorandum to all deans, directors, and department chairs, re minority recruitment, 12 October 1973, *Almanac* 20, no. 8 (16 October 1973): 1. A copy of the memorandum can also be found in Records of the Office of the Vice Provost, 1967–1975, UPA 6.7, box 20, folder 20 ("Black Presence"), UPA.

51. This was related to me in a conversation with Dr. Engs in June 1994.

52. Lori Feldman, "Houston Baker Joins U. English Department," *DP,* 13 September 1974, 6; "Afro-American Studies: Houston Baker Jr.," *Almanac* 21, no. 3 (10 September 1974): 1, 2.

Chapter 6. The Most Difficult Year, 1969–70

1. George Royal, "An Open Letter, Updated," *DP,* 31 October 1968, 2.

2. Bob Hoffman, "Legal Snafus Are Seen in Social Center," *DP,* 4 September 1969, 1, 3.

3. John Riley, "Directors to Sign Official Papers Incorporating Campus Black Center," *DP,* 11 September 1969, 1; "Black Center Organized; Council Weighs Black Studies," *Almanac* 16, no. 1 (September 1969): 1, 6.

4. See *West Philadelphia Black Pages* 1, no. 3 (25 February 1972), in Records of the Office of the Vice Provost, 1967–1975, UPA 6.7, box 20, folder 7 ("Afro-American Studies, 1967–1972"), UPA.

5. In 1972 the *West Philadelphia Black Pages* identified the members of "the Family" individually (apart from the editors already mentioned), ibid., 2.

6. Ruby Martin, memo to "Presidents of Institutions Of Higher Education Participating in Federal Assistance Programs," March 1969. A copy of the memorandum appears as an appendix on p. 45 in the Teller report ("Analysis of Selected Areas in Black Studies at the University"), 4 September 1969, in Records of the Office of the Secretary, UPA 8, University Council, Committee Files, box 156, "Afro-American Studies Committee, 1969–1970" folder, UPA.

7. Ibid.

8. Jonathan Talmadge, "Charge Alleges U. Civil Rights Violation," *DP,* 4 September 1969, 1.

9. Debby Jameson, "SAAS Is Subject to Questions," *DP,* 10 September 1969, 1.

10. Claudia Cohen, "HEW Reps Are Here Investigating SAAS," *DP,* 27 October 1969, 1, 3.

11. Ibid.

12. John Riley, "Blacks, Admissions Dept. Settle Dispute," *DP,* 13 December 1970, 1, 4; idem, "Editorial Perspective: April 13–20," *DP,* 20 April 1970, 2.

13. Riley, "Editorial Perspective: April 13–20," 2.

14. George Schlekat, Dean of Admissions, to Jack Aron, President of the Aron Charitable Foundation, 25 November 1969, in Records of the Office of the Vice Provost, 1967–1975, UPA 6.7, box 20, folder 8 ("Afro-American Studies 1969–1972"), UPA. This letter is attached as an appendix to a report from Dean of Students Alice Emerson, dated 9 February 1972.

15. Schlekat to Aron, ibid. See also AFE [Dean of Students Alice F. Emerson], "Advising Program for Black Freshmen," 17 February 1972, in Records of the Office of the Vice Provost, 1967–1975, UPA 6.7, box 20, folder 8 ("Afro-American Studies, 1969–1972"), UPA.

16. Minutes of the Trustees' Student Affairs Committee, 9 October 1970, in Records of the Office of the Secretary, UPA 8, Committees, box 178, "Student Affairs Committee, 1970–1971" folder, UPA.

17. "SAAS Advising Program, University of Pennsylvania, 1970–1971," p. 1, in Records of the Vice Provost. 1967–1975. This is appendix 2 of the report from Dean of Students Alice Emerson, dated 9 February 1972.

18. "Black Group Demands Release . . . ; Charges Repression," *DP,* 27 April 1970, 1, 5.

19. Ibid.

20. Ibid.

21. Phyllis Kaniss, "100 Black Students March through Campus; Call Administration Racist," *DP,* 17 April 1970, 1. I have deliberately refrained from giving the name of the associate dean in order to protect his identity, preserve his privacy, and avoid any potential embarrassment.

22. Ibid.

23. Ibid., 2.

24. Peter Eglick, Phyllis Kaniss, and Jonathan B. Talmadge, "3 More Fires Blaze; Damage Slight, Case Remains Unsolved," *DP,* 24 April 1970, 1, 3.

25. Ellen Weber and Peter Eglick, "Fire Damages College Hall; Former Administrator Is Charged with Arson: Saturday Morning Blazes Hit Rooms on Two Floors," *DP,* 27 April 1970, 1, 5.

26. Claudia Cohen, "Fire Damages College Hall; Former Administrator Is Charged with Arson: To Be Tried on 7 Counts of Arson," *DP,* 27 April 1970, 1, 5; idem, "Russell, Two U. Students Testify at Trial," *DP,* 12 October 1970, 1, 2; Peter Eglick, "State Probes for Holes in Defense Case," *DP,* 14 October 1970, 1, 2.

27. Weber and Eglick, "Fire Damages College Hall," 1, 5.

28. Anita Sama, "[X]Acquitted of All Charges in Spring Firebombing of College Hall," *DP,* 16 October 1970, 1; "[X]Refutes Friend's Report; Denies Guilt," *DP,* 13 October 1970, 2; Eglick, "State Probes for Holes in [X]Defense Case," 1, 2; Cohen, "Russell, Two U. Students Testify at Trial," 1, 2.

29. Phyllis Kaniss, "Agreement Reached on Black Advising," *DP,* 4 May 1970, 1, 2.

30. Ibid.

31. "SAAS Advising Program, University Of Pennsylvania, 1970–1971," p. 2, in Records of the Office of the Vice Provost, 1967–1975.

32. John Bracey Jr., "Black Nationalism since Garvey," in *Key Issues in the Afro-American Experience*, ed. Nathan Huggins, Martin Kilson, and Daniel Fox, vol. 2, 260.

Chapter 7. Confronting Class and Disadvantage

1. "Black Students in the College," 16 February 1971, in Records of the Office of the Vice Provost, 1967–1975, UPA 6.7, box 20, folder 8 ("Afro-American Studies, 1969–1972"), UPA.

2. See James M. O'Neill, "News Is Mixed on Minorities' SATs," *Philadelphia Inquirer*, 31 August 1997, E3.

3. Thus, for example, a hypothetical black student graduating from a public high school in Philadelphia with an SAT score of 1090 might have had the highest SAT score of any student in his class at his high school, in that year. He might be among the top five students in his high school class and be the recipient of both a Mayor's Scholarship and a Board of Education Scholarship from Philadelphia. But although his SAT score is a good 200 points lower than that of a white classmate, each is in the upper echelon of his respective ethnic group. Therefore, when groups are compared, these students are among the best qualified of their respective ethnic groups.

4. "Black Students in The College," 16 February 1971, in Records of the Office of the Vice Provost.

5. Scott Gibson, "Conrad Jones Resigns; Will Head State Office," *DP*, 22 November 1972, 1.

6. "Advising Program for Black Freshmen," Alice Emerson, 17 February 1972, in Records of the Office of the Vice Provost, 1967–1975. See also, Letters to the Editor, "White Perception," *DP*, 23 September 1970, 4.

7. Appendix 6, Report on Black Advising Program from Dean of Students Alice Emerson, 9 February 1972, in Records of the Vice Provost, 1967–1975.

8. Appendix 5, Summary of Black Advising Program for Summer of 1971, by Conrad Jones, 28 January 1972, on Black Advising Program from Dean of Students Alice Emerson, in ibid.

9. Appendix 6, Report on Black Advising Program from Dean of Students Alice Emerson, ibid.

10. Ibid.

11. Conrad Jones, "A Commitment to Minority Students," *DP*, 29 November 1972, 4.

12. "Advising Program Aids Blacks," *DP*, 3 November 1972, 3.

13. Claude Mayberry, "Support Services for Minority Students at Penn," *Almanac* 20, no. 32 (30 April 1974): 5–6; Carla Solomon, "Supportive Services: More than Remedial," *Almanac* 22, no. 8 (14 October 1975): 5.

14. Larry Field, "Wide Application Seen for Counseling Plan," *DP,* 23 October 1974, 1.

15. Ibid.

16. Peter Ginsberg, "New Position Studied to Cover Ugrad Life," *DP,* 10 September 1974, 1; Rick Dunham, "New Vice Provost to Coordinate Student Life," *DP,* 21 February 1975, 1, 5.

17. "Vice-Provost: Patricia A. McFate," *Almanac* 22, no. 4 (16 September 1975): 1.

18. "News in Brief: FAS: Dean Brownlee, Dr. Joullie," *Almanac* 21, no. 23 (25 February 1975): 1; Teri Gross, "Dean Brownlee Plans Retirement from U. Administrative Position," *DP,* 29 September 1975, 1, 2.

19. "Report of the Task Force on Black Presence," Presented to the Trustees of the University of Pennsylvania, July 9, 1977. Published in *Almanac* 24, no. 24 (21 March 1978); 17.

20. See Claude Mayberry, "Proposal for Improving Postsecondary Education," 5 February 1975, and "Qualitative And Prescriptive Design for Extending First-Semester Courses in Physics, Chemistry, Biology, and Mathematics," n.a, n.d, in Records of the Office of the Vice Provost, 1967–1975, UPA 6.7, box 24, folder 15 ("University Life Supportive Services, 1975"), UPA.

21. Susan Elman, "PENNCAP Recruiters Look to Inner City," *DP,* 16 October 1978, 1.

22. Carol Hutchinson, "Report on Admissions Indexes Performance," *DP,* 27 April 1976, 1, 2; Roger Walmsley, Chairman, Committee on Undergraduate Admissions, "The Prediction of Academic Performance: An Admissions Study," *Almanac* 22, no. 31 (27 April 1976): 2.

23. Robinson and Holland are graduates of the Magnet Program—and proof that the program works.

Chapter 8. Is a Black Dormitory "Voluntary Segregation"?

1. "Autonomy" as I use it here is adapted from Peter Eisinger, "Ethnic Conflict, Community-Building, and the Emergence of Ethnic Political Traditions in the United States," *Urban Ethnic Conflict,* ed. Susan E. Clarke and Jeffrey L. Obler, 1–34.

2. "Black Residence Center Announced," *Almanac* 18, no. 27 (14 March 1972): 1. See also Kathe Archdeacon, "Panel Reviews Proposal for All-Black Residential Center," *DP,* 18 February 1972, 1, 5. Cathy Barlow completed her undergraduate studies in 1971, and received her J.D. in 1976.

3. "Black Residence Demands," *DP,* 18 February 1972, 4.

4. Ibid.

5. Archdeacon, "Panel Reviews Proposal for All-Black Residential Center," 1.

6. "Background On Black Residence" [condensation of the proposal for a Black Residential Center], *Almanac* 18, no. 30 (4 April 1972): 7.

7. Letters to the Editor, "Black Residence," *DP,* 21 February 1972, 4.

8. Archdeacon, "Panel Reviews Proposal for All-Black Residential Center," 5.

9. In the fall of 1974, as an extreme example, enrollment in the introductory course in psychology exceeded four hundred, and it had to be held in Irvine Auditorium. The professor lectured from the stage, and students arriving late had to find seats in the balcony. Under these conditions, exams must be in multiple-choice format to be graded with op-scan readers. It is undoubtedly the most cost-effective way to teach students, but students and their parents alike may be forgiven if they think it resembles an educational assembly line. For a contemporary version of the same problem, see "Lining Up to Get a Lecture," *New York Times,* 17 November 2000, B1, 8.

10. D.T., 22 February 1972, letter to Martin Meyerson, in Records of the Office of the Vice Provost, 1967–1975, UPA 6.7, box 23, folder 17 ("President's Office"), UPA. This is taken from a photocopy of the original in the files of Vice Provost Humphrey Tonkin.

11. Martin Meyerson to D.T., 25 February 1972, in ibid. This is also from a photocopy of the original in the records of Vice Provost Humphrey Tonkin.

12. Steven Bell, "Experimental House Plan Okayed," *DP,* 26 March 1971, 1.

13. "A Program for Residential Living in the Seventies," *DP,* 21 January 1972, 8.

14. Louis Coles and Gary Galloway, "Black Problems," *DP,* 16 February 1972, 4.

15. Archdeacon, "Panel Reviews Proposal for All-Black Residential Center," 1.

16. Ibid.

17. Howard Lesnick, "Considering Residence Proposals," *DP,* 21 February 1972, 4.

18. John O'Brien, Letter to the Editor, "Black Residence," *DP,* 21 February 1972, 4.

19. "Black Residence Plan," editorial, *DP,* 25 February 1972, 4.

20. John Daniszewski, "Black Students Attack University Commitment to Minority Programs," *DP,* 1 March 1972, 1, 3.

21. Ibid., 1.

22. Committee of the Black Faculty and Administrators, "Open Letter to the University," *DP,* 2 March 1972, 4.

23. Arthur Graham and Richard Rogers, "Black Grievances," *DP,* 8 March 1972, 4.

24. Judy Appelbaum, "New Housing Projects Set for Operation in Dorms, S-block," *DP,* 8 March 1972, 1.

25. John Daniszewski, "Comm. Okays Black Dorm; Council to Hear Plan Today," *DP,* 8 March 1972, 1.

26. Ibid., 5.

27. "Minutes of the Meeting of the University Council," 8 March 1972, pp. 3–4, in Records of the Office of the Secretary, UPA 8, University Council Material, 1963–1989, Papers and Minutes of Meetings, box 283, folder 9 ("8 December 1971–17 May 1972"), UPA. See also John A. Russell Jr., Statement on Black Residence Proposal, March 8, 1872. Published as "The Council: Black Residence Program," in *Almanac* 18, no. 27 (14 March 1972): 4.

28. "Minutes of the Meeting of the University Council," 8 March 1972, 6.

29. John Daniszewski, "Modified Black Residence Plan," *DP,* 9 March 1972, 1, 5; "The Council: Black Residence Center Announced," *Almanac* 18, no. 27 (14 March 1972): 1.

30. Acel Moore, "Penn to Build Black Dorm as Orientation Center," *Philadelphia Inquirer,* 11 March 1972, 21.

31. "The Together Paradox," editorial, *Philadelphia Daily News,* 10 March 1972.

32. Ibid.

33. "U. Of P. Approves All-Black Dormitory and Student Center," 14 March 1972, *Philadelphia Tribune,* 2.

34. "Students Turning Back the 'Clock,'" editorial, ibid., 8.

35. Scott Gibson, "Future of Black Residence Plan at U. Uncertain as Administrators Decide," *DP,* 20 March 1972, 1.

36. William K. Mandel, "Move for All-Black Dorms Assailed by NAACP Head," *Philadelphia Bulletin,* 26 March 1972, A6. See also "NAACP Leader Raps All-Black Dorm Plan," *DP,* 24 March 1972, 1.

37. Jim Kahn, "Black Group Faults Housing Plan Delay," *DP,* 30 March 1972, 1; "Holding Back Black Residence," Statement of the Organization of Black Faculty and Administrators, ibid., 4.

38. Judy Appelbaum, "Black Dorm May Encounter Legal Problems, Counsel Says," *DP,* 31 March 1972, p. 1.

39. Ibid.

40. "Future Residents of All-Black Dorm Rap Delay over Decision," *DP,* 3 April 1972, 1.

41. "Statement Of Position," 3 April 1972, in Records of the Office of the Vice Provost, 1967–1975, UPA 6.7, box 20, folder 7 ("Afro-American Studies, 1967–1972"), UPA. See also Ben Ginsberg, "Blacks Protest Dorm Delay, Hit Faculty Senate, Admin." *DP,* 4 April 1972, 1; and "Open Letter to President Meyerson," ibid., 4.

42. Statement of the Black Faculty and Administrators on Residence Center Proposal, April 3, 1972, published in *Almanac* 18, no. 31 (11 April 1972): 7.

43. Michael Silver, "Changes Ordered for Black Dorm," *DP,* 5 April 1972, 1, 7.

44. "Taking Stock," editorial, *DP,* 6 April 1972, 2.

45. "Daily Pennsylvanian Theft," Statement of the Committee on Open Expression, *DP,* 13 April 1972, 2.

46. "Deliberate Speed," editorial, *DP,* 5 April 1972, 2.

47. Michael Silver, "Faculty Senate Accepts Black Residence Proposal," *DP,* 6 April 1972, 1, 8.

48. Ibid., 1.

49. Ibid., 8.

50. Ibid., 1.

51. Ibid.; "The Senate: Black Residence Proposal," *Almanac* 18, no. 31 (11 April 1972): 2.

52. Ben Ginsberg, "University Gives Final Approval to Plan for Black Residential Center," *DP,* 7 April 1972, 1, 5.

53. Ibid.; "News in Brief: Black Residence Center," *Almanac* 18, no. 31 (11 April 1972): 1.

Chapter 9. "A Program for Any Undergraduate of Any Race"

1. Ernest Dunbar, "Cornell's experience indicates why, all over the country, so much stress is being put on The Black Studies Thing," *New York Times Magazine,* 6 April 1969, 25–27, 60, 65, 68, 70, 75, 76–77.

2. Ibid., 65.

3. "NAACP Leader Will Sue to Stop Black U. of P. Dorm," *Philadelphia Tribune,* 22 April 1972, 10. See also Ed Silverman, "NAACP Seeks Legal Action to Prevent 'All-Black' Dorm," *DP,* 13 April 1972, 1.

4. "Minutes of the Meeting of the University Council," 12 April 1972, p. 3, in Records of the Office of the Secretary, UPA 8, University Council Materials, 1963–1989, Papers and Minutes for Meetings, box 283, folder 9 ("8 December 1971–17 May 1972"), UPA.

5. "Cole to Teach African History, Assist with Black Residence," *DP,* 21 April 1972, 8. The term "Residential Program" was still used for the first few years, especially as the program was initially established on an "experimental" basis. By 1977, however, it was referred to as Du Bois College House.

6. Ibid.

7. "Penn to Open Black Center with Integrated Dorm Unit," *Philadelphia Daily News,* 7 April 1972, 14.

8. William K. Mandel, "Penn Dorm for Blacks Reflects Steady Rise in Separatist Sentiment," *Evening Bulletin,* 16 April 1972, 35.

9. "Separatism at Colleges," editorial, *Evening Bulletin,* 15 April 1972, 6.

10. Iver Peterson, "Black Study Project, Open to All Races, Is Approved at Penn," *New York Times,* 7 April 1972.

11. Margot Cohen, "Ceremony Celebrates Du Bois Dedication," *DP,* 23 February 1981, 1, 6.

12. Ibid.

13. Bill Davenport, "background paper" on W. E. B. Du Bois House, prepared for Provost Eliot Stellar, 9 May 1973, in Records of the Office of the Vice Provost, UPA 6.7, box 22, folder 4 ("Du Bois" [House]); Humphrey Tonkin, statement entitled "The Du Bois Project," May 1972, ibid.; News Release, dated 18 August 1972, University of Pennsylvania News Bureau, UPF 8.5, News Bureau: Subject Files, Residences,

"W. E. B. Du Bois Resident Center, 1972–1982," box 176, folder 23, UPA; Tom Candor, "W. E. B. Du Bois House: Programs, Problems," *DP,* 20 February 1973, 1.

14. Davenport, "background paper" on W. E. B. Du Bois House.

15. "Three House Masters," *Almanac* 21, no. 5 (24 September 1974): 3.

16. "Undergraduate Studies Digest: A Digest of News from the Office of the Vice Provost for Undergraduate Studies," January 1975, p. 6, in Records of the Office of the Vice Provost, UPA 6.7, box 22, folder 2 ("Digest Items"), UPA.

17. Steven Fadem, Letters to the Editor, *DP,* 6 April 1972, 2. Michael Schwerner, Andrew Goodman, and James Chaney were three civil rights workers who disappeared in Mississippi in June 1964. President Lyndon Johnson sent the Federal Bureau of Investigation, and the navy, to find them. In August 1964, the bodies of the three men were found buried beneath an earthen dam. They had been murdered by Klansmen. Schwerner and Goodman were white, Jewish, and from the north. Chaney was an African American and a native of Mississippi. Schwerner and Goodman still symbolize white civil rights activists who died for the cause of desegregation and human rights for African Americans.

18. Michael Meyers, "Black Residence: Where It's Been . . . ," *DP,* 27 April 1972, 2.

19. Larry Fine, "And Where It May Go," ibid.

20. "Black Study Projects," editorial, *Chicago Daily Defender,* 20 April 1972.

21. Wilson Jones, "Defending the Black Dorm," *DP,* 19 April 1972, 2.

22. Mitchell Berger, "Pa. Attorney General Probes Du Bois House," *DP,* 26 February 1973, 1, 5.

23. Peter Grant, "HEW Closes Projects Elsewhere; Du Bois House Probe Pending," *DP,* 17 September 1975, 1.

24. I knew Marion Dorn when she lived at Du Bois House. I had hoped to interview her in connection with this chapter. Sadly, the Penn alumni magazine has reported her untimely death.

25. Marian Dorn and Kimberly Edmunds, "Examining a Case of Social Myopia and Affirmative Action," *DP,* 4 March 1977, 5.

26. Margot Cohen, "Du Bois House Living: Student Bridges Racial Barriers," *DP,* 2 April 1981, 1, 3. The *DP* article was written after Zagerman had applied to live at Du Bois and had been accepted but before he actually resided there in the academic year 1981–82.

27. Quoted in ibid., 1.

28. Ibid.

29. Conversation with Robert Zagerman, 22 August 2001.

30. "Black-Oriented Du Bois Program Begins Third Controversial Year," *DP,* 1 July 1974, 5.

31. President Sheldon Hackney, Provost Thomas Ehrlich, Vice Provost Janis Somerville, et al., "Rejecting Intolerance," *Almanac* 28, no. 7 (17 October 1981): 1.

32. Press release, dated 13 February 1974, University of Pennsylvania News Bureau,

UPF 8.5, News and Public Affairs, Subject Files, box 176, folder 23 ("Residences, W. E. B. Du Bois Residence Center, 1972–1982"), UPA.

33. Albert Gorden, "The Black and White of Campus Integration," *DP,* 4 December 1975, 4.

34. The residential "thematic" programs, as they existed in 1974, are described in a document prepared for the Middle States Evaluation. See "The SCUE [Student Committee on Undergraduate Education] Report," Appendix G, "The College House System: Description of the Programs," in Records of the Office of the Vice Provost, 1967–1975, UPA 6.7, box 23, "Middle States Evaluation" [of 1974] folders, UPA.

35. "The Masters," *Almanac* 22, no. 23 (11 May 1976): 1.

36. Mark Cohen, "Stellar Reaffirms U. Commitment to Blacks," *DP,* 25 September 1974, 2; Jeff Birnbaum, "House of the Family Decision Due Soon," *DP,* 18 November 1974, 1.

37. "Black Residence Demands," *DP,* 18 February 1972, 4.

38. Ibid.

39. An African American faculty member told me this anecdote. The "prank" occurred about 1972.

40. For two discussions of the concept of "cultural style," see Reginald M. Clark, *Family Life and School Achievement;* and Judith Thomas and Dana Flint, "Black Youth in Urban Schools: Attrition, Self-Concept, and Performance," in *The State of Black Philadelphia,* vol. 9, 1990, 37–48.

41. In a very different context, one author who alludes explicitly to the process of people and society becoming "middle-classified" is John Dollard, in *Caste and Class in a Southern Town.*

42. Again, the benefits and advantages that flow from the fortuitous accident of birth to wealthy parents can scarcely be described as having been "earned" by our own individual efforts. If our parents achieved something, *they* achieved it—not their children who merely inherit the benefits without, in many cases, having to do so much as to lift a silver spoon. We may be entitled to what our parents give us, but this is not the same as our having "earned" it.

43. John McGowan, "City Agency Threatens Suit against de Facto Black Center," *Pennsylvania Voice* (University of Pennsylvania), 12 April 1972, 1, 4.

Chapter 10. The Sit-in of 1978 and the United Minorities Council

1. A useful summary of Penn's budget difficulties can be found in the *Almanac* of November 1975, which sought to shed some light on the confusing issue of the university deficit. Trustee Robert Dunlop was quoted as indicating an *accumulated* deficit (as opposed to annual or yearly deficit) of $11 million in the operating budget, plus an accumulated deficit of almost $2 million in housing (the student dormitories), for a total in the neighborhood of $13 million. Comptroller J. Jerrold Jackson reported

that there was an accumulated deficit of $9.3 million for the university operating budget and the high-rise dormitories, and an accumulated deficit for the Graduate Hospital of $3.6 million, for a total of $12.9 million. The Coopers and Lybrand audit, which applied the reserves of the Hospital of the University of Pennsylvania against the "negative balance," reported the total accumulated deficit to be $12.3 million. See "What Is the Deficit?" *Almanac* 22, no. 12 (11 November 1975): 1, and note 6 below.

2. Lawrence Klein, Academic Planning Committee, "The Measurement of Excellence and Performance: Some Preliminary Investigations by the Academic Planning Committee," *Almanac* 21, no. 25 (18 March 1975): 6–7.

3. Martin Meyerson, letter to Executive Committee of the Trustees on tuition increase for 1975–76, 10 February 1975, published as "On the Undergraduate Tuition Increase," *Almanac* 21, no. 22 (18 February 1975): 4–5; John Hobstetter, chairman, University Budget Committee, letter recommending tuition increase, 10 February 1975, published as "From the Budget Committee," ibid., 4.

4. Larry Field, "Budget: Severe Financial Hardship Due to Expenses, Cuts in Support," *DP,* 6 April 1976, 4.

5. Seth Rosen, "University Officials Project Fiscal 1978 Budget Deficit," *DP,* 2 November 1976, 1.

6. Martin Meyerson, President, Report to the Trustees, 13 January 1978, published as "The State of the University: Achievement and Adversity," *Almanac* 24, no. 18 (31 January 1978): 2, 3.

7. Quoted in Susan Elman, "Annenberg Center Cuts," *DP,* 24 February 1978, 5.

8. Susan Elman, "Campus Expresses Anger over Annenberg Cutbacks," *DP,* 28 February 1978, 1.

9. Clemson Smith, "Hockey, Other Sports Ended in Cost-Cutting," *DP,* 24 February 1978, 1.

10. Elizabeth Wilson, "UA Vote Defeats Resolution Asking Meyerson to Resign," *DP,* 1 March 1978, 1.

11. Elizabeth Wilson, Jonathan Greer, Susan Coopersmith, Eric Jacobs, Keith C. Epstein, Larry Frohman, Gerri Sperling, Rob Dubow, Sue Laiken, Dom Manno, Noel Weyrich, Elizabeth Sanger, Steven Marquez, and others, "Student Protesters Occupy College Hall: Takeover Follows One-Hour Rally Protesting Hockey, Theatre Cuts," *DP,* 3 March 1978, 1, 6.

12. Ibid.

13. Ibid.

14. Susan Elman, "President, Trustee to Seek Funds to Continue Professional Theatre," *DP,* 6 March 1978, 1.

15. Keith C. Epstein and Greg Manning, "Franklin Bldg. Taken Over by Minorities," ibid.

16. Ibid.

17. I was an undergraduate at Penn in 1978 and was present at the College Hall sit-

in and the occupation of the Franklin Building by the BSL. My knowledge of the events described in this section is based on eyewitness observation (and participation), as well as published news accounts and documentary materials.

18. Epstein and Manning, "Franklin Bldg. Taken Over by Minorities," 1, 2; Eric Jacobs, Richard E. Gordon, and Larry Frohman, "Leaders Agree to 31 Demands," *DP*, 6 March 1978, 1, 3; Richard E. Gordon, "Original Six Demands Expand to 31 at Sit-In," ibid., 3.

19. Gordon and Frohman, "Leaders Agree to 31 Demands," 1, and Gordon, "Original Six Demands Expand to 31," 3; "Comprehensive Settlement Ends Student Sit-in," *Almanac* 24, no. 23 (7 March 1978): 1.

20. Greg Manning, "Minorities Meet with Stellar on Carrying out Proposals," *DP*, 7 March 1978, 1; "Agreements Reached during College Hall Sit-in," [text of agreements ending sit-in], ibid., 2; and Greg Manning, with the assistance of Noel Weyrich, "The Sit-in: What Happened?" *DP*, 25 September 1978, 3.

21. Kenny Birnbaum, "U. Acquires Minority Center: Building to House UMC Offices," *DP*, 29 October 1982, 1; William Molette, "Finally, the Intercultural Center Opens—University Optimistic about Its Future," *The Voice* 3, no. 1 (November 1983), 1, 4.

22. Greg Manning, "Faculty Creates Review Panel: New Confidence Sought by Assembled Faculty," *DP*, 1 May 1978, 1; "Faculty Senate Votes to Establish Review Panel," *Almanac* 24, no. 30 (2 May 1978): 1; "Resolution Passed by Faculty Senate," ibid.

23. Steven A. Marquez, "Meyerson Will Resign by 1981: President Tumbles into Credibility Gap," *DP*, 7 September 1978, 1, 7; Steve Dubow, "Meyerson Will Resign by 1981: Meyerson Announces Resignation after Consultation with Trustees," ibid., 1, 2.

24. Janet Novack, "Student Group Claims U. Neglects Chicanos," *DP*, 2 October 1974, 1.

25. Louis R. Escareno and Craig Inge, "Admission Office Crisis Concerns Students," *DP*, 4 October 1974, 4.

26. This supports the view of Robert Blauner: "Many of the ambiguities of American race relations stem from the fact that two principles of social division, race and ethnicity, were compressed into one. With their own internal ethnic differences eliminated, people of African descent became a race in objective terms, especially in the view of the white majority. Afro-Americans *became an ethnic group also,* one of the many cultural segments of the nation. The ethnicity of Afro-America, however, is either overlooked, denied, or distorted by white Americans, in part because of the historic decision to focus on the racial definition, in part because of the racist tendency to gainsay culture to people of color beyond what they may have assimilated directly from the European tradition. This merging of ethnicity with race, in the eyes of people of color as well as of whites, made it inevitable that racial consciousness among blacks would play a central part in their historic project of culture building, and that their

institutions, politics and social character would be misinterpreted in a restricted racial paradigm" (emphasis added). See Robert Blauner, *Racial Oppression in America*, 1972, 117.

27. For an early (1962) discussion of the emergent sense of black or African American ethnicity in the 1960s, see Larry Singer, "Ethnogenesis and Negro-Americans Today," in *Social Research* 20, no. 4 (winter 1962): 419–32.

28. For a discussion of the role of the concept of shared ancestry in shaping the sense of nationalism and ethnicity, see Walker Connor, "A Nation Is a Nation, Is a State, Is an Ethnic Group, Is a . . . ," in *Ethnonationalism: The Quest for Understanding*, 89–117. The essay originally appeared in *Ethnic and Racial Studies* 1, no. 4 (1978): 379–88.

29. Ibid.

30. See ibid.

31. Edward Shils, "Primordial, Personal, Sacred and Civil Ties," *British Journal of Sociology* (June 1957): 130–45; Clifford Geertz, "The Integrative Revolution: Primordial Sentiments, and Civic Politics in the New States," in Clifford Geertz, ed., *Old Societies and New States*, 107–13.

32. For a cogent discussion of black nationalism and cultural pluralism, see Harold Cruse, *Plural but Equal*.

Chapter 11. Assimilation, Pluralism, and Nationalism–Separatism

1. Jacqueline E. Wade, "Black College Students' Adaptive Modes: Making It at Penn" (Ph.D. diss., University of Pennsylvania, 1983).

2. William Van Deburg, *New Day in Babylon*, 25.

3. In deference to his chosen name, I will refer to him hereafter as Conrad Muhammad. As a student at Penn in 1986, however, he still used the name Tillard.

4. Jeffrey Goldberg, "Procedural Problems Mark BSL's Election," *DP*, 28 March 1986, 1.

5. Ibid., 7.

6. Robert Pasnau, "White Student Not Allowed in BSL," *DP*, 19 September 1986, 1.

7. Ibid., 1, 10.

8. Robert Pasnau, "BSL Will Address Incident," *DP*, 24 September 1986, 1.

9. Felipe Albuquerque, "Sid Ordem, Sem Progreso: A Nation of Hatred," *DP*, 16 September 1986, 4.

10. Conrad Muhammad, "A Nation of Love," *DP*, 19 September 1986, 4.

11. Jill Noel Robinson, "Black Student Supports Whites' Right to Join BSL," *DP*, 24 September 1986, 4.

12. Phillip A. Remaker, "Freshman Blasts Conrad Tillard for Separatist Views," ibid.

13. April Claytor, "Student Defends BSL's Black Only Admissions Policy," ibid., 4.

14. Statement of President Sheldon Hackney, Provost Thomas Ehrlich, and Vice

Provost James Bishop, "Administration Supports Discourse to End Conflict," *DP*, 25 September 1986, 4.

15. The Finance Committee of the Student Activities Council presided over the allocation of funds for recognized student organizations. Recognition also entitled those organizations to use campus facilities.

16. Robert Pasnau, "BSL Says Student Can Join," *DP*, 26 September 1986, 1, 5; Conrad Tillard Muhammad and Reuben Brown, "BSL's Chairman Defines Role of Minority Group," interview in ibid., 3. It should be noted that the limitation of full membership to African Americans remained the *practice* of the BSL as late as August 1997, although more recently I have heard some discussion of changing it.

17. Jeffrey Goldberg, "Student Turns Down BSL Offer," *DP*, 16 October 1986, 1.

18. Sydney Thornbury, "Questioning," *DP*, 26 September 1986, 4.

19. Ibid.

20. Ralph H. Turner and Lewis Killian, *Collective Behavior*, 2nd ed. (1972), 252.

21. Ibid., 261.

22. "Council: Elections: Ruth Ann Price, Charles Price," *Almanac* 20, no. 5 (25 September 1973): 1.

23. "Full disclosure" probably requires me to confess that, while a graduate student in fall 1988, I was a columnist for the *Daily Pennsylvanian* and received a plaque as columnist of the year. This might make me a little partisan toward the *DP*.

24. Helen Jung, "UA Veteran Harris Elected Chairperson," *DP*, 9 April 1990, 1; and "On the Record: Harris Hopes to Consolidate UA Power," interview with Duchess Harris, *DP*, 20 April 1990, 3.

25. Lauren Shaham, "Students Form Support Group for SAS Blacks," *DP*, 26 April 1989, 1.

26. Telephone Directory, 1990–91, University of Pennsylvania, 72–73.

27. Robert L. Allen, *Black Awakening in Capitalist America*.

28. Culture as "ornamental" is discussed by Maria Lugones and Joshua Price in "Dominant Culture: *El deseo por un alma pobre* (The desire for an impoverished soul)," in *Multiculturalism from the Margins,* ed. Dean A. Harris, 103, 104; Manning Marable discusses "corporate multiculturalism," which "celebrates diversity" but ignores questions of power, exploitation, racism, sexism, and homophobia—in contrast to "liberal multiculturalism," "racial essentialism," and "radical democratic multiculturalism." See Marable, "Black Studies, Multiculturalism and the Future of American Education," in *Beyond Black and White,* 117–30.

Conclusion: The Revolt against Assimilation

1. Harold Cruse argued that African Americans have oscillated between integration–assimilation on the one hand and nationalism–separatism on the other. I suggest

that implicitly there has been a third path running parallel to the other two. It is cultural and ethnic pluralism, with a pattern of ethnic group self-organization. See Cruse, *The Crisis of the Negro Intellectual,* 5–6, 264, 291, 333–34, 563–64.

2. The term "Anglo-conformity," or conformity to the dominant Anglo-Saxon culture, is taken from Milton Gordon, *Assimilation in American Life,* 85, 88–114.

3. Maria Lugones and Joshua Price, "Dominant Culture: *El deseo por un alma pobre* (The desire for an impoverished soul)," in *Multiculturalism from The Margins,* ed. Dean A. Harris, 103–27 (especially 107).

4. Ibid., 105.

5. Ibid., 105–6.

6. See Cheryl Zarlenga Kerchis and Iris Marion Young, "Social Movements and the Politics of Difference," in *Multiculturalism from the Margins,* 1–27; and Iris Marion Young, *Justice and the Politics of Difference.*

7. My use here of the terms "particularism" and "particularistic" is after Manning Marable, who offers a critique of the use of the terms by former Assistant Secretary of Education Diane Ravitch (during the first Bush administration). See Marable, *Beyond Black and White,* 14, 113–14. Wilson is quoted in Oscar Handlin, *The American People in the Twentieth Century,* 2d ed. rev. (Cambridge: Harvard University Press, 1966), 121.

8. The title of Schlesinger's book is *The Disuniting of America.* The references to fragmentation appear on pp. 16, 102, and 130. The "cult of ethnicity" is discussed on pp. 15 and 102. The danger of the "tribalization of American life" is described on p. 18, and on p. 56, John Kelleher is quoted as musing in a "satiric" fashion about "ethnic cheerleading."

9. Thus, Cheryl Zarlenga Kerchis and Iris Marion Young have written: "Assimilation always implies coming into the game after it has already begun, after the rules and standards have already been set. Therefore, disadvantaged groups play no part in making up the rules and standards by which they must prove themselves—those rules and standards are defined by privileged groups." See "Social Movements and the Politics of Difference," in *Multiculturalism from the Margins,* ed. Harris, 9.

10. Michael Parenti, "Assimilation And Counter-Assimilation: From Civil Rights to Black Radicalism," in *Power and Community: Dissenting Essays in Political Science,* ed. Philip Green and Sanford Levinson, 179.

11. The concept of superexploitation, as used here, is adapted from James Boggs, *Racism and the Class Struggle,* 154–53, 167; and George Hermon Jr, *American Race Relations Theory: A Review of Four Models,* 93, 106, 145, 157, 161, 170, and 204.

12. Iris Marion Young, defines "marginals" as the people whom "the system of labor cannot or will not use." She alludes to a growing underclass of people permanently consigned to lives of social marginality. These individuals are involuntarily unemployed, and, "via marginalization a whole category of people is expelled from useful participation in social life and thus potentially subjected to severe material deprivation

and even extermination." See "Five Faces of Oppression," in *Multiculturalism from the Margins*, ed. Harris, 76–77.

13. The concept of "cultural erasure," as used here, is adapted from a compelling essay by Maria Lugones and Joshua Price, entitled "Dominant Culture: *El deseo por un alma pobre* (The desire for an impoverished soul)," in ibid., 103–27 (especially 107).

14. See Iris Marion Young, "Five Faces of Oppression," in ibid., 81–82.

15. *Statistical Abstract of the United States, 1996,* Table Number 62, "Married Couples of Same or Mixed Races and Origins," 56.

16. Dr. Maria Farnsworth Riche, Director, Bureau of the Census, "Population: How America Is Changing—The View from the Census Bureau, 1995," in *The World Almanac and Book of Facts, 1996,* 382.

17. Patrick Buchanan, Lynne Cheney, former Secretary of Education William Bennett, former Assistant Secretary of the Department of Education Diane Ravitch, and former United Nations Ambassador Jeanne Kirkpatrick have been partisans of the view that seeks to "put America first" and asserts the superiority and universality of Western "values" against the dissonance of ethnic "particularism."

SELECTED BIBLIOGRAPHY

University Archival Sources

In preparing this book my focus was on black student activism. Therefore, I consulted a number of sources generated by students themselves, especially letters to the editor and other materials written by black students. These appeared in student publications, such as the *Daily Pennsylvanian, Summer Pennsylvanian,* and *The Voice* (the latter produced by the United Minorities Council). Over the years the Black Student League and United Minorities Council have issued written statements and letters, and on occasion chairpersons of the BSL, such as Craig Inge, Skip Knight, Sheryl George, Kenneth McNeil, Russell Brooks, Lorenzo Holloway, Conrad Muhammad, Traci Miller, Melissa Moody, and Reuben Brown have written open letters that appeared in campus publications. The campus association of black faculty members, administrators, and staff persons has issued written declarations and reports, and these too have been consulted.

Other campus organizations such as the Undergraduate Assembly and University Council have an extensive "paper trail." *Almanac* is the university's "journal of record," and the *Pennsylvania Gazette* is the alumni magazine. I have also consulted numerous sets of minutes and reports of university committees and the trustees, and formal statements from the offices of the president, provost, and vice provosts, and other primary sources housed in the University of Pennsylvania Archives. Among reports relating to "black presence," as it was called in the 1970s and 1980s, of particular importance are the Report of the University Development Commission, entitled "Pennsylvania: One University" (January 1973), the Report of the Task Force on Black Presence (July 1977), and the Provost's Response to the Report of the Task Force on Black Presence and Plans for Implementation (published in the *Almanac,* 21 March 1978, 20–23). Another critical document is the 1967 Report of the Committee on Undergraduate Admissions, known as the McGill Report. Detailed citations for the various news accounts, policy statements, reports, minutes, and archival documents can be found in the notes.

Secondary Sources

Allen, Robert L. *Black Awakening in Capitalist America: An Analytic History.* Trenton, N.J.: Africa World Press, 1990. Originally published, Garden City, N.Y.: Doubleday, 1969.

Anthony, Earl. *The Time of the Furnaces: A Case Study of Black Student Revolt.* New York: Dial Press, 1971.

Appiah, Kwame Anthony, and Henry Louis Gates Jr., eds. *Identities.* Chicago: University of Chicago Press, 1995.

Asante, Molefi. *The Afrocentric Idea.* Philadelphia: Temple University Press, 1987.

Baldwin, James. *The Fire Next Time.* New York: Dell, 1962.

Barbour, Floyd, ed. *The Black Power Revolt: A Collection of Essays.* Boston: F. Porter Sargent, Extending Horizons Books, 1968.

Barlow, Bill, and Peter Shapiro. "The Struggle for San Francisco State." In *Black Power And Student Rebellion,* edited by James McEvoy and Abraham Miller, 277–97. Belmont, Calif.: Wadsworth, 1969.

Barol, William, "Why They Choose Separate Tables." *Newsweek on Campus* (March 1983): 4–13.

Bell, Daniel. "Columbia and the New Left." In *Black Power and Student Rebellion,* edited by James McEvoy and Abraham Miller, 31–74. Belmont, Calif.: Wadsworth, 1969.

Berger, Bennett. "Soul Searching." Review of *Urban Blues* by Charles Keil. *Trans-Action* (June 1967): 54–57.

Berghe, Pierre van der. *Race and Racism: A Comparative Perspective.* New York: Wiley, 1967.

Blackburn, Robert T., Zelda F. Gamson and Marvin W. Peterson. "The Meaning of Response: Current and Future Questions." In *Black Students on White Campuses: The Impact of Increased Black Enrollments,* edited by Marvin W. Peterson, Robert T. Blackburn, Zelda F. Gamson, Carlos H. Arce, Roselle W. Davenport, and James R. Mingle, 309–21. Ann Arbor: University of Michigan, Institute for Social Research, 1978.

Blalock, Hubert M. *Toward a Theory of Minority Group Relations.* New York: Wiley, 1967.

Blauner, Robert. *Racial Oppression in America.* New York: Harper and Row, 1972.

Blum, John Morton. *Years of Discord: American Politics and Society, 1961–1974.* New York: Norton, 1991.

Blumer, Herbert. "Race Prejudice as a Sense of Group Position," *Pacific Sociological Review* 1, no. 1 (spring 1958): 3–7.

———. "The Future of the Color Line." In *The South in Continuity and Change,* edited by John C. McKinney and Edgar T. Thompson. Durham, N.C.: Duke University Press, 1965.

Boggs, James. *The American Revolution: Pages from a Negro Worker's Notebook.* New York: Monthly Review Press, 1963.

———. *Racism and the Class Struggle: Further Pages from a Black Worker's Notebook.* New York: Monthly Review Press, 1970.

Bracey, John H. Jr. "Black Nationalism Since Garvey." In *Key Issues in the Afro-American Experience,* vol, 2, edited by Nathan Huggins, Martin Kilson, and Daniel Fox, 259–79. New York: Harcourt, Brace, Jovanovich, 1971.

Bracey, John H., Jr., August Meier, and Elliott Rudwick. *Black Nationalism in America.* Indianapolis: Bobbs-Merrill, 1970.

Bradley, Michael. *The Iceman Inheritance.* Toronto: Dorset, 1979.

Breitman, George. *Malcolm X Speaks: Selected Speeches and Statements.* New York: Grove Press, 1965.

———. *The Last Year of Malcolm X: The Evolution of a Revolutionary.* New York: Pathfinder, 1967.

———. *February 1965: The Final Speeches* [of Malcolm X]. New York: Pathfinder, 1992.

Brisbane, Robert. *The Black Vanguard: Origins of the Negro Social Revolution, 1900–1960.* Valley Forge, Pa.: Judson Press, 1970.

Broderick, Frank. "The Gnawing Dilemma: Separatism and Integration, 1865–1925." In *Key Issues in the Afro-American Experience,* vol. 2, edited by Nathan Huggins, Martin Kilson, and Daniel Fox, 93–106. New York: Harcourt, Brace, Jovanovich, 1971.

Caplan, Nathan. "Identity in Transition: A Theory of Black Militancy." In *The New American Revolution,* edited by Roderick Aya and Norman Miller. New York: Free Press, 1971.

Carlisle, Rodney. *The Roots Of Black Nationalism.* Port Washington, N.Y.: Kennikat Press, 1975.

Carson, Clayborne. *In Struggle: SNCC and the Black Awakening of the 1960s.* Cambridge: Harvard University Press, 1981.

Cass, James. "Can the University Survive the Black Challenge?" *Saturday Review* 52, no. 25 (June 21, 1969): 68–71, 83–84.

Chrisman, Robert. "Observations on Race and Class at San Francisco State." In *Black Power and Student Rebellion,* edited by James McEvoy and Abraham Miller, 222–32. Belmont, Calif.: Wadsworth, 1969.

Christian, Charles M. *Black Saga: The African American Experience.* New York: Houghton Mifflin, 1995.

Clark, Kenneth B., and Mamie K. Clark. "Segregation as a Factor in the Racial Identification of Negro Pre-School Children: A Preliminary Report." *Journal of Experimental Education* 8, no. 2 (December 1939): 161–63.

Clark, Peter B., and James Q. Wilson. "Incentive Systems: A Theory of Organization." *Administrative Science Quarterly* 6 (June 1961): 129–66.

Clark, Reginald M. *Family Life and School Achievement: Why Poor Black Children Succeed or Fail.* Chicago: University of Chicago Press, 1983.

Cleage, Albert, Jr. *The Black Messiah.* New York: Sheed and Ward, 1968.

———. *Black Christian Nationalism.* New York: William Morrow, 1972.

Cone, James. *Black Theology and Black Power.* New York: Seabury Press, 1969.

———. *A Black Theology of Liberation.* Philadelphia: Lippincott, 1970.

———. *God of the Oppressed.* New York: Seabury Press, 1975.

Conniff, Michael L., and Thomas J. Davis. *Africans in the Americas: A History of the Black Diaspora.* New York: St. Martin's Press, 1994.

Connor, Walker. *Ethnonationalism: The Quest for Understanding.* Princeton, N.J.: Princeton University Press, 1994.

Cose, Ellis. *The Rage of a Privileged Class: Why Are Middle-Class Blacks Angry? Why Should America Care?* New York: HarperCollins, 1993.

Cox, Oliver C. *Caste, Class, and Race: A Study in Social Dynamics.* 6th ed. New York: Modern Reader Paperbacks, Monthly Review Press. Originally published, New York: Doubleday, 1948.

Cruse, Harold. *The Crisis of the Negro Intellectual.* New York: William Morrow, 1967.

———. *Rebellion or Revolution?* New York: William Morrow, 1968.

———. *Plural but Equal: A Critical Study of Blacks and Minorities and the American Plural Society.* New York: William Morrow, 1987.

Daniel, Jack. "Black Academic Activism." *Black Scholar* 4 (1973): 44–52.

Davis, James C. "The J-Curve of Rising and Declining Satisfactions as a Cause of Some Great Revolutions and a Contained Rebellion." In *The History of Violence in America: Historical and Comparative Perspectives,* edited by Hugh D. Graham and Ted R. Gurr. New York: Praeger, A New York Times Book, 1969.

de Graaf, Lawrence B. "Howard: The Evolution of a Black Student Revolt." In *Protest! Student Activism in America,* edited by Julian Foster and Durward Long, 319–44. New York: William Morrow, 1970.

Dollard, John. *Caste and Class in a Southern Town.* With a foreword by Daniel Patrick Moynihan. Madison: University of Wisconsin Press, 1988. Originally published, New Haven: Yale University Press, 1937.

Donadio, Stephen. "Black Power at Columbia." *Commentary* 46 (1968): 67–76.

———. "Columbia: Seven Interviews." *Partisan Review* (1968): 354–92.

Donald, Cleveland. "Black Students." In *Through Different Eyes: Black and White Per-*

spectives on American Race Relations, edited by Peter Isaac Rose, Stanley Rothman, and William Julius Wilson, 135–84. New York: Oxford University Press, 1973.

———. "Cornell: Confrontation in Black and White." In *Divided We Stand: Reflections on the Crisis at Cornell,* edited by Cushing Strout and David I. Grossvogel, 135–84. Garden City, N.Y.: Doubleday, 1971.

Draper, Theodore. *The Rediscovery of Black Nationalism.* New York: Viking Press, 1970.

Du Bois, W. E. B. "The Conservation of Races." In *W. E. B. Du Bois: Writings,* edited by Nathan Huggins, 813–26. New York: Library of America, Literary Classics of the United States, 1980. Originally published by American Negro Academy, *Occasional Papers* 2, (1897).

———. *The Souls of Black Folk.* With introductions by Nathan Hare and Alvin Poussaint, M.D. New York: Signet, New American Library, 1969. Originally published, 1903.

———. "Segregation in the North." In *W. E. B. Du Bois: Writings,* edited by Nathan Huggins, 1239–48. New York: Library of America, Literary Classics of the United States, 1980.

———. "Does The Negro Need Separate Schools?" *Journal of Negro Education* 4, no. 3 (July 1935): 328–35.

Eichel, Lawrence, Kenneth Jost, Robert Luskin, and Richard Neustadt. *The Harvard Strike.* Boston: Houghton Mifflin, 1970.

Eisinger, Peter. "Ethnic Conflict, Community-Building, and the Emergence of Ethnic Political Traditions in the United States." In *Urban Ethnic Conflict: A Comparative Perspective,* edited by Susan E. Clarke and Jeffrey L. Obler, 1–34. Chapel Hill, N.C.: Institute for Research in Social Science, 1976.

Elam, Julia C., ed. *Blacks on White Campuses: Proceedings of a Special NAFEO Seminar: Seminar Held at the Rayburn House Office Building and the Washington Hilton Hotel, March 25, 1982.* Lanham, Md.: University Press of America and Washington, D.C.: National Association for Equal Opportunity in Higher Education, 1983.

Engs, Robert F. *Freedom's First Generation: Black Hampton, Virginia, 1861–1890.* Philadelphia: University of Pennsylvania Press, 1979.

Epps, Edgar, ed. *Cultural Pluralism.* Berkeley, Calif.: McCutchan Publishing, 1974.

Essien-Udom, E. U. *Black Nationalism: A Search for an Identity in America.* Chicago: University of Chicago Press, 1962.

Exum, William H. *Paradoxes Of Protest: Black Student Activism in a White University.* Philadelphia: Temple University Press, 1985.

Fanon, Frantz. *The Wretched of the Earth.* Preface by Jean-Paul Sartre. Translated by Constance Farrington. New York: Grove Press, 1963. Originally published, Paris: François Maspero, 1961.

Flacks, Richard. *Youth and Social Change.* Chicago: Markham, 1971.

Fleming, Jacqueline. *Blacks in College*. San Francisco: Jossey-Bass, 1985.

Forman, James. *The Making of Black Revolutionaries*. New York: Macmillan, 1972.

Forman, Seth. *Blacks In The Jewish Mind: A Crisis of Liberalism*. New York: New York University Press, 1998.

Fossett, Judith Jackson, and Jeffrey A. Tucker, eds. *Race Consciousness: African American Studies for the New Century*. With a foreword by Nell Irvin Painter and Arnold Rampersad, and an introduction by Robin Kelley. New York: New York University Press, 1997.

Foster, Julian. "Student Protest: What Is Known, What Is Said." In *Protest! Student Activism in America*. Edited by Julian Foster and Durward Long, 27–58. New York: William Morrow, 1970.

Franklin, Vincent P. *Black Self-Determination: A Cultural History of African American Resistance*. With a foreword by Mary Frances Berry. 2nd ed. New York: Lawrence Hill Books, Chicago Review Press, 1992. Originally published, 1984.

——. *Living Our Stories, Telling Our Truths: Autobiography and the Making of the African American Intellectual Tradition*. New York: Oxford University Press, 1995.

Frazier, E. Franklin. *The Negro in the United States*. Rev. ed. New York: Macmillan, 1957. Originally published, 1949.

Gamson, Zelda F., and Carlos H. Arce. "Implications of the Social Context for Higher Education." In *Black Students on White Campuses: The Impact of Increased Black Enrollments*, edited by Marvin W. Peterson, Robert T. Blackburn, Zelda F. Gamson, Carlos H. Arce, Roselle W. Davenport, and James R. Mingle, 23–42. Ann Arbor: University of Michigan, Institute for Social Research, 1978.

Geertz, Clifford. "The Integrative Revolution: Primordial Sentiments and Civic politics in the New States." In *Old Societies and New States: The Quest for Modernity in Asia and Africa*, edited by Clifford Geertz, 107–13. New York: Free Press, 1963.

Genovese, Eugene. *Roll, Jordan, Roll: The World the Slaves Made*. New York: Random House, 1972.

George, Hermon, Jr. *American Race Relations Theory: A Review of Four Models*. Lanham, Md.: University Press of America, 1984.

Gerlach, Luther P., and Virginia Hine. *People, Power, Change: Movements of Social Transformation*. Indianapolis: Bobbs-Merrill Educational Publishing, 1970.

Gershwender, James, ed. *The Black Revolt: The Civil Rights Movement, Ghetto Uprisings, and Separatism*. Englewood Cliffs, N.J.: Prentice-Hall, 1971.

Gilliam, Reginald. *Black Political Development: An Advocacy Analysis*. Port Washington, N.Y.: Kennikat, 1975.

Gitlin, Todd. "On the Line at San Francisco State." In *Black Power and Student Rebellion*, edited by James McEvoy and Abraham Miller, 298–306. Belmont, Calif.: Wadsworth, 1969.

Glazer, Nathan, and Daniel Patrick Moynihan. *Beyond the Melting Pot: The Negroes,*

Puerto Ricans, Jews, Italians, and Irish of New York City. Cambridge: MIT Press, 1970. Originally published, 1963.

Goffman, Erving. *Stigma: Notes on the Management of Spoiled Identity.* Englewood Cliffs, N.J.: Prentice-Hall, 1963.

Gordon, Milton M. *Assimilation in American Life: The Role of Race, Religion, and National Origins.* New York: Oxford University Press, 1964.

Greer, Edward. *Black Liberation Politics.* Boston: Allyn and Bacon, 1971.

Greico, Elizabeth M., and Rachel Cassidy. "Overview of Race and Hispanic Origin: Census 2000 Brief." U.S. Census Bureau, March 2001. <www.census.gov>

Gurin, Patricia, and Edgar Epps. *Black Consciousness, Identity, and Achievement: A Study of Students in Historically Black Colleges.* New York: John Wiley, 1975.

Hall, Raymond. *Black Separatism in the United States.* Hanover, N.H.: University Press of New England, for Dartmouth College, 1978.

Harding, Vincent. "Black Students and Their Impossible Revolution." *Journal of Black Studies* (September 1970): 75–100.

———. *There Is a River: The Black Struggle for Freedom in America.* New York: Vintage/Random House, 1981.

Harper, Frederick D. "Media for Change: Black Students in the White University." *Journal of Negro Education* 40 (1971): 255–65.

Harris, Dean A., ed. *Multiculturalism from the Margins: Non-Dominant Voices on Difference and Diversity.* Westport, Conn: Bifocal Publications, Bergin and Garvey, 1995.

Heath, G. Louis, ed. *Off the Pigs! The History and Literature of the Black Panther Party.* Metuchen, N.J.: Scarecrow Press, 1976.

Henderson, Donald M. "Black Student Protest in White Universities." In *Black America,* edited by John F. Szwed, 157–70. New York: Basic Books, 1970.

Hermon, George, Jr. *American Race Relations Theory: A Review of Four Models.* Lanham, Md.: University Press of American, 1984.

Higham, John. *Strangers in the Land: Patterns of American Nativism, 1860–1925.* New Brunswick, N.J.: Rutgers University Press, 1955.

Hodgson, Godfrey. *America in Our Time.* New York: Random House, 1976; Vintage Books, 1978.

Holt, Thomas. "Marking: Race, Race-making, and the Writing of History." *American Historical Review,* 100, no. 1 (February 1995): 1–20.

Hornsby, Alton, ed. *The Black Almanac. Fourth Revised Edition.* Woodbury, N.Y.: Barron's Educational Series, 1977.

Horton, John. "Order and Conflict Theories of Social Problems as Competing Ideologies." *American Journal of Sociology* 71 (1966): 701–13.

Huggins, Nathan, ed. *W. E. B. Du Bois: Writings.* New York: Library of America, Literary Classics of the United States, 1980. Originally published by the American Negro Academy, 1897.

Huggins, Nathan, Martin Kilson, and Daniel Fox, *Key Issues in the Afro-American Experience* Vol. 2. New York: Harcourt, Brace, Jovanovich, 1971.

Hutchinson, John. *The Dynamics of Cultural Nationalism*. London: Allen and Unwin, 1978.

Hutchinson, John, and Anthony D. Smith, eds. *Nationalism. An Oxford Reader*. New York: Oxford University Press, 1994.

Immigration and Naturalization Service. Immigrants. Table C, "Immigrants Admitted from Top Twenty Countries of Birth: Fiscal Years 1996–1997." Available through <www.ins.usdoj.gov/aboutins/statistics/97immtxt>.

Jackson, George L. *Blood in My Eye*. New York: Random House, 1972.

Karenga, Maulana. *The Quotable Karenga*. Edited by Clyde Halisi and James Mtume. Los Angeles: Saidi Publications, 1967.

——. *Introduction to Black Studies*. Los Angeles: University of Sankore Press, 1982.

——. "Society, Culture, and the Problem of Self-Consciousness: A Kawaida Analysis." In *Philosophy Born of Struggle: Anthology of Afro-American Philosophy from 1917*, edited by Leonard Harris, 212–28. Dubuque, Iowa: Kendall-Hunt, 1982.

Kaurouma, Yusuf. "Right On! . . . Where? Historical Contradictions of the Black Student Movement." In *The Minority Student on Campus: Expectations and Possibilities*, edited by Robert A. Altman and Patricia O. Snyder, 63–73. Boulder, Colo.: Western Interstate Commission for Higher Education, 1970.

Kelman, Steven. *Push Comes to Shove*. Boston: Houghton Mifflin, 1970.

Killian, Lewis M. "Herbert Blumer's Contributions to Race Relations." In *Human Nature and Collective Behavior: Papers in Honor of Herbert Blumer*, edited by Tamotsu Shibutani, 179–90. Englewood Cliffs, N.J.: Prentice-Hall, 1970.

Killian, Lewis and Charles Grigg. *Racial Crisis in America*. Englewood Cliffs, N.J.: Prentice-Hall, 1964.

Kilson, Martin. "From Civil Rights To Party Politics: The Black Political Transition." *Current History* 67, no. 399 (November 1974): 193–99.

Kleinbaum, David G., and Anna Kleinbaum. "The Minority Experience at a Predominantly White University." *Journal of Negro Education* 45 (1976): 312–28.

Knowles, Louis, and Kenneth Prewitt. *Institutional Racism in America*. Englewood Cliffs, N.J.: Prentice-Hall, 1969.

Kornstein, Daniel and Peter Weissenberg. "Social Exchange Theory and the University." In *Protest! Student Activism in America*, edited by Julian Foster and Durward Long, 447–56. New York: William Morrow, 1970.

Kramer, Judith. *The American Minority Community*. New York: Crowell, 1970.

Lewis, David Levering. *W. E. B. Du Bois: Biography of a Race, 1868–1919*. New York: Henry Holt, 1993.

Long, Durward. "Black Protest." In *Protest! Student Activism in America*, edited by Julian Foster and Durward Long, 459–82. New York: William Morrow, 1970.

——. "Wisconsin: Changing Styles of Administrative Response." In *Protest! Student*

Activism in America, edited by Julian Foster and Durward Long, 246–70. New York: William Morrow, 1970.

Lyon, Marvin, Jr. "Blacks At Penn, Then and Now." In *A Pennsylvania Album: Undergraduate Essays on the 250th Anniversary,* edited by Richard S. Dunn and Mark F. Lloyd, 43–47. Philadelphia: University of Pennsylvania, 1990.

Malcolm X. *The Autobiography of Malcolm X.* With the assistance of Alex Haley. Introduction by M. S. Handler and epilogue by Alex Haley. New York, Grove Press, 1965.

Marable, Manning. *How Capitalism Underdeveloped Black America: Problems in Race, Political Economy, and Society.* Boston: South End Press, 1983.

——. *Race, Reform And Rebellion: The Second Reconstruction in Black America, 1945–1982.* Jackson: University of Mississippi Press, 1984.

——. *W. E. B. Du Bois, Black Radical Democrat.* Boston: Twayne Publishers, 1986.

——. *Beyond Black and White: Transforming African American Politics.* New York: Verso, 1995.

Matthews, Donald, and James Protho. "Negro Students and the Protest Movement." In *Black Power and the Student Rebellion,* edited by James McEvoy and Abraham Miller, 379–418. Belmont, Calif.: Wadsworth, 1969.

Matusow, Allen. *The Unraveling of America: A History of Liberalism in the 1960s.* New York: Harper and Row, 1984; Harper Torchback, New American Series, ed. Henry Steele Commager and Richard B. Morris, 1986.

Mbadinuju, C. Chinwoke. "Black Separatism." *Current History* 67, no. 399 (November 1974): 206–213 and 233.

McCormick, Richard P. *The Black Student Protest Movement at Rutgers.* New Brunswick, N.J.: Rutgers University Press, 1990.

McEvoy, James, and Abraham Miller. "On Strike . . . Shut It Down." In *Black Power and Student Rebellion,* edited by James McEvoy and Abraham Miller, 12–31. Belmont, Calif.: Wadsworth, 1969.

McGeveren, William A., ed. "Highest-Ranking Countries of Birth of U.S. Foreign-Born Population, 1998," 373. In *World Almanac and Book of Facts, 2001.* Mahwah, N.J., 2001.

Merton, Robert, and Alice S. Kitt. "Contributions to the Theory of Reference Group Behavior." In *Continuities in Social Research,* edited by Robert Merton and Paul F. Lazersfeld, 40–105. New York: Free Press, 1950.

Meyer, Marshall W. "Harvard Students in the Midst of Crisis." *Sociology of Education* 44 (1971): 245–69.

Moses, Wilson Jeremiah, ed. *Classical Black Nationalism: From the American Revolution to Marcus Garvey.* New York: New York University Press, 1996.

Muse, Benjamin. *The American Negro Revolution: From Nonviolence to Black Power.* New York: Citadel Press, 1970. Originally published, Bloomington: Indiana University Press, 1968.

Nairn, Tom. "The Maladies of Development." In *Nationalism. Oxford Reader,* edited by John Hutchinson and Anthony D. Smith, 70–76. Oxford: Oxford University Press, 1994.

Napper, George. *Blacker than Thou: The Struggle for Campus Unity.* Grand Rapids, Mich.: Eerdmans, 1973.

Newsweek. "The 'Bust' at Harvard," 21 April 1969, 102–3.

——. "It Can't Happen Here—Can It?" 5 May 1969, 26–30.

Newton, Huey. *Revolutionary Suicide.* With the assistance of J. Herman Blake. New York: Harcourt Brace Jovanovich, 1973.

Novak, Michael. *The Rise of the Unmeltable Ethnics.* New York: Macmillan, 1971.

Obatala, J. K. "Black Students: Where Did Their Revolution Go?" *The Nation,* 2 October 1972, 272–74.

——. "Black Studies Stop the Shouting and Go to Work," *Smithsonian* 5, no. 9 (December 1974): 46–53.

Obear, Frederick W. "Student Activism in the Sixties." In *Protest! Student Activism in America,* edited by Julian Foster and Durward Long, 11–26. New York: William Morrow, 1970.

Parenti, Michael. "Assimilation and Counter-Assimilation: From Civil Rights to Black Nationalism." In *Power and Community: Dissenting Essays in Political Science,* edited by Philip Green and Sanford Levinson, 173–94. New York: Pantheon Books, 1969.

Perkins, W. E., and J. E. Higginson. "Black Students: Reformists or Revolutionaries?" In *The New American Revolution,* edited by Roderick Aya and Norman Miller, 195–222. New York: Free Press, 1971.

Peterson, Marvin W. "Conflict Dynamics of Institutional Response." In *Black Students on White Campuses: The Impact of Increased Black Enrollments,* edited by Marvin W. Peterson; Robert T. Blackburn, Zelda F. Gamson, Carlos H. Arce, Roselle W. Davenport, and James R. Mingle, 147–60. Ann Arbor: University of Michigan, Institute for Social Research, 1978.

——. "Environmental Forces: The Crucial Context." In *Black Students on White Campuses: The Impact of Increased Black Enrollments,* edited by Marvin W. Peterson, Robert T. Blackburn, Zelda F. Gamson, Carlos H. Arce, Roselle W. Davenport, and James R. Mingle, 105–25. Ann Arbor: University of Michigan, Institute for Social Research, 1978.

——. "Stage I: The 13 Colleges and Universities." In *Black Students on White Campuses: The Impact of Increased Black Enrollments,* edited by Marvin W. Peterson, Robert T. Blackburn, Zelda F. Gamson, Carlos H. Arce, Roselle W. Davenport, and James R. Mingle, 67–104. Ann Arbor: University of Michigan, Institute for Social Research, 1978.

Peterson, Marvin W., Robert T. Blackburn, Zelda F. Gamson, Carlos H. Arce, Roselle W. Davenport, and James R. Mingle, eds. *Black Students on White Campuses: The*

Impact of Increased Black Enrollments. Ann Arbor: University of Michigan, Institute for Social Research, 1978.

Peterson, Marvin W., and Roselle W. Davenport. "Student Organizations and Student Life." In *Black Students on White Campuses: The Impact of Increased Black Enrollments,* edited by Marvin W. Peterson, Robert T. Blackburn, Zelda F. Gamson, Carlos H. Arce, Roselle W. Davenport, and James R. Mingle, 195–208. Ann Arbor: University of Michigan, Institute for Social Research, 1978.

Pettee, George S. *The Process of Revolution.* New York: Harper Bros., 1938.

Podhoretz, Norman. "My Negro Problem—And Ours." *Commentary* (February 1963): 93–101.

Pothier, Dick. "Black Students Want Penn Teacher Fired." *Philadelphia Inquirer,* 15 February 1985, B2.

Redkey, Edwin S. *Black Exodus: Black Nationalist and Back to Africa Movements, 1890–1910.* New Haven: Yale University Press, 1969.

Rosovsky, Henry. "Black Students at Harvard: Personal Reflections concerning Recent Events." *American Scholar* 38 (autumn 1969): 562–72.

Rubenstein, Richard E. "Rebels in Eden." In *The New American Revolution,* edited by Roderick Aya and Norman Miller, 97–172. New York: Free Press, 1971.

Runciman, W. G. *Relative Deprivation and Social Justice.* Berkeley: University of California Press, 1966.

Schafer, Boyd C. *Nationalism: Myth and Reality.* New York: Harcourt, Brace, 1955.

Schlesinger, Arthur, Jr. *The Disuniting of America.* New York: Norton, 1992.

Shils, Edward. "Primordial, Personal, Sacred, and Civil Ties." *British Journal of Sociology* (June 1957).

Singer, Lawrence. "Ethnogenesis and Negro-Americans Today." *Social Research* 29, no. 4 (winter 1962): 419–32.

Sitkoff, Harvard. *The Struggle for Black Equality, 1954–1980.* New York: Hill and Wang, 1981.

Smedlowe, Jill. Reported by Peter Hawthorne, Johannesburg, and Bruce W. Nelan, Durban. "Harsh Words, Harsh Actions." *Time,* 25 August 1986, 32–33.

Smelser, Neil. *Theory of Collective Behavior.* New York: Free Press, 1963.

Snyder, Louis. *Varieties of Nationalism: A Comparative Study.* Hinsdale, Ill.: Dryden Press, 1976.

Stark, Rodney. "Berkeley: Protest + Police = Riot." In *Black Power and Student Rebellion,* edited by James McEvoy and Abraham Miller, 167–196. Belmont, Calif.: Wadsworth, 1969.

Strout, Cushing, and David I. Grossvogel, eds. *Divided We Stand: Reflections on the Crisis at Cornell.* Garden City, N.Y.: Doubleday, 1971.

Thomas, Judith, and Dana Flint. "Black Youth in Urban Schools: Attrition, Self-Concept, and Performance." In *The State of Black Philadelphia,* vol 9, 37–48. Urban League of Philadelphia.

Thompson, E. P. "Eighteenth-Century English Society: Class Struggle without Class?" *Social History* 3 (May 1978): 133–65.

Time. "Harvard and Beyond: The University Under Siege," 18 April 1969, 49–54.

Ture, Kwame [Stokely Carmichael], and Charles V. Hamilton. *Black Power: The Politics of Liberation in America.* New York: Random House, 1967.

Turner, James. "Social Origins of Black Consciousness." In *The New American Revolution,* edited by Roderick Aya and Norman Miller, 166–94. New York: Free Press, 1971.

Turner, Ralph H. "Determinants of Social Movement Strategies." In *Human Nature and Collective Behavior: Papers in Honor of Herbert Blumer,* edited by Tamotsu Shibutani, 145–64. Englewood Cliffs, N.J.: Prentice-Hall, 1970.

Turner, Ralph H., and Lewis Killian. *Collective Behavior,* 2d ed. Englewood Cliffs, N.J.: Prentice-Hall, 1972.

Unger, Irwin. *The Movement: A History of the American New Left, 1959–1972.* With the assistance of Debi Unger. New York: Dodd, Mead, 1974.

Van Deburg, William. *New Day in Babylon: The Black Power Movement and American Culture, 1965–1975.* Chicago: University of Chicago Press, 1992.

———. *Modern Black Nationalism: From Marcus Garvey to Louis Farrakhan.* New York: New York University Press, 1997.

Wade, Jacqueline E. *"Black College Students' Adaptive Modes: Making It at Penn."* Ph.D. diss., University of Pennsylvania, 1983.

Wallace, Anthony. "Revitalization Movements." *American Anthropologist* 58, no. 2 (April 1956): 264–81.

Welsing, Frances Cress. "The Neurochemical Basis for Evil." In *The Isis (Yssis) Papers: The Keys to the Colors,* 231–38. Chicago: Third World Press, 1991.

Wideman, John Edgar. *Brothers and Keepers.* New York: Holt, Rinehart and Winston, 1984.

Wildavesky, Aaron. "The Empty-Headed Blues: Black Rebellion and White Reaction." *Public Interest* 11 (Spring 1968): 3–16.

Williams, Juan, with the Eyes on the Prize Production Team. *Eyes on the Prize: America's Civil Rights Years, 1954–1965.* With an introduction by Julian Bond. New York: Viking Penguin, 1987.

Williams, Raymond. *Marxism and Literature.* London: Oxford University Press, 1977.

Willie, Charles Vert. *The Ivory and Ebony Towers: Race Relations and Higher Education.* Lexington, Mass.: Lexington Books, 1981.

Wilson, Kendall. "Ivy League's First Black Captain Honored by Univ. of Penn's Dental School," *Philadelphia Tribune,* 4 March 1980, 11.

Wilson, William Julius. *Power, Racism and Privilege: Race Relations in Theoretical and Sociohistorical Perspective.* New York: Free Press, 1973.

———. "The Significance of Social and Racial Prisms." In *Through Different Eyes: Black and White Perspectives on American Race Relations,* edited by Peter I. Rose, Stanley Rothman, and William Julius Wilson, 395–409. New York: Oxford University Press, 1973.

———. *The Declining Significance of Race: Blacks and Changing American Institutions.* Chicago: University of Chicago Press, 1978.

Wolters, Raymond. *The Burden of Brown: Thirty Years of School Desegregation.* Knoxville: University of Tennessee Press, 1984.

———. *The New Negro on Campus: Black College Rebellions of the 1920s.* Princeton, N.J.: Princeton University Press, 1975.

Young, Iris Marion. *Justice and the Politics of Difference.* Princeton, N.J.: Princeton University Press, 1990.

Zald, Mayer N., and Roberta Ash. "Social Movement Organizations: Growth, Decay, and Change." *Social Forces* 44 (1966): 327–40.

Zald, Mayer N., and Michael A. Berger. "Social Movements in Organizations: Coup d' Etat, Insurgency, and Mass Movements." *American Journal of Sociology* 83, no. 4 (1978): 823–61.

INDEX

WAYNE GLASKER is associate professor of history and director of the African American Studies Program at Rutgers University, Camden, New Jersey, campus. He received his Ph.D. from the University of Pennsylvania and, as a graduate student there, was active in the anti-apartheid movement. This experience shaped his determination to become an "activist scholar" and public intellectual. His areas of interest include the civil rights movement, cultural pluralism, ethnic studies, and educational reform. He has published more than a dozen book reviews in the journal *Choice* and works with faith-based programs and alternative Christian schools to promote quality urban education.